BRITAIN'S X-TRAORDINARY FILES

BRITAIN'S X-TRAORDINARY FILES

DAVID CLARKE

BLOOMSBURY
LONDON · NEW DELHI · NEW YORK · SYDNEY

First published in the United Kingdom in 2014
Copyright © David Clarke, 2014

The National Archives logo © Crown Copyright 2014.
The National Archives logo device is a trademark of The National Archives
and is used under licence.

Bloomsbury Publishing Plc
50 Bedford Square
London
WC1B 3DP

www.bloomsbury.com

London, New York, Delhi and Sydney

A CIP record for this book is available from the British Library.

ISBN: 9-781-4729-0493-5

Design by Fiona Pike, Pike Design, Winchester
Typeset by Hewer Text UK Ltd, Edinburgh
Printed and bound in the United Kingdom by CPI Group (UK) Ltd, Croydon CR0 4YY

CONTENTS

LIST OF ILLUSTRATIONS

ACKNOWLEDGEMENTS

I am very grateful to the numerous individuals and members of staff at archives, libraries and other public institutions who have assisted in the research for this book, especially reference staff at The National Archives, The British Library and the Imperial War Museum.

In particular I would like to thank Laura Simpson and Ed Field at The National Archives, Kew, and Alison Lindsay at The National Archives of Scotland, Edinburgh; the staff at The British Library reading rooms, St Pancras and the Newspaper Library at Colindale; Daisy Dalrymple at The Natural History Museum, London; Bridget Gillies of Archives and Special Collections, University of East Anglia; Valerie Hart of the Guildhall Library, London; and Sarah Ralph of Inverness Reference Library.

Individuals who deserve special mention for sharing material, providing references and supporting this project include Mark Pilkington, Andy Roberts, Bob Rickard, Janet Bord, Mark Vivian, Gary Anthony, Joe McGonagle, Ian Ridpath and Nick Redfern.

For assistance in providing and sourcing images, many thanks to the Fortean Picture Library, Mary Evans Picture Library, The National Archives, The National Archives of Scotland, The British Library, Warwickshire County Records Office, West Glamorgan Archive Service, , Edinburgh Castle and the late James Templeton.

INTRODUCTION

From time immemorial, Man has inhabited two worlds: one, the objective world about him which he could see and touch; the other, the realm of dreams and fancies, in the exploration of which his eager mind found fascinating employment. Although the frontiers of the Unknown have continued to recede before the advancement of scientific knowledge, there still remains a wide domain, where Mystery allures and beckons, and Man, ever delighting in that which eludes and baffles, still pursues.

Charles Eden Fay[1]

Unsolved historical mysteries have always fascinated the public and attracted the attention of writers and journalists. In an earlier book I explored the contents of the British government's formerly secret files on 'unidentified flying objects' (UFOs). These papers, described by the media as Britain's 'real X-files', were released to the public by the UK National Archives as part of a five-year open government programme that ended in 2013.[2] But the Ministry of Defence's records of UFO sightings are just one example of a range of uncanny phenomena that are documented in the official records.

My research at The National Archives in Kew has identified files on many other anomalies and historical mysteries. These include references to mysterious 'lightwheels' observed by the crews of merchant ships and 19th-century reports of 'sea serpents' reported to the Admiralty. Other mysteries recorded in the archives include the unexplained disappearance of the crew of the *Mary Celeste*, and a string of other mysterious 'vanishings' of both ships and aircraft that have puzzled investigators and resisted explanation. The official records also throw new light on many wartime legends and rumours. In some cases their contents offer rational explanations for events long considered inexplicable. In other examples, mystery continues to reign and has given rise to a range of theories encompassing everything from the supernatural to extra-terrestrial forces.

The rise and fall of belief in the supernatural is often linked to social upheavals, including changes in attitudes towards religion and the impact of mass loss of life during wartime. Certainly the spread of spiritualism from its origins in the United States during the 1850s coincided with the publication of Darwin's theory of evolution. For many people at that time, the new movement appeared to provide empirical proof of life after death; the Christian church, on the other hand, asked for faith rather than the evidence that was demanded by a new world ruled by scientific principles. A fresh revival of interest in spiritualism (along with a range of medieval omens and similar 'prodigies') emerged in response to the slaughter of the First World War. This febrile atmosphere of loss and yearning gave birth to enduring legends such as the Angels of Mons.

The popularity of supernatural beliefs among ordinary people can be gauged by the Mass Observation survey. This social research project was launched in 1937 and aimed to record snapshots of everyday life in Britain.[3] During the Second World War, the project conducted a series of surveys on levels of belief in the paranormal, using questionnaires and focus groups. One of these, completed by 100 people in 1942, revealed that a third of respondents said they believed in ghosts and five per cent reported a personal experience of something they could not explain.[4] Two years after the war, another panel of 100 Mass Observation volunteers was asked their opinion of a range of uncanny phenomena that were categorised as 'supernatural' including spiritualism, fortune-telling, 'second sight', telepathy and ghosts. Ten per cent said they had a personal experience of at least one category of uncanny phenomena that were not recognised by science.[5]

More recent opinion polls (see p.64) have revealed even higher levels of belief. Combining these results, it becomes apparent that belief in, and experience of, the paranormal appears to be hard-wired into the human condition. The pervasive nature of these phenomena has left a distinctive mark upon the written records that form the foundation stones of British history. For example, although the existence of uncanny powers such as Extra Sensory Perception (ESP) and Remote Viewing (RV) cannot be established using current scientific methodologies, both the US and UK, along with the countries of the former Soviet Union, have invested public money in attempts to develop new techniques that could be used to spy upon military secrets in foreign countries. There have also been many claims that police forces have used information provided by psychics in their attempts to solve murders and other serious crimes.

So while such phenomena do not exist officially, they still have credence for some people; indeed the archival record suggests some highly placed politicians and military officers were inclined to believe in them. Unfortunately, the popularity of the word 'paranormal' introduces linguistic problems in the way we interpret these types of anomalous human experience. 'Paranormal' is defined by the *Oxford English Dictionary* as something that is outside of any current scientific explanation. By using the word we implicitly refer to something that is, by definition, unscientific and has no objective existence except in the mind of those who believe in such manifestations.

Some of those who study and investigate extraordinary beliefs and experiences prefer to use the word 'supernatural' but even that has negative connotations. Non-Western societies, for instance, do not recognise any clear separation between the 'natural' and 'supernatural' worlds. Folklorist Bob Trubshaw prefers the word 'uncanny' to refer to a range of anomalous phenomena, including ghosts and extraordinary experiences. 'Uncanny' is defined as something 'partaking of a supernatural character; mysterious weird, uncomfortably strange or unfamiliar'.[6]

'Uncanny' accurately describes the many disparate stories and legends collected together for this book. My research in Britain's official archives has uncovered numerous occasions during the past 200 years when uncanny phenomena erupted into the wider public consciousness, despite protestations from those who disbelieved. Sometimes these events occurred as a result of media reporting on investigations by the police, fire service or the military into strange phenomena reported by members of the public. On other occasions members of the police or the armed forces were themselves eyewitnesses to anomalous phenomena, or became the subject of internal inquiries as a result of their own demonstrations of dowsing or clairvoyance. Occasionally, uncanny beliefs have featured in court proceedings and these have become part of the official record preserved by The National Archives.

As a direct outcome of their advisory role to ministers and Parliament, the paper trail produced by civil servants is a rich source of information on a range of anomalous phenomena. During the Cold War, the Air Ministry (until its disestablishment in 1964) and subsequently the Ministry of Defence became the default experts on all kinds of unexplained aerial phenomena sighted visually or recorded by radar in the UK. Decades earlier, the Admiralty, the Natural History Museum and the Scottish Office were drawn into debates on the existence of mysterious creatures such as the sea serpent and its landlocked cousin, the Loch Ness Monster. When news of the latter reached the national media in 1933, Scottish MPs demanded action by police to protect their 'monster' from the activities of big game hunters. More recently, armed police – and on one occasion, the Royal Marines – have been drawn into hunts for elusive 'big cats' that many people believe are living wild in the British countryside.

The thread that connects all these disparate experiences, beliefs and legends are the traces they have left in written records, primarily the public archives of the British Isles. This book investigates legends and mysteries via the medium of original source material using, where possible, the narratives produced by eyewitnesses or participants in the events described. Some stories and legends may be familiar, but even those with a deep interest in these subjects will realise how archive material can open new doors and reveal unexpected historical perspectives and insights. A substantial cache of hitherto secret records, generated by a range of UK government departments, have begun to emerge into the public domain since the introduction of the Freedom of Information Act (FOI) in 2005.

One common denominator shared by stories explored in this book is the disconnect between what the archive sources actually tell us and the elaborate legends that have grown up around them as a result of their dissemination to a wider audience. A legend is a story about an extraordinary object, person or event that is usually told as if it were 'true'. Despite this distinction, we instinctively recognise that the reality status of many legends is, to put it mildly, questionable. Many legends exist only in the oral tradition and have never been committed to writing. Some are based upon personal accounts of extraordinary experiences. Others have been created by either media stories or invented narratives that were intended to be fictional, humorous or ironic.

Linda Degh has described one of the functions of legends as being to express 'fundamental ideas concerning human existence'.[7] Legends make extraordinary claims that draw the audience into a debate over their truthfulness. Once stories and traditions appear in print as a ghost story connected with a stately home, for example, they become 'fixed' in literature. Once they become part of popular culture, legends feed back into the oral tradition, generating more beliefs and experiences. During this process the meaning and functions of legends adapt to fit modern preoccupations, such as the obsession with labelling stories as either 'true' or 'false'. For that reason, they have become the subject of long-running and often heated debates between believers and sceptics.

THE LEGEND OF JACK THE RIPPER

Archival evidence can be an invaluable tool for exploring the historical events that give rise to popular legends. However, the contents of archives, like any other types of historical evidence, have to be interpreted carefully. A good example are the stories that have grown up around the Jack the Ripper murders in Victorian London. The basic facts are that five prostitutes were murdered and horribly mutilated in the East End of the metropolis by a serial killer, or killers, between August and November 1888. The identity of the murderer has never been established and, after 150 years, it is unlikely the 'truth' will ever emerge. According to historian William Rubinstein, it is the very elusiveness of the solution to the Ripper mystery that makes it attractive. Reviewing the literary hunt for the Ripper in *History Today*, Professor Rubinstein wrote: 'Most believe that some rearrangement of the evidence combined with a lucky new find will enable them to crack the secret'.[8]

A small cottage industry, 'Ripperology', has grown up around the mystery, with its adherents dedicated to sifting through the written evidence in order to identify a 'prime suspect'. While the most plausible theory remains that the murderer was an ordinary working man living in or around Whitechapel, a series of extraordinary claims have been made for a more complex Masonic link to the murders, all wrapped up in a wider conspiracy involving the royal family and the British authorities.

When in the 1970s the Metropolitan Police began to open the Scotland Yard files on the killings to public scrutiny, letters sent to police by individuals claiming to be the murderer became available to scholars for the first time. These became the subject of intense scrutiny by those hoping to find a clue that would solve the mystery. One version of the Ripper conspiracy theory is based upon a story that a Victorian spiritualist, Robert James Lees, was plagued by psychic visions of the murderer (see p.98). Lees led police to a West End mansion where the Ripper was identified as none other than the Physician to the Queen, Sir William Gull. According to versions of this story, the deranged doctor was himself protecting a member of the royal family, the Duke of Clarence, who was being blackmailed by Mary Kelly, one of the Ripper's victims.[9]

This Ripper legend has such widespread popular appeal that it became a staple part of the narrative in films and TV dramas. The character of Lees was played by actor Donald Sutherland in the 1979 film *Murder by Decree*, which pitted Sherlock Holmes and Doctor Watson against a Masonic conspiracy. In 1988 the story reappeared in the form of an ITV miniseries, *Jack the Ripper*, starring Michael Caine and Ken Bones, who played Robert Lees. His character also appears in Alan Moore's graphic novel, *From Hell*, where he again plays the role of a psychic helping police identify the murderer.

Despite its popularity, this version of the Ripper legend appears to be, in the words of Professor Rubinstein, 'palpable nonsense from beginning to end, without a shred of evidence to support it'. Apart from a diary entry that confirms that Lees did visit the police to report his visions (see p.99), but was turned away, there is not a shred of contemporary evidence to link him with either the murders or the police investigation.

Journalist Melvin Harris traced the origins of the legend to a story published by a Chicago newspaper in 1895 that was exposed as a hoax. The story resurfaced again in 1931 when the *Daily Express* ran a series that claimed Lees was 'The Clairvoyant who tracked the Ripper'.[10] No further evidence emerged for a link between the Victorian clairvoyant and the Ripper murders until 1976, when Stephen Knight's best-selling book *Jack the Ripper: the Final Solution* was published. This contained fresh contemporary evidence for Lees' involvement, sourced from the Ripper letters themselves. One of the handwritten letters transcribed by Knight from the Scotland Yard archives, dated 25 July 1889, and signed 'Jack the Ripper', contained the line: 'Dear Boss, You have not caught me yet with all your cunning, with all your "Lees", with all your blue bottles.'[11] For believers in the Masonic/royal link to the murders, this was the clue that completed the circle. For the Ripper to have been aware of Lees' work assisting the police, news must have reached the public domain via a leak from Scotland Yard.

A serious flaw in this theory was none of the Victorian newspapers that covered the murders, often in a sensational fashion, contained any hint of a link between the police and John Lees. When the letter transcribed by Knight was carefully examined, the truth emerged. In 2001 Stewart Evans and Keith Skinner published facsimiles of more than 200 letters from the files of Scotland Yard in their book *Jack the Ripper: Letters from Hell*. All were carefully transcribed and their contents evaluated. Many were clearly hoaxes and details in others have been misinterpreted, often as a result of genuine mistakes, by journalists and historians. The letter linking John Lees with the Masonic/royal conspiracy is a good example. When Evans and Skinner scrutinised the word 'Lees' in the original document it became obvious this had been wrongly transcribed. The word was not 'Lees' but 'tecs', the contemporary slang for 'detectives'. Read in context, the sentence in which it appears makes much more sense.

Evans and Skinner point out just how important such small details, taken from original sources, can be when they are used as the building blocks for elaborate theories. 'In this case an error of transcription led to a repetition of the mistake in later books,' they wrote. 'The true content of the letter also underlines how important it is for writers and historians to access primary resources . . . only that way can they avoid perpetuating the mistakes of others.'[12]

SOURCES AND METHODOLOGY

Legends such as those surrounding the Ripper murders are constructed from two distinct categories of written resources: primary and secondary. Many of the significant primary resources for the stories in this book were located among records at The National Archives at Kew, in south-west London. The UK government archives are the official repository for millions of documents covering more than 1,000 years of British history. In addition to unique individual documents such as the Domesday Book, the archives also contain material relating to the work of government departments, the courts and armed forces as well as information about the life and work of the individuals that served in them.

Since the arrival of the Internet, many of the more important records at The National Archives have been digitised and can be read online or downloaded by anyone with access to a computer and a broadband connection. Extended access to original records has helped to reduce the reliance upon secondary sources of information. A common theme in the literature of anomalous phenomena is the desire to solve an intractable mystery by the presentation of sensational 'new' evidence on the part of an author or presenter, driven by a favourite theory or hypothesis, as was the case with the Jack the Ripper conspiracies. This can lead to reliance upon material that is not contemporary or that has been collected second- or third-hand. Such 'evidence' undoubtedly has a place in historical reconstructions but again it has to be carefully interpreted. Some re-writings of history based upon newly-discovered documentary evidence, for example the infamous Hitler Diaries or the *Alien Autopsy* film, have been revealed as pranks or hoaxes. Other legends have grown out of avowed fiction that has been recycled and presented, for a variety of reasons, as faithful retellings of 'the truth'.

Although massively influential, mainstream media accounts of modern legends such as the *Mary Celeste* and the Loch Ness Monster have themselves been overtaken by the spread of legends online. Social media is now the most important forum in which information about anomalous phenomena is shared and circulated. Stories that once took decades or even centuries to percolate through the collective imagination can now be spread around the world at the click of a mouse. The full implications of the changes are only just beginning to be felt and time will tell how they will affect the function and meaning of legends for future generations.

During the research for this book, I relied upon the excellent search engine developed by The National Archives that allows direct access to records held at Kew. Although my primary source material is the content of British archives, I have also drawn where necessary upon the holdings of other public archives including those available at The National Archives of Scotland in Edinburgh and the national archives of the United States and Australia. Other archives consulted include those at the Imperial War Museum and the Churchill Archives at the University of Cambridge. In addition, a number of private archives, including collections of correspondence and records kept by companies such as Lloyds of London, have provided supplementary information. Other more recent material, including recently declassified papers on the MoD's Remote Viewing study, have been obtained by requests made by the author and others under the Freedom of Information Act. These papers will, in due course, be opened at The National Archives.

THE MISSING FILES

The stories in this book are a representative sample selected by the author from a large collection of original records that have survived the process of review and destruction. Although the first Public Record Office opened in London in 1838, there was no statutory arrangement for the preservation of government papers until the first Public Records Office Acts of 1877 and 1898. As a result it was left to individuals in government departments to decide which documents might be of interest to future generations and those that should be destroyed. Before the arrival of modern record management systems staffed by trained archivists, decisions on how documents were preserved were made by civil servants on a case by case basis. This subjective process resulted in the loss of many papers that were not regarded as being of historical interest. Among these were naval records of sea serpent sightings and the original proceedings of the Vice-Admiralty Court of Inquiry at Gibraltar into the disappearance of the crew of the *Mary Celeste* (see Chapter 6).

The Public Record Act of 1958 introduced a more formal and accountable system of review for all documents generated by government departments. Even so, the Grigg Committee that reviewed the system suggested that around 90 per cent of papers could be destroyed at first review, usually five years after a file was closed. The remainder, which contained information deemed to be of historical importance, were retained for second review at the 30-year mark. Under this system, files on UFOs and other anomalies that fell outside the formal retention schedules which listed subjects deemed to be of interest, were marked for destruction. In the words of the American collector of anomalies, Charles Fort, these subjects were categorised as 'damned data'.

The introduction of the Freedom of Information Act in 2005 allowed researchers to request access to documents less than 30 years old. This obliged reviewers to improve their record-management systems and to introduce more transparent and inclusive retention schedules. FOI works because it allows members of the public to request direct access to records and encourages governments to release them in a proactive way. In the UK, one direct outcome of the use by journalists and other interested individuals of FOI has been the re-discovery of many documents once believed to have been 'lost'. In 2011 UFOs were added to the MoD's retention schedule for documents identified as having special historical interest.[13] Two years later, it was revealed that 4.7 million people across the world had visited the website created by The National Archives to read and download files on UFOs and other anomalous phenomena.[14]

This book has been designed to continue the process of opening these files to the wider public and facilitating scholarly discussion of their contents. The chapters that follow are arranged thematically and deal mainly, but not exclusively, with events and experiences that occurred during the last two centuries.

Chapter 1 investigates the stories surrounding the Angels of Mons and other legends of the Great War; Chapter 2 examines the rumours concerning mysterious death rays that preoccupied Western powers before the outbreak of the Second World War, while Chapter 3 deals with accounts of ghosts and poltergeists that have been documented in official records and court proceedings. Chapter 4 scrutinises government interest in ESP and other special powers that some individuals have claimed to have used to find underground water sources, locate murder victims or to remotely view far-off people and places. Chapters 5 and 6 deal with a variety of strange phenomena reported both in the sea and in the air that have found their way into government archives, from phantom helicopters to the great sea serpent of the Victorian era. The final chapter scrutinises official interest in the infamous Loch Ness Monster of Scotland and the 'Beast of Bodmin'.

CHAPTER 1

WAR AND THE WEIRD

THE ANGELS OF MONS

...the threatening sky, the restless symmetrical movements...the whole scene reminded me in some strange way of Milton's description of the legions of dark angels practising for giant warfare with St Michael on the plains of Hell...

Captain Arthur Osborn of the 4th Dragoon Guards, BEF, describing the retreat from Mons to Le Cateau, 24/25 August 1914[1]

The Angels of Mons was the most popular and inspiring legend to emerge from the First World War. At a time of great national crisis it inspired thousands to carry on the struggle against Germany, in the belief that God was fighting on the side of the British troops. The battle of Mons in Belgium was the first action British soldiers had fought on European soil since the Duke of Wellington's troops defeated Napoleon's forces at Waterloo in 1815. In August 1914 a small Allied force was all that stood in the way of a numerically superior German army and the tactical victory they achieved seemed, at the time, to be nothing short of miraculous. There are many versions but the basic story is that the British Expeditionary Force (BEF) were surrounded by the advancing Germans. At this moment of peril a shining figure (or figures) in white appeared, causing the enemy to hesitate or withdraw in confusion. This vision appeared to throw a protective curtain around the BEF, saving it from annihilation. Today the story sounds like a modern version of a medieval legend, but in the dark days of 1915 many thousands of people across the world accepted it as a fact. During the war it became unpatriotic, even treasonable, to doubt it. The Angels of Mons brought hope to the Home Front and comforted those who wanted to believe the British Army was fighting a just cause on behalf of God, king and country against a ruthless and godless enemy.

By the end of the war the angels had become the centre of a small cottage industry and an integral part of national folklore, to be invoked just a few decades later when the UK's armed forces faced new perils at Dunkirk and during the Battle of Britain. Sermons were preached about the angels, paintings were produced of scenes from the legend and poems written. Many books, pamphlets and tracts were published arguing for their existence. The legend was set to music and became the theme of one of the first silent movies produced in 1915 (now lost). Written and oral histories of the war testify to its popularity among ordinary soldiers and their families. The historian A.J.P. Taylor was so impressed by the 'evidence' that he felt confident referring to Mons, in his seminal 1963 history of the Great War, as the only battle where 'supernatural intervention was observed, more or less reliably, on the British side'.[2]

The battle of Mons was not the first time that supernatural intervention had occurred on the battlefield, and nor were the British especially singled out for supernatural assistance. This theme can be traced back thousands of years into the myths, legends and oral traditions of many peoples. Similar stories occur in the Greek myths and in the *Iliad*, the gods frequently intervene on behalf of favoured humans. Herodotus describes two occasions when supernatural beings appear in battle to pursue and slay enemy soldiers during the Persian Wars.[3] In the Old Testament there are stories that describe angels who protect the Israelites from their persecutors. From the Middle Ages English kings drew upon these traditions to encourage the idea that their troops, like the Israelites in the Old Testament, enjoyed divine protection. During the Crusades, medieval chronicles refer to a vision of St George who appeared to save the Christian army from the Saracens at the Battle of Antioch.[4] Three centuries later, soldiers fighting for King Henry V were encouraged by a vision of the saint who appeared in the sky, leading on the English and Welsh archers at the battle of Agincourt.

The medieval genre that depicted both St George and St Michael as warrior angels, protecting Christian soldiers, re-appeared as powerful images in Victorian art and culture. By the 20th century, belief that supernatural forces would intervene on the side of the British at times of peril or danger in battle was deeply implanted in the national psyche, so much so that it re-emerged in the middle of a ferocious modern war, fought on an industrial scale with machine guns, aircraft and poison gas. To understand the origins of the legend it is necessary to examine the primary evidence in the accounts of the battle of Mons and its immediate aftermath. Although there is no specific reference to the appearance of 'angels' in the records of the British Army in Flanders, the story is mentioned in diaries, memoirs and oral testimonies in the archives of the Imperial War Museum.[5]

THE BATTLE OF MONS

Britain declared war on Germany on 4 August 1914. Within days an 80,000-strong force composed of four infantry divisions and one cavalry division under the command of Sir John French crossed the English Channel to support the French 5th Army. The German High Command had anticipated the Allied strategy and under the Schlieffen Plan had already mobilised two million troops. German armies stormed through neutral Belgium, sweeping across the frontier. Their aim was to encircle and capture Paris, forcing France to surrender within a matter of weeks. The speed of the advance and the size of the German armies took the Allies by surprise and the French forces fell into a retreat. This left the small but well-trained BEF to make a stand outside the Belgian city of Mons against 14 German divisions. It should have been a massacre, but the small British force appeared to have survived the collision, 'as if by a miracle', or so it seemed back in the UK at the time.

The Battle of Mons took place on 23 August 1914. The British troops were outnumbered three to one along a 20-mile front along the Mons–Conde canal. For 24 hours they held onto their positions as the German army attempted to capture the canal bridges. As losses mounted on both sides, the BEF struggled on, mowing down the advancing lines of enemy troops with a hail of rifle fire. This proved to the decisive factor. The British troops were professional soldiers and many were veterans of the Boer War. They were trained to fire 15 rounds per minute on their Lee Enfield rifles and as their men fell, the German commanders came to believe they faced a wall of machine guns. In fact, there was only one machine gun per British regiment. In spite of their deadly firepower, however, the British troops were slowly overwhelmed and forced to pull back. By the end of the first day, 1,600 men were killed before the order came to retreat. Then followed the 'retreat from Mons' to the River Marne where the Kaiser's army was finally halted before it could reach Paris. The hungry and exhausted remnants of the BEF marched without a break for 200 miles through the French countryside with little food and no sleep. During the retreat the men endured oppressive August weather and fought rearguard battles with the advancing Germans.[6]

Dramatic and exaggerated accounts of the plight of the retreating British soldiers were sent back to England by the few journalists who were embedded within the army. Here they came to the attention of the War Office's Press Censor who held a stranglehold on the flow of real news about what was happening in France and Belgium. The most important was Arthur Moore's account of the fighting at Mons, published in *The Sunday Times* one week after the battle. Moore wrote of 'very great losses' suffered by the BEF, which he said was 'a retreating, broken army'. His dispatch from the front referred to waves of German troops so numerous 'that they could no more be stopped than the waves of the sea'.[7]

Normally the content of Moore's story would have been blocked by the Censor, but he quickly realised its potential propaganda value at home. It was approved for publication, with the addition of a final paragraph: 'England should realise, and should realise at once, that she must send reinforcements . . . we want men and we want them now.' Lord Kitchener used it to great effect in his famous appeal for 100,000 new recruits. Within eight weeks, three quarters of a million young men had enlisted and by the end of the year the number was approaching one million.

The fast-moving events on the Continent had two outcomes in England. First, starved of news about what had really happened at Mons, people on the Home Front were led to believe the BEF had escaped annihilation as a result of a miracle. Second, the news headlines inspired Arthur Machen, a Welsh writer of supernatural fiction, to draw upon the myths and legends of Britain – including the inspiring story of St George – to account for the British Army's escape from its clash with the Germans.

Fortuitously Machen had joined the staff of the *London Evening News* shortly before the war broke out. Inspired by news of desperate battles that were fought in the defence of Paris, Machen produced a series of short stories that were published alongside factual news from the front. These included first-person accounts from Allied soldiers. In his memoirs Machen recalled seeing the newspaper billboards announcing the retreat from Mons, and that morning took his thoughts to St Mark's Church in Marylebone Road. Here the story of *The Bowmen* occurred to him. In writing it, he drew upon Kipling's story *The Lost Legion* and his belief in the moral rightness of Britain's stand against Germany. Reflecting on the crisis in 1915, he felt the British army had divine support: '. . . I seemed to see a furnace of torment and death and agony and terror seven times heated, and in the midst of the burning was the British Army . . . So I saw our men with a shining about them . . .'[8]

THE BOWMEN

The Bowmen was published by the London *Evening News* on 29 September 1914. Whether by coincidence or design, this fell upon the feast day of St Michael and All Angels. Like St George, for believers the archangel Michael was a dragon-slayer and the protector of Christian troops against pagan hordes in battle. Both were depicted in artistic contexts as luminous beings sent from heaven to defend the righteous. As the Germans were depicted by Allied propaganda as godless devils who had murdered innocent civilians in Belgium, it seemed appropriate that warrior angels would be fighting alongside the Allied troops and defending civilisation against them.

The Bowmen was a work of fiction but it appeared alongside factual news from the Western Front. The narrative is told through the voice of an unnamed soldier, as this was the style that readers of the *Evening News* recognised. It opened in the middle of a battle that is not named, but a stand is about to be made by a single regiment of the BEF against the relentless advance of the German infantry. Blown apart by an artillery barrage and reduced to half their strength, the men have given up hope of survival as columns of grey-uniformed troops advance towards their trenches. Then, in the heat of battle, one of the soldiers remembers an image of St George he saw in a London restaurant before he crossed the English Channel. As the end draws near, in desperation he cries out a Latin invocation that was attached to the image: *Adsit Anglia Sanctus Georgius* ('St George, help the English!').

Immediately he feels 'something between a shudder and an electric shock pass through his body'. The deafening roar of battle dies away and is replaced by a multitude of voices shouting the name of the saint. Before the British lines, beyond the trenches, appears a long line of ghostly figures 'with a shining about them'. These are the ghosts of the bowmen who fought against the French for Henry V during the Hundred Years' War. Drawing their longbows, the medieval army lets loose a cloud of arrows that darken the sky above the battlefield. The stunned British troops then watch as the Kaiser's army crashes to the ground, scythed down by the deadly arrows . Machen concludes his inspiring story with a final paragraph that interrupts the narrative with a startling denouement:

> In fact, there were 10,000 dead German soldiers left before that salient of the English army . . . and in Germany, a country ruled by scientific principles, the Great General Staff decided that the contemptible English must have used turpinite [poison gas], as no wounds were discernible on the bodies . . . but the soldiers knew that St George had brought his Agincourt bowmen to help the English.[9]

In today's world, dominated by the Internet and 24-hour news, Machen's story sounds quaint and dated. At the outbreak of the First World War, newspapers were the only reliable source of news from the front and the latest information on battles and troop movements often took weeks to arrive in London. Starved of real news, Machen's story had an immediate impact among the wives and girlfriends, parents and children waiting for news of loved ones serving abroad. But what transformed a piece of ambivalent fiction into a legend that was believed by many across the British Empire?

As noted above, this type of short story was in fact typical of Machen's contributions to the *Evening News*. It was not even his first to draw upon the legend of St George as a figurehead in the struggle against the Germans. Machen was fond of mixing first-person narratives with supernatural fiction drawn from his imagination. This was a heady and volatile fuel and it directly stoked the flames of anxiety, fear and hope that blazed at home. The context of the tale, set in a real wartime situation and apparently told by an 'eyewitness', reinforced the impression of many readers that this was a story with solid foundations. Given the censorship of news, it seemed plausible to many people that only now, a month after the battle, was the 'truth' being told.

Within days of the appearance of *The Bowmen*, the editor of the *Evening News* began to receive letters from readers asking for the identity of the soldiers who witnessed the miracle on the battlefield. Requests also came from the editors of the spiritualist magazines that were popular during the Great War. They wanted to republish Machen's story, and asked for the authorities upon which he had drawn. Machen was taken aback by the reaction. In 1930 he recalled: 'I could not give my authorities . . . because I had none, the tale being pure invention.'[10]

BOWMEN INTO ANGELS

After a pause of six months, by St George's Day in 1915 Machen's tale of St George and his Agincourt bowmen re-appeared as a new rumour that told of angels appearing at Mons. Across the country, in churches of every denomination, clergymen began drawing upon the story as proof of the rightness of the Allied cause. Patriotic, uplifting sermons kept hope alive as the war became bogged down in the trenches of the Western Front. During this bleak time, new versions of Machen's story began to appear in newspapers and magazines. One of the earliest came from an anonymous 'military officer' who called at the offices of *Light: A Journal of Psychical, Occult and Mystical Research* in April with an account of a battlefield vision. He said:

> It took the form of a strange cloud interposed between the Germans and the British . . . Other wonders were heard or seen in connection with this cloud which, it seems, had the effect of protecting the British against the overwhelming hordes of the enemy.[11]

The editor of *Light* described the story as 'fascinating' and said 'we should like to hear more of it'. This account was swiftly followed by the story of a Catholic officer whose men had been saved from certain death at the hands of the Germans by a vision of St George on horseback leading an army of bowmen. And there were rumours about corpses of German soldiers found without a mark of violence on their bodies. Had they been killed by poison gas or invisible arrows?

Angels were not mentioned in these rumours initially. Mysterious clouds did figure, as did phantom bowmen and reinforcements that were seen by the Germans but were invisible to the British soldiers they protected. What these stories had in common was that they were all told by 'a friend of a friend' and none could be traced to a single named eyewitness. This was made apparent by the story told by a respectable young lady, Sarah Marrable. She was the daughter of a senior canon of the church and by all accounts a trustworthy and credible witness. Miss Marrable's account of her meeting two officers who had been present during the retreat from Mons was widely published in British and Commonwealth newspapers. Versions of Miss Marrable's story were repeated in letters sent home from the front. This account appears in the letters of Captain John Drury, who was killed in action in 1916, to his family in Derbyshire:

> [One] said he had seen them himself . . . while he and his company were retreating, they heard the German cavalry tearing after them. They saw a place where they thought a stand could be made . . . but before they could reach it the German cavalry were upon them. They turned round and faced the enemy, expecting nothing but instant death, when to their wonder they saw, between them and the enemy, a whole troop of angels. The German horses turned round terrified and regularly stampeded. The men tugged at their bridles, while the poor beasts tore away in every direction from our men . . . he swore they saw the Angels whom the poor horses saw plainly enough . . . this gave them time to reach safety.[12]

Miss Marrable's story was enthusiastically taken up as the proof that would confound those who found the story difficult to believe. Unfortunately, when journalists questioned her further it was found that she had been misquoted. She explained she actually heard the story second-hand and had no idea who the officers were. Miss Marrable was understandably annoyed that her name had been widely published as the first-hand source of the something that she admitted she knew nothing about. Nevertheless, in subsequent versions of the story, her denial was ignored and her name removed as the source.

Hoaxes added to the growing body of rumour. The most audacious of these was a story told by Private Robert Cleaver of the 1st Cheshire Regiment who declared: 'I personally was at Mons and saw the Vision of Angels with my own eyes. The men were in retreat and lying down behind tufts of grass for cover. Suddenly the vision came between them and the German cavalry like a FLASH. The cavalry horses rushed in all directions . . . allowing the British troops to escape.'[13]

Cleaver's evidence took the form of a legal affidavit sworn on oath before a Justice of the Peace at Chester. His testimony was seized upon by those who were promoting the angels story, until a check on regimental records revealed Cleaver's regiment did not leave for France until a month *after* the battle of Mons was fought.

With the perspective of hindsight it appears all these stories can be categorised as examples of 'urban legends' or FOAF-tales, an acronym that is based upon the way narrators attribute the source of the story to 'a friend of a friend'. Or as Machen put it at the time: 'Someone (unknown) has met a nurse (unnamed) who has talked to a soldier (anonymous) who has seen angels. But THAT is not evidence.'[14] Urban legends were first recognised as a distinct legend type by folklorists in the 1940s. Like traditional legends, they contain ancient and modern elements and are told as if they are true. Their subject matter can be sinister or uncanny but always reflects the fears and anxieties circulating within groups and wider society.

In his book *The Bowmen and other Legends of the War*, published at the height of the controversy in 1915, Arthur Machen mused on how his story about phantom bowmen evolved into the legend of the Angels of Mons. He believed the link between the two versions was his use of the word 'shining'. He concluded: '. . . in the popular view shining and benevolent supernatural beings are angels and nothing else . . . and so, I believe, the Bowmen of my story have become the Angels of Mons.'

As the legend evolved and circulated on the Home Front, subtle changes occurred in the narrative structure. In the early versions, the vision appears when the soldier invokes St George to help the English. In the later versions the angels appear without an invocation, in a flash. They throw a protective curtain around the British soldiers, whilst the Germans are startled, as if they have come upon an invisible barrier.

FIGURE 1.2 THE COVER OF ARTHUR MACHEN'S BOOK, *THE BOWMEN AND OTHER LEGENDS OF THE WAR,* PUBLISHED IN 1915 AT THE HEIGHT OF THE CONTROVERSY SURROUNDING THE ANGELS OF MONS (COURTESY OF THE FORTEAN PICTURE LIBRARY).

For the remainder of his life Arthur Machen continued to believe he was the author, not the historian, of the Angels of Mons. For a time during the Great War, no one would believe him. This was indeed a cruel irony given the obsession with the supernatural that permeates much of Machen's writing and his hatred of the materialism that he believed had brought the world to the brink of disaster. Initially he appears to have encouraged belief in the story out of a sense of patriotism, but found it took on a life of its own. By the summer of 1915, when the *Evening News* reissued his story in book form he wrote in the foreword: 'It began to dawn on me that if I had failed in the art of letters, I had succeeded, unwittingly, in the art of deceit . . . the snowball of rumour that was then set rolling has been rolling ever since, growing bigger and bigger, till it is now swollen to monstrous size.'[15]

ON THE SIDE OF THE ANGELS

One outcome of this controversy was the portrayal of Arthur Machen as the arch debunker by those who believed in 'divine intervention' during the war. From the summer of 1915 a series of books and pamphlets appeared arguing the case for the angels as fact. Chief among them was a book by Harold Begbie, *On the Side of the Angels*, which included the subtitle 'An Answer to Arthur Machen'.[16] In his book Begbie claimed there was independent evidence that soldiers experienced supernatural visions at the front weeks before Machen's story was published by the *Evening News*. Begbie felt the Angels of Mons was good for morale and should be defended. He accused Machen of exploiting a true and beautiful legend for his own egotistical and commercial ends. One of his more bizarre theories was that Machen's inspiration for *The Bowmen* could be explained by a telepathic vision from the brain of a dying soldier on the battlefield at Mons.

Begbie's book relied heavily upon the evidence of Phyllis Campbell, who had joined the nurses caring for wounded and dying soldiers in field hospitals in northern France at the outbreak of war. Her writings show that she was an occultist driven by an intense hatred of the Germans.[17] She mixed her angel stories with first-hand accounts of atrocities in which women and babies were bayoneted and mutilated by the enemy. Nurse Campbell also claimed dying soldiers had confided with her how they had seen winged angels and giant figures on horseback leading them against the enemy. The English soldiers identified the figures as St George, whereas the French had seen Joan of Arc.

Campbell had connections in the British establishment and friends in the Russian royal family. They sent similar stories of angels inspiring the Czar's forces fighting on the Eastern Front. But she could not provide a single name of a soldier as evidence of her claims. Machen used his position as a lead writer for the *Evening News* to challenge Begbie and

Campbell. He demanded they produce the names of the soldiers who had made these statements before they could be accepted as evidence. Unable to answer, Campbell claimed there was a British government cover-up to hide the truth. The soldiers who had seen the angels could not be named, she claimed, because of a conspiracy by the War Office to hide the facts from the public. Those who had witnessed wonders on the battlefield were forbidden by the Army from discussing what they had seen. In her book *Back of the Front*, published in 1915, Campbell promised that 'the evidence exists . . . and when the war is over and the embargo of silence is removed, Mr Machen will be overwhelmed with corroborative evidence.'[18]

Despite the conspicuous lack of first-hand testimony from eyewitnesses, popular belief that angels had appeared at Mons and saved the British Army from defeat continues to the present day.[19] The longevity and persistence of the legend can partly be explained by the influence of what appears to be an official endorsement in the memoirs of a high-ranking officer who served with the Army. A letter written on 5 September 1914 by Brigadier General John Charteris to his wife Noel refers to: '. . . the story of the "Angels of Mons" going strong through the 2nd Corps, of how the angel of the Lord on the traditional white horse, and clad all in white with flaming sword, faced the advancing Germans at Mons and forbade their further progress. Men's nerves and imagination play weird pranks in these strenuous times.'[20]

If genuine, this letter would be the earliest contemporary written evidence for the Angels of Mons. Not only does it predate publication of *The Bowmen* by 14 days, its existence appears to destroy Machen's claim that his piece of fiction was the single and only source for the legend.[21] During my research I set out to establish if this – and a second diary entry dated 11 February 1915 that mentions the angels – were genuinely contemporaneous. I was suspicious because Charteris' expertise lay in the shadowy fields of counter-intelligence and propaganda, and his testimony is regarded as unreliable by historians of the war. Transcripts of the letters and diary entries made by Charteris appear in *At GHQ*, a book published in 1931 that was assembled from an enormous collection of his correspondence from the war. Charteris was a compulsive writer, and produced more than 1,200 separate letters describing his experiences during the campaign, sometimes several in one day. These were gathered by his wife after the war and edited into the form in which they appear in the book.

Did Charteris really have advance knowledge of stories circulating amongst the BEF during the retreat from Mons, as his book implies? Or did he recycle rumours that appeared months later? To answer these questions I examined microfilm copies of Charteris' papers, including letters, postcards and telegrams to his wife that were donated to the Liddell Hart Centre for Military Archives at King's College, London. The collection for September 1914 does not contain any reference to the Angels of Mons or anything that resembles the diary entry in the form published in 1931.[22] While it is impossible to prove beyond doubt, it seems likely this was based upon rumours heard later in the war. Charteris admits in his book that he did not keep a formal diary at the outbreak of the conflict but kept notes of his views from day to day. He relied upon these notes when writing his memoirs and 'where records were incomplete, I have amplified them by my recollections'.[23]

In 1914, Charteris travelled to France with the intelligence branch of the British Expeditionary Force. He soon became a trusted and close friend of General Douglas Haig, who promoted him to Chief Intelligence Officer at British General Headquarters (GHQ). In the early weeks of the war, he watched as the British Army retreated from Mons to the Marne and wrote detailed and eloquent accounts of the battles and their aftermath. The absence of accurate news encouraged those left behind in England to believe many false stories and rumours, and these were spread back to the soldiers overseas in letters from loved ones. The War Office Censor took action to block those that were felt to be harmful, but others were quietly encouraged by the War Office's nascent intelligence branch for use in the propaganda war against Germany.

Military historian James Hayward has shown how certain useful rumours were spread to confuse the German High Command during this period. In August and September 1914, a story that thousands of Russian troops 'with snow on their boots' had secretly travelled through England was overheard by the spy Carl Lody. British intelligence allowed him to pass this information to his handlers in the German High Command. Subsequently two divisions were detached from the Battle of the Marne to protect the Belgian coast against the phantom Cossacks. This was a decision that some believe altered the course of the war at a crucial moment.[24] Ironically, General Charteris wrote in his memoirs of having heard the story of the Russians from a colleague on the Western Front but found it impossible to persuade his informant of its falsity.

The extent of the Intelligence Corps' role in spreading rumours about Russians and angels will probably never be known. Even in the midst of a ferocious war, such a tactic would hardly tax the resources of a banana republic, let alone those of the British Army. It was, after all, the visit by a mysterious and unnamed 'military officer' to a spiritualist magazine that had rekindled press interest in The Bowmen and the Angels of Mons after a hiatus of six months. St George's day in 1915 coincided with the bad news from the front. With the failure of Allied forces to break the German army at the first battle of Ypres and the first use of poison gas all adding to the air of gloom and despair, what better way of raising the nation's spirits than a story claiming angels had intervened to save British soldiers?

THE FIRST 'URBAN LEGEND'?

As the Imperial War Museum concluded in their account of the Angels of Mons: '. . . to pursue the supporting stories to source is to make a journey into a fog'.[25] The Society for Psychical Research conducted a detailed investigation of the rumours in 1915. The Society's officers sent out questionnaires to people quoted in the press. In her report on the investigation held in the SPR archives at the University of Cambridge, psychologist Helen Salter admits 'the whole history of the case throws an interesting light on the value of human testimony and the growth of rumour'. She realised this was important because the SPR relied upon human testimony for its investigations. Summing up, she wrote:

> In the main . . . the result of our enquiry is negative, at least as regards the question of whether any apparitions were seen on the battlefield, either at Mons or elsewhere. Of first-hand testimony we have received none at all, and of testimony at second-hand none that would justify us in assuming the occurrence of any supernormal phenomenon.[26]

During the past century many dedicated researchers have tried and failed to pursue the accounts to source and find a single named soldier who claimed to have fought at Mons and seen the angels. As Salter realised, there appears to be no first-hand account of the Angels of Mons that can be traced back to 1914. For his part, Arthur Machen found himself in a difficult position. He was a mystical and deeply religious man and yet he found himself obliged to debunk the claims of supernatural intervention at Mons that he realised had no basis in reality. In his later years, Machen was less patient or polite with those who asked about the origins of the story than he had been during the war. Before his death he wrote one final article about the legend where he said: 'It was strong evidence, as I say. Or rather it would have been strong evidence but for one circumstance – there was not one word of truth in it. Or, in the stronger phrase of Wemmick, these stories were lies: Every one of 'em lies, sir!'[27]

Nevertheless, as the war progressed Allied soldiers came to believe that the spirits of the dead continued to fight alongside them as 'angel helpers' at times of great peril. Occultists such as Ralph Shirley, author of *Angel Warriors at Mons: An Authentic Record* (1915) remained convinced of divine intervention not only at Mons but also at the second battle of Ypres as well as at Loos and elsewhere. But as the Imperial War Museum account points out, 'it may have seemed strange to some that, with all this angelic aid, our General Staff did not make a better go of things!'

The function these stories played in comforting soldiers and their families back in the UK became apparent to Vera Brittain as she nursed wounded troops at a field hospital in Etaples in 1917. She published verbatim accounts of her conversations with some of them in *Testament of Youth* (1933). Brittain was present at the hospital in the aftermath of the slaughter on the Somme. On the first day, 1 July 1916, 20,000 British troops were killed and the carnage dragged on for five months, claiming hundreds of thousands more lives. During her service, Brittain frequently overheard soldiers talking about encounters with dead pals who acted as guardian angels for the living. After collecting several similar accounts, curiosity led her to ask a group of wounded soldiers if these stories were true. She wrote: '. . . there was an awed silence in the ward, and I turned from the dressing I was doing to ask rather breathlessly: "Do you really mean that in the middle of the battle you met those men again who you'd thought were dead?" The reply left her stunned: "Aye, Sister, they're dead right enough. They're our mates as was knocked out on the Somme in '16. And it's our belief they're fightin' with us still."'[28]

THE BATTALION THAT VANISHED

. . . as the Sandringham Company advanced onto the battlefield, a strange mist was seen to descend and engulf them – almost as though God was wrapping them up and taking them from the terror that awaited . . .

BBC trailer for the TV drama *All The King's Men* (1999)[29]

Another legend that emerged from the First World War – and which rivals the Angels of Mons in its persistence – tells of an entire battalion of British troops swallowed by a 'mysterious cloud' during one of the fiercest battles at Gallipoli, in present-day Turkey. In the *Book of Kings*, the prophet Elijah is said to have been taken up to heaven from a hilltop in a whirlwind accompanied by a chariot of horses and flames. Stories about mysterious clouds and mist that hid British troops at times of peril were common during the war, and these were often associated with divine intervention.

Today angels have been replaced by extra-terrestrials as the supernatural agency responsible for the 'battalion that vanished'. The link between the 'vanished' battalion and alien abductions did not arise during the Great War itself but half a century later, in 1965, on the 50th anniversary of the Allied assault on the Gallipoli peninsula. During a reunion of ANZAC veterans, three former sappers from the New Zealand Expeditionary Force spoke of a 'strange incident' that occurred during the most severe fighting at Suvla Bay in 1915. The story was overheard by a UFOlogist, Gordon Tuckey, who felt it should be recorded for posterity.

FIGURE 1.3 'THE CROSS IN THE HEAVENS OVER THE TRENCHES', BY A.C. MICHAEL, INSPIRED BY A STORY THAT SPREAD THROUGH THE BRITISH TRENCHES PRIOR TO THE BATTLE OF THE SOMME IN JULY 1916. A LETTER SENT HOME BY A SERGEANT REPORTED 'A MOST BEAUTIFUL WHITE CROSS IN THE SKY' BEFORE THE BATTLE THAT 'SAILED ALONG BEFORE IT TOUCHED THE MOON'. THIS VISION – ONE OF MANY REPORTED DURING THE WAR – WAS GREETED WITH 'ABSOLUTE SILENCE ON BOTH SIDES . . . NOT A SHOT WAS FIRED'. (COURTESY OF THE MARY EVANS PICTURE LIBRARY).

Afterwards Sapper Frederick Reichart produced a signed statement, witnessed by two fellow veterans. This described how, on a morning they identified as 28 August 1915, they saw six or eight odd-looking 'loaf of bread' shaped clouds, light grey in colour and all exactly alike, hovering in the sky above a position known as 'Hill 60' that was held by the Turks. At the time the men were in trenches on Rhododendron Spur, 300ft above the fighting around Hill 60. As they watched, the peculiar looking clouds remained perfectly still and never changed position despite the presence of a prevailing wind. Beneath them was another cloud, more dense and solid-looking. Roughly 800ft long and 200ft high, it seemed to straddle a dry creek bed or sunken road. From a distance of around 2,500 yards, the men then saw what appeared to be an entire British regiment marching up the sunken road that led through the valley directly towards Hill 60. The statement continued:

> . . . when they arrived at this cloud, they marched straight into it, with no hesitation, but no one ever came out to deploy and fight at Hill 60. About an hour later,

after the last of the file had disappeared into it, this cloud very unobtrusively lifted off the ground and, like any fog or cloud would, rose slowly until it joined the other similar clouds . . . On viewing them again, they all looked alike 'as peas in a pod'. All this time, the group of clouds had been hovering in the same place, but as soon as the singular 'ground' cloud had risen to their level, they all moved away northwards . . . In a matter of about three-quarters of an hour they had all disappeared from view.[30]

The account identified the missing regiment as 'the First Fourth Norfolks' and added:

> . . . on Turkey surrendering in 1918, the first thing Britain demanded of Turkey was the return of this regiment. Turkey replied that she had neither captured this Regiment, nor made contact with it, and did not know that it existed. A British Regiment in 1914–18 consisted of any number between 400 and 800 men. Those who observed this incident vouch for the fact that Turkey never captured that Regiment, nor made contact with it.[31]

The 'First Fourth' referred to by Reichart was actually a battalion that formed part of the Norfolk regiment and consisted of approximately 266 officers and men. This was just the first error to creep into the story. Reichart's statement appeared first in a small-circulation UFO magazine called *Spaceview*, published in New Zealand, in 1965, but the news quickly captured the imagination of American researchers who were collecting examples of humans abducted by UFOs. From 1966 onwards a more sensational version of the story began to appear in the UFO literature,that gave credence to the idea of a 'paranormal' explanation for the mystery. In some of these accounts, the sappers' statement was corroborated by an extract from an 'official history' of the Gallipoli campaign that said the Norfolks were swallowed up by an 'unseasonable fog'. The fog reflected the sun's rays in such a way that artillery observers were dazzled by it and were unable to fire in support of the infantry.[32]

What was it that the three New Zealand soldiers saw that fateful day in 1915? Did UFOs or mysterious aerial phenomena really play a part in the disappearance of a battalion of British soldiers at Gallipoli? And if that was the case, which battalion was it and what really happened to them? Despite the confusion that has surrounded these events for decades, it is possible to use primary documents, including the war diaries of the soldiers involved in the campaign, to reconstruct the true sequence of events that gave birth to the legend of the vanishing battalion.

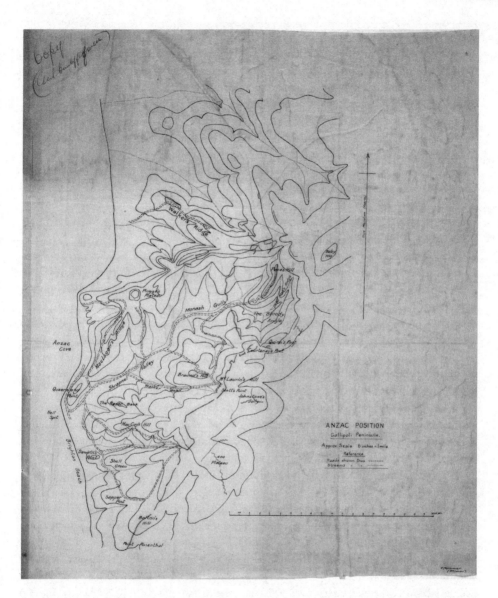

FIGURE 1.4 MAP SHOWING POSITIONS OF ANZAC TROOPS DEPLOYED ON THE GALLIPOLI
PENINSULA, IN PRESENT DAY TURKEY, FOLLOWING THE ATTACK ON THE DARDENELLES
IN AUGUST 1915. DURING ONE OF THE ALLIED ADVANCES NEW ZEALAND SAPPERS ON
RHODODENDRON SPUR (TOP CENTRE) REPORTED SEEING A BRITISH REGIMENT, OR IN
SOME VERSIONS A BATTALION, DISAPPEAR INTO A 'MYSTERIOUS CLOUD' (CROWN
COPYRIGHT, THE NATIONAL ARCHIVES: WO 153/1050)

THE GALLIPOLI CAMPAIGN

To place the ANZAC veterans' story in context, it is necessary to understand the historical background to the Gallipoli campaign. This was a second front opened by the Allies in 1915 in an attempt to break the deadlock in Western Europe. The campaign was launched to gain control of the Dardanelles, a narrow 40-mile channel connecting the Mediterranean with the Black Sea. The Gallipoli Peninsula, through which the channel ran, was controlled by the Ottoman Empire, which was then allied to Germany. The Allied plan was to relieve pressure on Russia by landing troops on the peninsula to capture Constantinople and then force the Germans' Turkish allies out of the war. The landings, in April, were preceded by a naval bombardment and at first it seemed the plan might achieve some success. Hesitation and poor judgement on the part of the Allied command, combined with stubborn resistance by the Turks, led to stalemate and appalling loss of life. The Allies eventually withdrew from the peninsula in December.[33]

Among the thousands of British infantry sent to Gallipoli were two battalions of the Royal Norfolk Regiment, the 1/4th and the 1/5th (Territorial), which formed part of the 163rd Infantry Brigade. The 1/4th were wrongly referred to as a regiment in Reichart's statement. The regimental diaries record how the Norfolks left Liverpool aboard the SS *Aquitainia* on 29 July 1915 and arrived at Suvla Bay in Gallipoli on 10 August. Two days later, the 1/5th battalion were ordered to clear Turkish positions on the Anafarta Plain prior to the Allied advance. Their sister battalion, the 1/4th, waited in reserve and were not involved in the events that followed. The outcome was typical of the bad planning and general confusion that characterised the Allied campaign.

The British attack was made in broad daylight, in the heat of the afternoon and without adequate maps; the well-prepared defenders, on the other hand, were firmly dug in along a ridge of hills overlooking the bay. The Norfolk battalion was made up of 16 officers and 250 men and was led by a veteran of the campaign in the Sudan, Colonel Sir Horace Proctor-Beauchamp. As they left their positions, the Norfolks were joined by soldiers from battalions of the Suffolk and Hampshire regiments.

During the advance the Norfolks turned slightly to the right, opening up a gap between them and the other British troops from whom they became separated. As the Norfolks overtook the Turkish positions on the Kavak Tepe ridge, they were surrounded by the enemy and picked off by snipers. Col. Proctor-Beauchamp was last seen leading his men into burning scrubland from which they never emerged. As night fell a few survivors, wounded and exhausted, began to filter back to the British positions at Suvla Bay. The war diary of the 1/5th Norfolks simply refers to 'a frontal attack on strong Turkish positions' during which men from the battalion, along with soldiers from the Suffolk and Hampshire regiments, 'met strong opposition and suffered heavily' losing 22 officers and 350 men.[34]

In 2002, historians Tim Travers and Birten Çelik examined British and Turkish military archives in search of the truth about the fate of the men. They were surprised to find the British official history of the campaign 'actually reinforced the myth of the disappearance of the 1/5th Norfolk Battalion'.[35] In his memoirs, Brigadier General Cecil Aspinall-Oglander refers to a portion of the battalion that pressed forward, '[but] was not supported, and was never seen again'. [36] This extraordinary explanation was first introduced into the public domain early in 1916 after the Allies abandoned the campaign. In his 'final dispatch from the Dardanelles' the Commander in Chief of the Mediterranean Expeditionary Forces, Sir Ian Hamilton, accounted for the loss of the 1/5th Norfolks in the following way:

> . . . in the course of the fight . . . there happened a very mysterious thing . . . against the yielding forces of the enemy Colonel Sir H. Beauchamp, a bold, self-confident officer, eagerly pressed forward, followed by the best part of the battalion. The fighting grew hotter . . . [and] at this stage many men were wounded or grew exhausted . . . but the Colonel, with 16 officers and 250 men kept pushing forward, driving the enemy before him . . . nothing more was seen or heard of any of them. They charged into the forest and were lost to sight or sound. Not one of them ever came back . . .[37]

Hamilton's account was based upon reports from British officers who had watched from a distance as the disaster unfolded. One of these was a brigade major, Lt Col. Charles Villiers-Stuart, who watched the assault made by the Norfolk battalion through field glasses. He said the men appeared to advance without support towards Turkish positions on Kvak Tepe. Before he could do anything to help them, 'immediately the Turks debouched from their cover and attacked our men in the flank and rear. It was soon too dark to see the issue of the fight, but at the time I was afraid they would be destroyed'.[38]

After the war, yet another explanation emerged in letters sent to the official historian of the campaign, a British officer. He claimed the soldiers from 1/5th Norfolks who had been captured by the Turks were all shot in the head. This claim later resurfaced as an established 'fact' in a BBC dramatisation of the abortive attack by men from the Sandringham company that formed part of the 1/5th Norfolk battalion, *All the King's Men* (shown on television on Remembrance Sunday, 1999). Travers and Çelik believe this story grew out of work carried out in 1919 by the Commonwealth War Graves Commission on the battlefields at Gallipoli. Officials from the commission discovered a cap badge belonging to a soldier of the Norfolk regiment hidden in sand 800 yards behind the Turkish lines at Suvla Bay. Further investigations found a mass grave containing 180 bodies from the 163rd Infantry Brigade, from which the remains of 122 were identified as members of the missing battalion. They included those of their commanding officer, Col. Proctor-Beauchamp, who was identified by the distinctive shoulder flashes on his uniform. Of the men reported as missing, 144 remained unaccounted for, but a number of these had been captured after they were wounded during the assault.

The evidence collected by Travers and Çelik suggested that British soldiers who did not fall into enemy hands after they were injured were bayonetted during hand-to-hand fighting with the Turkish defenders. Summarising the facts, they conclude the 1/5th Norfolks did not disappear, but were 'simply overwhelmed in bayonet fighting by the Turkish counterattack, after a praiseworthy but poorly organized and overly ambitious advance'.[39]

Their investigation of the archive sources found no evidence to support what they called 'the mythic explanation' of the battalion's fate that included the idea of their capture by aliens and their death in a wartime atrocity. So how did these explanations become so widely believed?

MYSTERIOUS CLOUDS AND PEARLY MISTS

From the 50th anniversary of the battle, when the New Zealand soldiers first spoke publicly about the events they had witnessed, the legend of the battalion that vanished has refused to go away. Soon after it appeared in the UFO literature, the Ministry of Defence and the Imperial War Museum began to receive letters from members of the public asking if the story about the soldiers kidnapped by extra-terrestrials was true.[40]

Responding to inquiries about 'the vanishing Norfolks' in 1977, the Imperial War Museum produced a factsheet setting out what was known about the mystery. This confirmed that the 'First Fourth Norfolk regiment' identified by the New Zealand sappers *was* a battalion of the Norfolk Regiment. Their movements were accounted for by the war diaries and although they took part in several actions at Gallipoli '. . . they did not vanish and all the men remained in active service for the remainder of the war!'.[41] If any British battalion could truly be described as having 'vanished', it was the 1/4th's sister battalion, the 1/5th. These were the men referred to by Sir Ian Hamilton in his dispatch as having charged into a 'forest' never to be seen again. But why would the ANZAC soldiers have made such a fundamental error?

The answer is that 50 years separated the events of 1915 and the reunion of veterans where Reichart first told his story. It refers not to 12 August 1915 but 28 August, but by his own account, Reichart did not keep a diary and accepted even this date was a guess because: 'I lost count of time during that week of severe fighting.'[42] A further clue emerged from the testimony of another New Zealand soldier, Gerald Wilde. He also witnessed the attack on Hill 60 but did not see any mysterious clouds. In a letter published by *Spaceview* he said that after the fighting died down, there was a persistent rumour that a completely different group of soldiers from the Sherwood Foresters 'completely disappeared in a cloud of smoke and apparently no trace of them was ever found'.[43]

In his book *All the King's Men* (1992), Nigel McCrery points out that the sappers were four and a half miles from the action on 12 August and 'even with binoculars their power of observation must have been phenomenal if they could see through the dust and conditions of a major battle, and identify the units taking part in the attack'.[44] McCrery believes the ANZAC soldiers did not invent the story but were describing something uncanny that happened in a different action during the Gallipoli campaign. This began on 21 August 1915 when 3,000 ANZAC soldiers were involved in an assault against Turkish positions on Hill 60.

The involvement of Hill 60 sits more comfortably with Reichart's statement as the sappers had a clear view of this objective from their positions. The battle to capture the hill from the Turks continued for a week and again ended in confusion and massive loss of life. It coincided with another assault by the Sherwood Rangers Yeomanry, led by Sir John Milbanke VC, on nearby Scimatar Hill, a small spur that stuck out into Suvla Bay. The British troops advanced into a thick 'pearly mist' and could not see their objective, whilst the Turks could see the advancing Allies plainly. Milbanke became one of the many casualties in the slaughter that followed. Was this 'pearly mist' connected with the oddly shaped clouds seen by the ANZAC sappers from their trenches overlooking the hills?

In his account of this assault, Sir Ian Hamilton says that 'by some freak of nature Suvla Bay and plain were wrapped in a strange mist' on the afternoon of 21 August. 'This was sheer bad luck as we had reckoned on the enemy's gunners being blinded by the declining sun and upon the Turks' trenches being shown up by the evening sun with singular clearness,' he wrote. 'Actually, we could hardly see the enemy lines this afternoon, whereas to the westward targets stood out in strong relief against the luminous light.'[45] The reference to 'a strange mist' is too redolent of the incident witnessed by the ANZAC soldiers for them to be unconnected. Author Paul Begg noticed the significance of the fact that the official accounts of the loss of the 1/5th Norfolks and the story of the 'freak of nature' appear on facing pages of the report by the Dardenelles Commission.[46] Even more significant is the fact that the final version of the report was declassified in 1965, the same year that Sapper Reichart told his story.

The cumulative evidence suggests the ANZAC sappers conflated an incident they witnessed during the attack on Hill 60 with rumours they overheard concerning the disappearance of a British regiment. The troops they saw marching into the freak mist were probably the Sherwood Rangers mentioned by Gerald Wilde. In the fog of war they were confused with a battalion of the Norfolk regiment who had been wiped out in a futile attack a week earlier. As the years passed memories of the two events became combined and as Nigel McCrery noted: '. . . once the story had been told it undoubtedly became embellished [and] with each re-telling . . . over fifty years [it] became totally confused.'[47]

In the aftermath of the First World War, the disappearance of a whole battalion in one assault was dwarfed by the total losses of nine million soldiers from both sides. The campaign to capture the Dardanelles lasted more than eight months and cost the lives of 34,000 British and Commonwealth troops. To place this loss in context, the Commonwealth War Graves Commission's memorials contain the names of 771,982 dead of the two world wars who have no known grave. Of those who died in the Gallipoli campaign, a large percentage have no known grave and as Paul Begg commented in his account of the legend: '. . . when faced with such staggering numbers, is the fate of 144 missing in one of the worst theatres of war imaginable really all that mysterious?'[48]

The vanishing battalion was just one of a collection of rumours and legends that have persisted in the mythology of the Great War to the present day. The reason why the story has endured can be only partly explained by its more recent incorporation into the UFO literature. Long before the reunion of the veterans set that story running, the idea that the men had disappeared 'without trace' had been seeded by the generals who were responsible for the failure to capture the Gallipoli peninsula. Many of the missing men were royal servants recruited from the Sandringham estate of King George V. The king made inquiries about their fate on behalf of relatives from his company. Among them was Captain Frank Beck, who led a company of territorials into the battle never to return. The fate of Beck and his company played a key role in *All the King's Men*, mentioned above, with David Jason playing the role of Captain Beck.[49] The film depicted the captain and his men surrendering to the Turks only to be disarmed and then shot in the back of the head. Philip Dutton described the drama as 'from the historical perspective near 100% tripe . . . [but] nonetheless a great many people who watched the programme went to work the following morning feeling that they knew what had happened to the Norfolks'.[50]

Sir Ian Hamilton, the Allied commander responsible for the assault on the Gallipoli peninsula, clearly had a personal interest in making the disappearance of the battalion appear more mysterious than it actually was. As we have seen, in his 'final dispatch' from the Dardanelles he implied the disappearance of the battalion was inexplicable. In September the king had written to him asking for information about the fate of Captain Beck and his Sandringham company. In his response Hamilton explained the loss in less mysterious terms: '. . . the Battn and their leader were filled with ardour and dash and on coming into contact with the enemy pressed ahead of the rest of Brigade into close broken country where [their commander] entirely lost touch with them.'[51]

Shortly after the disaster at Gallipoli, Hamilton was relieved of his command and was never offered another. In the years that followed, the mystery he helped to set running became transformed into a fully-fledged legend of the 'war to end all wars'.

THE PHANTOM
MENACE

The Secret Service Bureau was created as a single organisation in 1909 to counter fears that Germany was planning an invasion of England via an elaborate (and largely imaginary) network of spies. In March of that year the Committee for Imperial Defence warned that 'an extensive system of German espionage exists in this country, and we have no organisation for keeping in touch with that espionage and for accurately determining its extent and objectives'.[1]

Early in its history, the bureau was split into two sections dealing with home and foreign espionage. By the outbreak of the First World War, Captain (later Major General) Vernon Kell became head of the agency responsible for counter-espionage on the British mainland. In 1914 the military intelligence branch that later became MI5 had a small office in London and a staff of just 14. By the Armistice, this had grown to 844. During the First World War, Kell's force, working closely with the Metropolitan Police's Special Branch, acted swiftly to break up a real network of spies who were working for German Naval Intelligence. His agents were also drawn into investigations of wilder stories including claims the enemy had established a secret base for aircraft in Scotland.[2]

On the outbreak of the Second World War, the security service was once again called upon to deal with a fresh 'spy scare' against a background of continuous air raids and the threat of invasion. From 1939 its agents investigated thousands of fresh reports of suspected German espionage in the UK. As the Battle of Britain raged in the skies above, fears grew that a 'fifth column' of Nazi sympathisers were busily at work in the countryside below. (The phrase is said to have been coined during the Spanish Civil War when General Emilio Mola claimed to have four columns of troops waiting to capture Madrid for the fascists and a fifth already inside the city waiting to rise up in support of General Franco.[3])

Earlier in the war many people, including some MI5 officers, felt this was a real possibility as it was common knowledge that enemy agents had played an important role in the invasions of France and Belgium. By far the most common 'fifth column' activity investigated by MI5 was 'light signalling' by enemy agents to German aircraft. A report on this phenomenon compiled by B Division, who were responsible for 'investigations and inquiries', revealed that a special unit was set up to investigate hundreds of reports describing mysterious lights in the sky. It said: 'The files containing them stand five feet high, and during 1940 and 1941 there were five officers dealing with lights cases alone, two of them in the office and three in different parts of the country making investigations on the spot.'[4] Typical observations included lights flashed from the ground to guide aircraft, red Verey lights allegedly used to signal to paratroopers and patterns of lights marking a secret landing strip.

In 1939 MI5 officer Guy Liddell was promoted to the director of B Division. During his time as head of counter-espionage, he developed an overview of the whole 'fifth column' syndrome. Liddell kept a daily diary and on 28 November of that year he noted 'large numbers of reports . . . that lights in the sky have been seen flashing at various parts of the country'.[5] His agents worked closely with police Special Branch and the Air Ministry to check all these reports against known Luftwaffe air raids. In December the Observer Corps were brought in to plot sightings on a map and all reports were listed in a book and indexed using a punch-card system. Agents were sent to parts of the country, including the Thames Estuary and East Anglia, where they were most common. Here the MI5 report says 'they would live in the neighbourhood, smell out local gossip in the pubs, co-operate with the police in getting a line on any individuals suspected, and very often sit on church towers through the night keeping watch'.[6]

Liddell's team quickly began to realise that even the most 'credible witnesses' were poor observers. Their report says crucial details required by MI5 such as colours, rough compass bearings and time were often missing and, when investigated on the spot 'very often a flashing light 30 miles away would be reported a suspicious flashing light five miles away'. Agents carefully followed up each report and it sometimes took weeks of painstaking work before solutions were found. One example was a 'strange waving light' that was visible for miles even out at sea. As police approached, it disappeared. Eventually it was traced to an old shepherd who, crossing the moor at night, would sling his lantern on the end of a pole and carry it swinging across his shoulder. Similar 'mysterious lights' had been investigated by MI5 agents on Dartmoor during the First World War.[7]

These problems were brought sharply into focus early in 1941 when MI5 were called in to investigate a spy scare in Yarmouth, Norfolk. Senior military officers there, including an Admiral, were convinced that fifth columnists were signalling to enemy aircraft with Verey lights 'and they were sure that Yarmouth was full of German agents'. On arrival an agent decided to stage a detailed experiment to recreate the lights that had been seen in the sky. Working with the Army, Navy, police and civil defences he chose a clear night in March and placed observers on rooftops around the town. From 7.30 five white Verey lights were put up from Gorlestone pier and during the 20 minutes that followed, bursts of anti-aircraft and machine gun tracer shells were fired into the sky from the harbour and points around the coast.

Each observer was given a piece of paper and asked to guess what they had seen, noting directions, distance and colours. The results confirmed how poor even trained observers were in estimating the correct time, direction, distance and even basic characteristics of lights seen at night. Few got the colours right and one round of white machine gun tracer fired from Yarmouth harbour was reported by individual observers as a green tracer, red tracer, yellow Varey light, blue recognition lights and amber flares. Of the civilian observers the police did best but even they achieved only 33 per cent accuracy and one sergeant became convinced spies were at work trying to break up the experiment. The most accurate observers were those from the Army, but even they failed to identify tracer rounds from Bofors and pom-pom guns and none judged their distance correctly.

Reporting back to Liddell, the agent said: 'it will be seen that the experiment showed that very often only one man in fifty was likely to report correctly on these lights when he saw them, and, at the best, one man in two or three.' Although no fifth columnists were found, 'we put the minds of the Services at rest and enabled them to continue their jobs undisturbed by the thought that they were riddled with enemy agents'.[8] On 2 October 1942, Liddell wrote in his diary that not a single case of light signalling had been traced to Nazi agents. As for the 'fifth column', he concluded 'there is no evidence to show the existence of a widespread organisation, either controlled or uncontrolled by the Germans but that in time of crisis there might be more people than we know about who would be prepared to give assistance to the enemy'.[9]

Nevertheless, during the invasion of France and Norway in 1940, real fifth columnists *had* used both lights and ground markings to guide bombers and parachutists to their targets. MI5 believed spies parachuted into England might follow this strategy by the 'cutting of cornfields into guiding marks for [German] aircraft'. In his memoirs, wartime intelligence officer R.V. Jones records how the scare about fifth columnists spread to Britain, and '. . . our countryside was scanned by aircraft of the RAF looking for suspicious patterns laid out on the ground which might serve as landmarks to aid the navigation of German bombers'.[10] During this 'scare' several unusual ground markings that might today be called 'crop circles' were spotted from the air and led to inquiries by MI5. In May 1941 one such 'unusual mark', 33 yards long and in the form of the letter G, was spotted by the RAF in a field of growing corn in South Wales. From the air it appeared the tail of the marking pointed towards the Royal Ordnance Factory at Glascoed. When questioned, the farmer, 'a man of good character', explained the marking was created by surplus barley that he had sown transversely across a field of growing corn in April, so that he could return a drilling machine to its owner. The MI5 report concludes: 'He agreed to plough up this part of the field [and] as a satisfactory solution had been reached, the case was carried no further.'[11]

Examples of Ground Markings Investigated.

1.   Field at Little Mill, Monmouthshire.

      In May 1941 a report was made that an unusual mark was visible amongst the growing corn.   Near one of the gates was a mark in the form of the letter 'G', some 33 yards long.   (See photograph)   This mark had been made by sowing barley transversely through the grain.   Air photographs were taken and it was seen that the tail of the marking pointed towards the Ordnance factory at Glascoed.

      The farmer, a man of good character, was interviewed, and admitted that he had sown the field himself.   He explained that he had sold the field in April.   Shortly after, having a drilling machine nearby which had a small quantity of barley seed in it, and wishing to empty it as he had to return it to the farmer from whom he had borrowed it that night, he turned his team of horses into

- 6 -

PANEL FIGURE 1.1 A PAGE FROM A MI5 REPORT ON 'UNUSUAL GROUND MARKINGS' PHOTOGRAPHED BY THE RAF DURING THE SPY SCARE THAT GRIPPED BRITAIN FOLLOWING THE OUTBREAK OF THE SECOND WORLD WAR. IN THIS CASE THE MARKING IN A WELSH FIELD WAS FOUND, ON INVESTIGATION, TO HAVE AN INNOCENT EXPLANATION. (CROWN COPYRIGHT, THE NATIONAL ARCHIVES KV4/11)

In October 1943, a RAF aircraft spotted a crop circle in a field near Staplehurst in Kent, with the word 'Marden' inscribed within it. Inquiries discovered the field had been used before the war as an emergency landing ground for aircraft. All similar examples investigated by MI5 during the war turned out to have innocent explanations. In one case a circular white swirl in a growing crop, photographed from the air, was found to be caused by sacks of manure laid out in the field. The urge to attribute unusual crop marks to sinister or supernatural forces was nothing new. References to swirled circles in fields of crops have been found in records dating back as far as the 17th century. At that time they were attributed to the work of the devil.

In 2013 an Australian researcher found what appeared to be further examples 'of circular features that can be reasonably confirmed as crop circles' on aerial photographs taken by the RAF towards the end of the Second World War. None of these simple circles resemble the elaborate formations and pictograms that have become characteristic of the modern 'crop circle' phenomenon.[12]

CHAPTER 2

THE DEATH RAY

. . .it was sweeping round swiftly and steadily, this flaming death, this invisible, inevitable sword of heat. . .

H.G. Wells' description of the Martian heat ray from *The War of the Worlds* **(1898)**[1]

Richard Nixon once told a colleague that Winston Churchill was the only political leader in history 'who had his own crystal ball'. The Prime Minister's predictions, including the outbreak of both world wars and development of chemical and nuclear weapons, has often been attributed to an uncanny ability to perceive patterns in history.[2] Churchill's reputation for prophecy might have been connected with his interest in science fiction. He was a fan of H.G. Wells and adopted the phrase 'the gathering storm' from *The War of the Worlds* as the title of his first book about the Second World War. Churchill also appears to have drawn upon Wells' ideas about weapons of the future as the inspiration for an article published by *Pall Mall* magazine in September 1924. With the provocative title 'Shall We All Commit Suicide?', it quoted a German informant who warned the next war would be fought with 'electrical rays which could paralyse the engines of motor cars, could claw down aeroplanes from the sky and conceivably be made destructive of human life or vision'.[3]

Secret inventors and their devilish new machines were a favourite theme for writers and journalists during the Victorian age. Ideas for the next scientific break-throughs took shape in works of fiction long before they became a reality. The static carnage of the First World War set inventors around the world thinking about how the impasse of trench warfare could be broken. All the talk was of some kind of deadly 'ray' that would be able to disable men and machines at great distances, of the type described by Churchill's informant.

FIGURE 2.1 IN 1924 WINSTON CHURCHILL PREDICTED THE NEXT WAR WOULD BE FOUGHT WITH ADVANCED WEAPONS SUCH AS DEATH RAYS THAT 'COULD PARALYSE THE ENGINES OF MOTOR CARS'. HE MAY HAVE BEEN INSPIRED BY H.G. WELLS' DESCRIPTION OF THE MARTIAN HEAT RAY FROM *THE WAR OF THE WORLDS.* (CROWN COPYRIGHT, THE NATIONAL ARCHIVES: INF 2/44/2804).

Soon after 1919, when the Treaty of Versailles was signed and the war formally ended (fighting itself had ceased when the Armistice was declared), the idea of a 'death ray' also began to obsess many of the finest military minds in Europe. Two years later the Air Ministry began to receive reports from agents of the Secret Intelligence Service (MI6) who had collected rumours about such a 'ray'. These implied the Germans were 'evolving a machine for projecting by means of electromagnetic rays, considerable electrical power on some distant object'.[4] Similar rumours reached the British press in the autumn of 1923, eight months after French and Belgian troops marched into the Ruhr Valley in order to force the German Weimar Republic to honour war reparations agreed with the Allies at Versailles. As tension rose along the border in September of that year, the *Daily Mail* claimed more than 30 French aircraft had been forced to land whilst flying over German territory. They had suffered engine trouble in an area of southern Germany between Prague and Strasbourg. Some were carrying passengers and mail and the 'pilots and passengers were at once arrested and the machines confiscated', but the crews were not allowed to investigate the cause of the mechanical problems. The rumours implied that some new kind of 'electrical ray' developed by the Germans had interfered with the aircraft's magnetos, causing their engines to fail.[5]

This claim was dismissed as 'far-fetched' by two of Britain's most respected physicists, Professor Archibald Low and Sir Oliver Lodge. They told the paper that it was possible to focus a beam of electrical energy that could melt a small coil of wire two feet away. 'But there is a wide difference between transmitting such power over a distance of a foot or two and a distance of one or two thousand yards,' said Professor Low. He was confident such a device might be possible 'in 50 or 60 years' time' but not with the technology then available to scientists. The *Daily Mail* then turned to a 'British air expert' who was convinced the Germans were working on an advanced electrical ray. He said the rumours were based on fact and claimed: 'In one of the machines captured at Furth the pilot was able to discover that an inexplicable hole several inches wide had been made in the aluminium oil-tank and that the lead solder of the copper pipes had been melted.'[6]

The story grew stranger in a follow-up article published by the paper. Inquiries by its reporters found that scientists at a radio laboratory at Nauen in northern Germany had been working on a project 'with the object of sending out concentrated wireless rays in the same way as the beams of a searchlight are directed along a certain path'. The plant's director denied any link between his laboratory and the mishaps suffered by French aircraft. But he was said to have been furious when a story leaked out 'about a number of motor cars having been brought to a dead stop on a lonely road at night by a wireless beam focussed across a stretch of country by the Nauen station'. The paper added that French Secret Service agents confirmed this experiment did take place and was followed by desperate attempts by the Germans to cover it up.[7]

While the British government remained sceptical in public, papers at The National Archives reveal that senior military officers were by now convinced the Germans really were working on a 'death ray'. Evidence of high-level concern appears in a secret memo sent by the Chief of the Air Staff, Sir Hugh Trenchard, to the Director General of Scientific Research on 12 April 1922. In it the founder of the RAF says he had returned from discussions at the War Office about 'the formidable Air menace to this country which exists'. The nature of that menace was revealed in the next paragraph: 'The General Staff enquired from us whether we were making any efforts towards electrical interference with aeroplanes in the air or explosives.' This was the genesis of the British military's quest for its own 'death ray'. Trenchard said the General Staff had referred the issue to the Industrial Research Committee who were 'making investigations with regard to a ray to produce electrical interference. Although this did not look a practical proposition at present the idea must not be ruled out . . .'[8]

Two years later, MI6 reported back on their investigations of the 'wild stories' published by the *Daily Mail*. It was likely, they concluded, 'the German authorities were responsible for exaggerating the non-essential parts of the story in order to draw attention away from the localities where the real experimental work was going on'.[9] In effect, they were disinformation planted by the Germans themselves. With the benefit of hindsight, we now know that a working example of a directed energy weapon (DEW) of the type imagined during the 1920s did not exist. Yet throughout the 1920s and 30s, a number of governments and maverick inventors busied themselves developing 'death rays' and were convinced that a breakthrough was imminent. The press lapped up these stories and the inventors were often portrayed as paranoid eccentrics who worked in secrecy and seclusion to perfect their mysterious devices.

A survey of the British government archive on 'death rays', published in 1997, revealed that 'several workers claimed to have achieved weapon demonstrations that would be considered useful today, although most of the available reports lack the detail or clarity required for critical analysis'.[10] In his paper, Ministry of Defence scientist Gari Owen wrote that clear descriptions of the principles by which these weapons operated is lacking in the surviving records, but a number of ideas attracted both interest and financial backing from Western governments.

One of the earliest proposals for a 'death ray' came from the Serbian-American inventor and electrical genius Nikola Tesla (1856–1943), who is best known today for his work on alternating current. He also experimented with X-rays and radio communication and invented the Tesla coil at his power plant in New York state. During the First World War, he claimed to have worked on a particle gun that 'may be used to destroy property and life'. In 1934 the *New York Times* said Tesla had boldly claimed this invention could 'send concentrated beams of particles through the free air, of such tremendous energy that they will bring down a fleet of 10,000 enemy airplanes at a distance of 200 miles from a defending nation's border and will cause armies to drop dead in their tracks'.[11]

Despite its destructive powers, Tesla preferred to refer to this super-weapon as a 'peace ray' and believed it would 'put an end to all war'. This was a laudable aim that was articulated by other inventors at the time. Later in his life Tesla tried to persuade the US War Department, the Soviet Union and the British War Office to fund his research on the ray and claimed several attempts had been made to steal the plans from his workshop. These did not succeed because the idea existed in his head rather than on paper. Nevertheless, fears that rival powers employed an army of spies that were constantly plotting to steal blueprints of the 'death ray' run like a thread through the story of this putative device.

'DEATH RAY' MATTHEWS'

Britain produced its own answer to Nikola Tesla in the form of the inventor Harry Grindell-Matthews. The press preferred to call him 'Death Ray Matthews' and although he did not select that name himself, his invention became the subject of heated debate at the highest levels of the British Government. The controversy it generated is chronicled by an Air Ministry file at The National Archives. By any standards Matthews led a remarkable life.[12]

Born in 1880 at Winterbourne in Gloucestershire, he was educated at the Merchant Venturers' School in Bristol before training as an electrical engineer. During the Boer War he enlisted in the Baden-Powell South African Constabulary and was wounded twice. On his return to Britain, he pursued his interest in electronics and began to first visualise, and later produce, a remarkable series of inventions. Matthews was also fascinated by the possibilities offered by radio. Following in the footsteps of Tesla, in 1911 he staged a demonstration of radio telephony, sending a message from the ground to the pilot of an aircraft flying two miles away at 600ft.

FIGURE 2.2 A PHOTOGRAPH OF HARRY GRINDELL-MATTHEWS TAKEN FOR PATHÉ NEWS IN 1924. MATTHEWS WAS KNOWN TO THE PRESS AS 'DEATH RAY MAN' FOR HIS MOST FAMOUS INVENTION THAT WAS INSPIRED BY STORIES OF MYSTERIOUS ENGINE-STOPPING RAYS IN GERMANY. (COURTESY OF WEST GLAMORGAN ARCHIVE SERVICE)

During this period he was invited to Buckingham Palace and met members of the royal family. Fame and fortune awaited those who could successfully demonstrate new inventions that could be useful to the armed forces. With the First World War approaching, the British government was seeking new devices that would help defend the empire against the Kaiser's most advanced technology. Two inventions interested them. The first was a weapon which could destroy Germany's fleet of Zeppelin airships before they could reach Britain's coastline. The second was a design for a remote-controlled boat or aircraft: in modern parlance, a remotely piloted aircraft or 'drone'. A reward of £25,000 was offered to the person who came up with either. Matthews was convinced he could provide the latter and claimed he had developed an effective remote control system using selenium cells.

After a successful test of his invention on Edgbaston Reservoir, it was demonstrated to Admiralty officials on Richmond Park's Penn Pond. They were so impressed that Matthews received the prize offered, a considerable sum of money in 1915. Yet there was something unusual about this event. The Admiralty, for whatever reason, chose not to pursue Matthews' selenium control system which, besides operating boats remotely, was claimed to detonate explosives at a distance. This was the first intimation in official records that Matthews was not to be trusted.[13]

MATTHEWS UNDER THE SPOTLIGHT

In 1923, Matthews turned his attention to the 'death ray' after he read reports of French airplanes being forced from the sky over Germany. Like Churchill and Trenchard, he appeared to give credence to the story. Noting the proximity of the interference to high-powered radio aerials, he told the press: 'I realised that the Germans had found an invisible ray that put the magnetos of the aircraft out of action. I concentrated on efforts to discover what it was, and with the electric ray now at my command I think I have succeeded.' Early in 1924, a group of journalists were treated to a demonstration of Matthews' 'ray' stopping a motor cycle engine at a distance of 50ft. 'I am confident,' Matthews informed them, 'that if I have facilities for developing it I can stop aeroplanes in flight – indeed I believe the ray is sufficiently powerful to destroy the air, to explode powder magazines, and destroy anything on which it rests'.[14]

Matthews was charismatic and confident and he cultivated his popularity with the press to his personal advantage. Rather than approach the government directly, he preferred to force their hand by manipulating public opinion via newspaper headlines. For their part, the press knew stories about 'death rays' were popular with readers, and soon fanciful accounts of Matthews' invention began to fill the columns of newspapers and magazines. The fantastic 'ray' could, it was claimed, 'melt plate glass, light lamps, explode gunpowder, kill vermin at 64 feet and stop a motorcycle engine'.

Fearful that the publicity Matthews was enjoying could lead a rival power to make a successful bid for his invention, the authorities were forced to act. The Air Ministry's scepticism was based on their past experience negotiating with 'inventors'. They had been duped or conned many times before by those who made astonishing claims but failed to deliver the promised goods. They may have even been duped by Matthews himself. In the Air Ministry file, a memo by Wing Commander James Bowen suggested that Matthews' wartime payment of £25,000 was largely due to the influence of one particular member of the House of Lords and was not entirely deserved. Bowen suggested that enquiries should be 'instituted with the police records as to Mr G Matthews' past history'. Mention is also made in the file of a report by the Security Service, MI5, that scrutinised Matthews' claims and his career to date.[15] This report, if it exists, is not available at The National Archives.

Swallowing their pride and suspending their disbelief, in February 1924 the Air Ministry offered Matthews the opportunity to demonstrate his 'death ray' to them. He ignored their advances initially as he was now involved in negotiations to sell his invention to France, but in May he was persuaded to return home to demonstrate his device before a gathering of Britain's leading military scientists. This event proved something of an anti-climax. After being ushered into Matthews' laboratory at Harewood Place in Mayfair, the officials were shown two examples of the ray's wonderful powers. An Osglim light bulb was held in its path and when the ray was switched on, the bulb lit up. A small motor mounted on a bench was then started and immediately brought to a halt by the ray. When Matthews was asked to move the motor to another part of the room and repeat the test he refused and said he was in 'a great hurry'. If the inventor expected to win the confidence of the British government with this performance, he would be disappointed.

Immediately afterwards, the Air Ministry convened a meeting of those who had attended the demonstration. The ministry's scientific advisor, Major Harry Wimperis, said it was an 'entirely unconvincing test [as] it is a simple matter to make such lamps glow by bringing them near a powerful electric machine of high frequency and high voltage'. Wimperis added that he was 'rather surprised to find the inventor should imagine that one would be impressed'. Sir Frank Smith, director of the Admiralty's Experimental Department, was equally lukewarm. He did not believe any of Matthews' claims. Smith also mentioned a visit made to the Admiralty by a mysterious 'Mr Appleton', possibly an MI5 agent, who claimed that Mathews had no scientific knowledge as such but liked to experiment with 'all sorts of gadgets'. Appleton suggested that Matthews 'brought things up to a certain stage and no further, he would then raise money on what he had achieved'. In short, he was a scientific confidence trickster. Appleton claimed Matthews was 'working the press, but had now lost control of it'. The conclusion of this meeting was that the government did not trust Matthews, yet they did not wish to dismiss his ideas completely as no government wanted to turn down the opportunity to obtain the 'death ray', only for it to turn up later in the arsenal of an enemy.[16]

Soon afterwards, Air Vice-Marshal Geoffrey Salmond, the Air Member for Supply and Research on the Air Council, wrote to Matthews suggesting a second, more detailed test of his device in the open air. Matthews refused to provide it and told the press he had lost patience with England. He was again offering the 'ray' to the French who were more respectful of his status and achievements. Following the breakdown of communications with British officials, events took a dramatic turn. Early on the morning of 27 May 1924, the High Court in London granted an injunction to Matthews' investors who moved to stop him from selling the rights to his device abroad. At 10.45 am, Matthews, who was unaware of this legal challenge, set off for Croydon aerodrome to catch the lunchtime flight to Paris. Three minutes later, Major Wimperis arrived at Matthews' laboratory in an attempt to broker a deal. As he was leaving, Matthews' financial backers and their solicitor arrived, holding the injunction. Finding Matthews had left, they hired the fastest car available and sped to Croydon in an attempt to stop him leaving for France. But once again he eluded them. They reached the runway seconds too late and could only watch as the small mail plane headed towards the Channel. Questioned later, a Mr Gubbins, one of Matthews' investors, remained convinced of the ray's potency, saying: '. . . the ray is the most terrible invention which has been created in recent years. It is of such a nature that it will make wars impossible. Other countries could not hope to combat a power armed with such a weapon.'[17]

Faced with a growing public uproar, on 28 May the government of Labour Prime Minister Ramsay MacDonald was forced to make a statement in the House of Commons. The Under Secretary for Air, William Leach, was questioned by MPs who demanded to know what steps were being taken to prevent an invention of the death ray's magnitude from leaving the country. Leach simply re-iterated the government's position: 'We are not in a position to pass judgment on the value of this ray, because we have not been allowed to make proper tests. Therefore whether there is anything in it or not still remains unexplored,' he explained.

'The Departments have been placed in a difficult position in dealing with the matter partly because of the vigorous Press campaign conducted on behalf of this gentleman, and partly because this is not the first occasion on which the inventor has put forward a scheme for which extravagant claims have been made,' he went on. 'The result is the Departments are not able to accept Mr Matthews' statement about this invention without a scrutiny which he is not prepared to face.'[18]

Leach diplomatically explained that: 'the conditions under which the demonstrations were made by Mr Matthews were such that it was not possible to form any opinion as to the value of the device [and] the departmental representatives were shown nothing which would lead them to credit the statements which have appeared in the Press as to the possibilities of the invention.'

Unfazed by this scepticism, Matthews, who was still in France, announced he now had eight separate bids under consideration. The Air Ministry file contains a letter from Charles Dick of the British Consulate in Paris who met with the inventor during his trip. Dick had made inquiries into the background of his French backer, Eugene Royer, finding him to be untrustworthy and on the point of bankruptcy. An Air Ministry official summed up the problem succinctly, writing: 'This invention is either worth a large sum of money or it is worth nothing. No inventor could reasonably expect the Government to pay a large sum of money for a patent until it had been fully tested. If the invention fulfils all that is claimed for it the inventor has nothing to fear from official sources.'[19]

THE DEATH RAY FILM

Despite the press hype, as yet few people outside Matthews' inner circle had actually seen his 'death ray' at close quarters. This was rectified in the summer of 1924 with the release of the film with the ambitious title of *The Death Ray – The Most Startling and Breath Taking Motion Picture Ever Made!* Made by Pathé and released in Britain and the US, the 25-minute movie made entertaining viewing. It was an effective advertisement both for Matthews' inventions and his acting skills, yet there was no evidence that the subject matter of the film had any basis in reality. Stills from the film show a fantastic apparatus, said to be *the* death ray. In appearance it resembles a searchlight, with three megaphone-like 'ears' attached to its sides. But this device bore no relation to the small machine demonstrated to the British government earlier in the year. As the film's star pulled levers, a rat falls dead in its cage, a motorcycle engine stalls and aircraft are seen crashing to the ground in flames.[20]

Poetic licence was clearly at work and S.R. Littlewood, writing in *The Sphere*, said he learned nothing new about the scientific basis of the 'ray' by watching the film. He did, however, find himself enthralled by what he called 'the remarkable personality of Mr Matthews himself', adding: 'One cannot help being at least bewildered by the psychology of a scientist who can enter into the spirit of a piece of mummery like this so completely that it is quite clear he was acting for all he was worth. In view of his many experiments it can evidently have been no great emotional strain to Mr Matthews to pull a lever with the intention of doing nothing worse than stopping a bicycle-wheel. Yet he pulls that lever with as much impressive gravity as if he were about some operation upon which life and death depended.'[21]

The mass press coverage of the 'death ray' captured the public imagination. The film allowed them to 'see' it for themselves. Its release marked the point at which Matthews abandoned the quest to sell his invention to European governments and in July 1924 he left for the United States. Once again he set about publicising his device, announcing he would develop a more advanced version of it that would convince the world that his 'dream deserves a place among the great inventions of history'. But in December, when he was offered $25,000 to demonstrate the ray to the Radio World Fair at Madison Square Gardens he declined, claiming that he was not permitted to demonstrate his invention outside Britain. This was a curious statement as there is no evidence he was under any such constraint, legal or political. He continued to tantalise the American public, saying he would return to Britain and set up a research station so that, 'in eighteen months I can perfect my apparatus so that it will be the most formidable war weapon of the future'. US scientists were not impressed. A physicist, Professor Robert Woods, was so scornful he offered to stand in front of the ray, confident it would do him no harm. 'Nothing,' he said, 'has been done that could lead a scientist or engineer to place the slightest credence in the death ray'.[22]

Matthews never managed to successfully demonstrate his death ray to the satisfaction of any Western government. Research by his most recent biographer, Jonathan Foster, uncovered a patent registered in Paris for 'remote projection of invisible high frequency electricity' in October 1924 under the name of Eugene Royer, Matthews' French business partner.[23] Matthews' name disappears from British records until 1931 when he faced proceedings for bankruptcy. High Court papers at The National Archives reveal a series of loans and investments, none of which made money. That said, they allowed him to live in hotels and luxury rented accommodation whilst he developed his various inventions.[24]

Despite his financial problems, by 1934 Matthews had raised sufficient funds from new financial backers to relocate his laboratory to South Wales. There he became a semi-recluse, living in a fortified laboratory with private airfield on the summit of Tor Cloud, near Swansea. From this point on, the inventor's activities became the subject of strange rumours. The West Glamorgan Archive Service website describes how the inventor 'ended his days living on Mynydd y Gwair near Clydach, where his house, heavily guarded by security systems of his own devising, became the focus of stories of odd goings-on up on the moor: animals suddenly dying [and] car engines stopping for no reason'.[25]

With the Second World War looming, Matthews began to develop an idea for aerial mines fired by rockets or suspended from barrage balloons. These, he claimed, could create an effective aerial ring of defence round cities such as London. This idea was discussed seriously by the War Office but never taken up as a practical proposal. Matthews then came up with the idea of a 'stratosplane' that could fly on the edges of space. He became a member of the British Interplanetary Society, pushing forward ideas that led eventually to the development of rockets that could leave Earth's atmosphere. There were many more inventions, including a system for detecting submarines, that were offered to the government departments. Unfortunately, Matthews' reputation preceded him and his past history meant his major contributions to science and technology were destined to fall into obscurity. He died from a heart attack on 11 September 1941.

Today the inventor of Britain's 'death ray' has been largely forgotten, but whether Harry Matthews was a genius or a charlatan is a question that remains unanswered. Some of his ideas and inventions such as early talking films, the aerophone and the Sky Projector, were genuinely innovative and years ahead of their time (see panel, p.60). Although he was best known as the inventor of a 'death ray', the scientific principles upon which it worked were always glossed over in reports of its capabilities. 'Ionized air carrying an electrical current' was mentioned by some newspapers while others talked of 'exceptionally short radio waves'. Matthews refused to elaborate but a confidential document in the Air Ministry file explains the invention in terms of the transmission of electrical energy through the atmosphere along a 'carrier beam'. The wavelength of the beam was said to be somewhere between X-rays and ultraviolet in the electromagnetic spectrum.[26]

In 1997 a Ministry of Defence scientist, Gari Owen, looked for clues in contemporary photographs of the device operated by Matthews in his central London laboratory.[27] These were published in a biography, *The Death Ray Man*, written by the inventor's friend, Ernest Barwell, two years after his death. One image in the book shows Matthews and his assistants wearing white lab coats, watching closely as the 'death ray' is tested.[28] Owen said this photograph raises 'more questions than it answered' as the demonstration 'could not be easily achieved using present-day technology'. Owen could not account for how Matthews achieved the 64-foot operating range he claimed, 36 years before the first functioning laser was operated at a laboratory in California.

FIGURE 2.3 THE MYSTERIOUS 'DEATH RAY' IS DEMONSTRATED BY HARRY GRINDELL MATTHEWS AT HIS LABORATORY IN LONDON IN THESE IMAGES PUBLISHED IN 'LECTURES POUR TOUS', NOVEMBER 1924 (COURTESY MARY EVANS PICTURE LIBRARY).

Another problem identified by Owen was how Matthews generated the very high voltages that would be required to produce such a 'ray' using the power sources available in the early 1920s. The photograph in Barwell's book appears to a show a discharge or some form of combustion at the target itself, but Owen noted there was no evidence of any conducting channel between the device and the target. 'The recombination and decay of ions in the channel would be expected to produce visible emissions and these would be very strong if the channel had transferred sufficient energy to produce the dramatic effects seen at the target,' he wrote. 'Of course, the photograph may have been taken just *after* the equipment was operated.'[29]

What happened to Matthews' equipment after his death is not known. All that remains of his remarkable life is a collection of scrap books, press cuttings and photographs about his life and experiments, by the Glamorgan Archive Service preserved in South Wales.[30]

MOST SECRET WEAPONS

Harry Grindell-Matthews was not the only person who claimed to be working on directed energy weapons shortly before the outbreak of the Second World War. The press furore that followed his claims in 1924 prompted a number of other 'inventors' to offer their services to the British authorities. One of the most interesting claims was that made by Dr T.F. Wall, who taught physics at the University of Sheffield. He was described by the press as one of Matthews' main competitors in the quest to discover an effective death ray. Dr Wall told the *Sheffield Independent* his experiments were 'within reach of breaking down and releasing the energy of the atom' so that it could be directed and focussed 'in any desired direction'.[31] Unfortunately, no records of his work appear to have survived. Yet another proposal for a three component 'anti-aircraft' system based upon a device described as 'death torch' was offered to the Air Ministry in 1926. The inventor, Bateman Scott, claimed it would be effective at a range of seven miles. The ministry was unconvinced and refused to pay the £23,000 he requested to develop his idea.[32]

The British scientist R.V. Jones had access to a number of secret MI6 files on 'death rays' when he joined the intelligence branch of the Air Ministry at the outbreak of war in 1939. Jones was one of the few scientists assigned by Winston Churchill's wartime government to assess intelligence on enemy capabilities, including secret weapons. He had little time for the colourful claims made by Matthews and other 'cranks' . In his book *Most Secret War*, Jones mentions how, on one occasion, MI6 agents funded the work of a Dutch inventor. Unfortunately for them, he continued to present excuses for his lack of progress up to the outbreak of hostilities:

At last, when it was clear that even the [MI6] was not being fooled any longer and would therefore give him no more money, his final report stated that although the apparatus had been a failure as a death ray, he had discovered that it had remarkable properties as a fruit preserver, and he therefore offered this invention for exploitation by [MI6] in any venture that it might think appropriate.[33]

After he had debunked the more fantastic rumours, Jones was left with a number of intelligence reports on futuristic weapons 'of which some must be considered seriously'. The summary he produced for Churchill's government included bacterial warfare, flame weapons, 'gliding bombs' and 'death rays, engine-stopping rays and magnetic guns'. The uncertain situation that existed before 1939 ensured that the Allied and Axis powers continued to place their faith in the discovery of a secret weapon that would give their military forces a technological advantage over their adversaries. In Britain the War Office were said to have offered a standing reward of £1,000 to anyone who could build a death ray that could kill a sheep at 100 yards. A proposal from Nikola Tesla 'for a form of death ray' was rejected in 1937 when inquiries in Washington found the inventor 'was of an advanced age and had not produced anything of significance' since the 1914–18 war.[34] Another proposal that reached the British Treasury came from a German inventor, Herr Krause, who claimed *his* death ray had killed animals at a distance of a few hundred yards. In his case, the War Office decided that although 'he has convinced himself of the validity of his claims . . . no scientific evidence of any value is yet available'.[35]

None of these early experiments with directed energy 'rays' formed the basis for an offensive weapons system that was operational in time to be used during the war. They were not all in vain, however, as the quest for a working death ray was to have one long-lasting spin-off benefit. As an aerial attack from the Luftwaffe appeared inevitable, the British government was desperate to find an effective form of defence against the threat from enemy bombers. To prepare the public for the horrors that lay ahead, in 1932 the Conservative Prime Minister, Stanley Baldwin, told the House of Commons that 'it is well for the man in the street to realise that there is no power on earth that can protect him from being bombed . . . the bomber will always get through'.[36]

During the same year, the Air Ministry set up the Committee for the Scientific Survey of Air Defence. CASSAD contained some of the brightest minds of the day. Chaired by the Oxford-trained scientist, Sir Henry Tizard, the committee scrutinised a number of inventions and ideas, from acoustic mirrors to barrage balloons. Inevitably they were led to consider the 'death ray' that many officials feared the Germans already possessed. Faced with a decade of false trails, on 18 January 1935 the Air Ministry's Director of Scientific Research, Harry Wimperis, approached the scientist Robert Watson-Watt to provide advice 'on the practicability of proposals of the type colloquially called "death ray"'. The Tizard committee wanted to know if it was possible to create a directed beam of electromagnetic energy that

FIGURE 2.4 A CARTOON DEPICTING A 'HEATH ROBINSON' DEATH RAY THAT APPEARS IN THE BRITISH AIR MINISTRY FILE ON HARRY GRINDELL MATTHEWS. A CAPTION HAD BEEN ADDED BY HARRY WIMPERIS (1876–1960), DIRECTOR OF SCIENTIFIC RESEARCH, WHO WAS INSTRUMENTAL IN THE DEVELOPMENT OF BRITAIN'S RADAR DEFENCES BEFORE THE SECOND WORLD WAR. (CROWN COPYRIGHT, THE NATIONAL ARCHIVES AIR 5/179)

could kill enemy pilots and detonate bombs before enemy aircraft could reach British cities, just as Harry Grindell-Matthews had proposed a decade earlier.[37]

Watson-Watt delegated the problem of calculating the amount of power required to his assistant, Arnold 'Skip' Watkins. He concluded the proposed ray was way ahead of anything that could be achieved using technology available to British scientists. According to R.V. Jones, when Watson-Watt first saw the calculations, he asked Watkins: 'Well then, if the death ray is not possible, how can we help them?' Watkins replied that he was aware that Post Office engineers had noticed that whenever aircraft flew in the vicinity of BBC radio masts, they created disturbances to the radio signal. The two scientists then began to ponder whether this phenomenon could be utilised for detecting enemy aircraft before they crossed the British coastline. On 26 February 1935, the day that Adolf Hitler created the Luftwaffe, Watson-Watt and his team set up an experiment at Daventry in Northamptonshire that proved it *was* possible to detect aircraft by the use of radio waves. As the RAF flew aircraft backwards and forwards between two BBC radio masts, the two men sat inside a Bedford van watching as a tiny glowing green line flared and swelled on the cathode-ray display. 'Radar' (Radio Detecting And Ranging) had been born. Watson-Watt was so impressed by the results that he declared Britain had 'become an island once more'.[38]

The death ray may never have been a practical weapon, but those who had taken Matthews' advice to 'think outside the box' and employ their imaginations had stumbled upon a defensive weapon with far greater – indeed world-changing – possibilities.

FALSE RUMOURS AND URBAN LEGENDS

Before the beginning of the Second World War, intelligence officers and politicians both played a role in spreading rumours about 'secret weapons'. Scare stories of this kind were often used to justify increased public spending on preparations for war. Following the invasion of Poland in 1939, Adolf Hitler stoked the fire in a speech that announced the Nazis had developed a 'secret weapon against which no defence would avail'. Many feared this could be a type of deadly gas or death ray and much time and energy was spent by intelligence officers like Professor R.V. Jones investigating possible counter-measures against them. In this respect, the idea of a threat posed by the imaginary 'death ray' can be compared with more recent obsessions that have led both politicians and intelligence officers down false trails. The quest for the non-existent 'Weapons of Britain's coastline before the war. Although the setting and characters had changed, this

FIGURE 2.5 THE RAF'S CHAIN HOME ANTI-AIRCRAFT RADAR DEFENCES, SUCH AS THESE AT DOVER, FORMED A PROTECTIVE RING AROUND BRITAIN'S COASTLINE BEFORE THE OUTBREAK OF THE SECOND WORLD WAR. TO CONCEAL THEIR TRUE PURPOSE BRITISH INTELLIGENCE PLANTED A STORY THAT SUGGESTED THEY WERE TESTING A DEATH RAY. (CROWN COPYRIGHT, THE NATIONAL ARCHIVES AIR 2/2216)

Mass Destruction' that came to obsess Western governments before and during the second Iraq War is the most recent example.

In his memoirs Jones reveals how British intelligence was inundated with stories about an 'engine-stopping' ray in the years before 1939. The version of the legend he heard told how an English family on holiday in Germany were travelling in a car when its engine inexplicably failed on a country road on the edge of a wood. A German sentry stepped from the trees and told the family 'special tests' were in progress and they would soon be able to continue their journey. Soon afterwards the sentry reappeared and told them they could continue their journey. When the ignition was started, the engine immediately fired and they were able to drive away.[39]

A similar story, with the German sentry replaced by an RAF officer, was frequently overheard in the vicinity of the secret Chain Home radar stations that were built around appeared to be the same rumour that was reported by the British press during 1923. All these stories may have originated from sources in German intelligence. They were believed by Churchill, though, and they also inspired Harry Grindell-Matthews to build his own 'death ray'.

The 'engine-stopping' death ray was such a persistent and effective rumour that the British secret services decided to concoct their own version of it. It was, according to Jones, 'deliberately spread, hinting that we, too, had a ray'. Gordon Kinsey, in his book *Bawdsey: Birth of the Beam* (1983), notes that before the war, motorists in Suffolk recalled 'authentic rumours', never first hand, but always from 'reliable sources' that told of car engines that refused to work near the coastal radar stations, despite efforts to repair them. Sometimes an RAF officer appeared who informed the perplexed driver that 'at such and such a time' the car would work again.[40] A letter from GCHQ in Jones' archive at the University of Cambridge implies the British rumour may have been set running when the Air Ministry began experimental work on radar at Bawdsey Manor, Suffolk, in 1936. It refers to 'the reported high incidence of stopped cars around Felixstowe, in the early days of Bawdsey'. At the time, the experiments on early radar at the experimental station were top secret. But from 1936, the appearance of eight 360ft tall steel masts 'disclosed to the public that our activities included the transmission of electromagnetic energy'. Soon afterwards a letter appeared in a local newspaper 'describing how six cars became inactive in a distance of a quarter of a mile on the Felixstowe–Ipswich road'. The letter-writer said there was 'no rational explanation for this occurrence'.[41]

Soon rumours were rife that the tall towers under construction at secret military bases on the East Coast 'could inhibit the ignition of car engines'. Jones wrote that British intelligence were astonished by the success of their operation. Within a short time they were 'flooded out' with stories of similar events elsewhere in England. These contained circumstantial details from members of the public who then repeated the story to others. One version, from Salisbury Plain, was singled out as being genuine because the occupants of the car were a family of Quakers, 'and Quakers, it was added, were well known for telling the truth'.

In his papers Jones explains how he 'got to the bottom of the story' that triggered this urban legend when he interviewed a Jewish radio announcer from Frankfurt. All the locations mentioned in the early German 'death ray' stories were in the regions around the Brocken Mountains and the Feldberg near Frankfurt, both sites of the first television towers in Germany. With a chuckle, his informant explained how the story could have arisen:

In the days before the television transmitters had been erected, the engineers made field strength surveys, but these surveys were rendered difficult by interference from the engines of motor vehicles. Under an authoritarian regime such as that of the Nazis it was simple to eliminate this trouble by stopping all cars in the area around the survey receiver for the period of the test. Sentries, who were probably provided by the German Air Force, were posted on the road, and at the appointed hour would emerge to stop all vehicles.[42]

Jones came to believe that a simple transposition in the stories told by the drivers was all that was required for the idea to arise that car engines had failed *before* the sentry appeared. Once the rumour was seeded, the German authorities may have decided it was useful to encourage it as it implied their scientists were working on an 'engine-stopping' death ray. Versions of these rumours have proved so resilient they occasionally surface in the present day.

In the 1951 science-fiction film *The Day the Earth Stood Still*, a humanoid alien arrives on earth in a flying saucer, accompanied by a powerful robot. Towards the end of the film the robot demonstrates his power to paralyse all electrical apparatus on the planet, including car engines. Following the film's release, accounts of UFO encounters from motorists occasionally mentioned that vehicle engines inexplicably failed before the appearance of the flying saucer, only to return to life once the 'object' departed. Examples of alleged 'car stops' reported to the US Air Force 'UFO project' Blue Book were reviewed by scientists from the University of Colorado in 1968. They assumed that such engine failures must be attributed to magnetic fields, but in the one example studied by the project no evidence could be found that the car involved had been exposed to such a field. Their final report said that of all the physical effects attributed to the presence of UFOs 'the alleged malfunction of automobile motors is perhaps the most puzzling'.[43]

Rumours of invisible rays that can stop vehicle engines are not confined to UFOlogy: as noted above, they have also been linked with secret experiments at military bases such as RAF Bawdsey and other locations around the British coastline. Soon after the ballistic missile early warning radar station RAF Fylingdales opened on the North York Moors in 1963, stories spread about a 'death ray' that incapacitated cars in the vicinity of the base. Again in 2006, motorists experienced electrical problems whilst passing the 'golf ball' radar domes at RAF Trimingham on the north Norfolk coast. A report in the *Eastern Daily Press* revealed that around 30 motorists had suffered weird malfunctions when passing the domes including reports of engines and lights cutting out, dashboard dials going haywire and alarms going off. Speedometer dials swung alarmingly up to 150mph and several motorists required replacement fuse boards after seeking help at a nearby garage. It later emerged that the military radars at the base, which plays a key role in the UK's air defence system, were 'out of alignment' at the time the problems reached their peak.[44]

The Ministry of Defence eventually paid compensation to the drivers of five cars affected and a board of inquiry report concluded: 'It is not possible to exactly determine the radar effects on motor vehicles . . . [but we] cannot dismiss the apparent coincidence of radar faults on the Type 93 radar at Trimingham and a dramatic increase in vehicle electromagnetic interference.'[45] Tests by the ministry's scientists found there was no evidence that residents had been exposed to hazardous levels of radiation as a result of the fault but the MoD said it recognised the fears that some residents continued to have . As a result, one of the recommendations made by the inquiry was the removal of signs that warned 'a micro-wave radiation hazard exists beyond this point' from the fence that separates the base perimeter from the winding B1159 coastal road.

STAR WARS AND THE LEGACY OF THE 'DEATH RAY'

After the capitulation of Germany in 1945, research into directed energy weapons continued afresh as relations between the West and the Soviet Union continued to deteriorate. The best known outcome of the high-tech arms race that characterised the Cold War was the multi-million dollar Strategic Defence Initiative (SDI). This was launched by President Ronald Reagan in 1984 as an elaborate global shield to protect Western nations against the threat posed by Soviet intercontinental ballistic missiles. SDI planned to use high-energy beam weapons, based on X-ray lasers, to destroy nuclear-armed missiles long before they could reach their targets. Many scientists doubted the extravagant claims made by the US military and decided that, like the death ray, they could not be achieved with the technology available at that time. As a result SDI came to be described by the press as 'Star Wars' after the 1977 science-fiction film directed by George Lucas.

Although the SDI system has yet to be successfully demonstrated, according to one MoD analysis the investment it stimulated in advanced technology 'provided a strong stimulus in the field of lasers and optics which brought several new capabilities to fruition'[46]. The existence of one secret British military project of this kind was revealed when Cabinet Office papers written in the aftermath of the Falklands War were opened at The National Archives in 2013. In a letter to Prime Minister Margaret Thatcher, the then defence secretary, Michael Heseltine MP, revealed that since 1972, Britain had been co-operating with the Americans on the development of high-powered lasers for use on the battlefield. Heseltine said such 'death rays' were unlikely to be effective against tanks and aircraft, but could be used against humans: 'You may recall,' he wrote in 1983, 'that we developed and deployed with very great urgency a naval laser weapon, designed to dazzle low-flying Argentine pilots attacking ships, to the Task Force in the South Atlantic. This weapon was not used in action and knowledge of it has been kept to a very restricted circle.'[47] The naval 'dazzle' weapon resembles the device tested, but apparently never used in anger, by British forces defending the Suez Canal during the Western Desert Campaign in 1941 (see panel, p.61).

ANGELS IN THE CLOUDS

One of the more unusual explanations for the Angel of Mons (Chapter 1) explained the 'visions' as projections from magic lanterns mounted on German aircraft. This theory appeared in 1930 when the London *Daily News* published an interview with Colonel Friedrich Herzenwirth 'of the Imperial German Intelligence Service'. He claimed visions seen by Allied soldiers in Flanders were lantern slides projected onto cloudbanks from German aeroplanes. The officer said that the German plan was to create 'superstitious terror' among the troops so they would refuse to fight. But the plan unravelled because: 'what we had not figured on was that the English should turn the vision to their own benefit . . . This was a magnificent bit of counter-propaganda, for some of the English must have been fully aware of the mechanism of our trick. Their method of interpreting our angels as protectors of their own troops turned the scales completely upon us.'[1]

Col. Herzenwirth said the Germans were more successful when they projected images of the Virgin Mary onto clouds above the Eastern Front before a night assault. He said: 'A dense snowbank in the sky above the German Army was used as a screen. Entire regiments who had beheld the vision fell upon their knees and flung away their rifles . . . The trick was repeated several times on the Russian front and was invariably successful. We knew from prisoners we took that in some cases companies actually killed their officers and flung their rifles away, shouting that they would not be guilty of firing upon an army over which the Mother of God hovered in protection.'

When the Germans tried to use the same tactics against the French Army in Picardy, they miscalculated. He explained: 'Instead of taking the figure of a woman that we threw upon the clouds one night as that of the Virgin or a saint protecting our army, the French promptly recognised Joan of Arc. The tables were turned upon us once more when we changed from a woman to a man in Flanders. The British said it was St George.'

This story appeared superficially plausible because during the 1930s new and ever more ingenious inventions were appearing on a daily basis. Before questions could be asked about the logistics of the German operation, however, Col. Herzenwirth's tales were exposed as fiction. The day after they were published, a message arrived from Berlin: 'A prominent member of the War Intelligence Department in the present German Ministry declares that the story is a hoax: Herzenwirth himself is a myth, or, if existing, a liar. It is officially stated that there is no such person.' Furthermore, the *News* was assured by the British War Office that their files 'contained no record to support any statement that an apparition was seen at Mons'.[2]

This story may have been a publicity stunt that was inspired by the activities of inventor Harry Grindell-Matthews. Among his more successful inventions was one of the first processes for talking films and a patented device that was capable of projecting still images onto clouds. On one occasion, the inventor used his 'Sky Projector' to shine his name and the Stars and Stripes 10,000ft above New York City. Then on Christmas Eve 1930 – just six weeks after the Angels of Mons hoax – he stunned shoppers in London by projecting the ghostly image of an angel onto clouds above Hampstead Heath. The scene was described in his biography, *The Death Ray Man*: '. . . the busy shoppers, hurrying home with festive fare, forgot everything as they watched, more and more fascinated, a mysterious steely beam of light shooting through one cloud into another. At first it looked to be part of the mythical underside of dark patches of storm cloud, but the radiance intensified, and focussed, taking shape all at one in the form of a beautiful mystic figure with hair flowing out into the wind . . . The apparition appeared to glide across the sky at terrific speed, with wings outstretched, lost at one moment in a cloud, only to reappear again from another one a moment later. She was formed out of mist, became real, and then vanished into the mist again . . .'[3]

According to Ernest Barwell, some observers fell to their knees in prayer, believing they were watching a real angel. They soon realised their mistake when the image was replaced by a message which read 'Happy Christmas'. The Sky Projector consisted of a large searchlight mounted on a motor chassis, with a truck carrying the power linked to the electricity supply at a nearby cinema. Whilst the projector failed to bring Matthews the success he craved, it captured the imagination of someone in the British intelligence service. As war with Germany approached, the British War Office was searching for a 'secret weapon' that could produce panic or fear among enemy soldiers of the type described by the mysterious Col. Herzenwirth. During the 'Phoney War' of 1939–40, British intelligence discussed using the projector against the advancing Wehrmacht. In February 1940, a propaganda committee examined a War Office suggestion to deploy a projector that would 'throw messages or images on to clouds', although the messages 'must be short and the images simple'. Brigadier Ronald Penney of the Royal Signals told the committee: 'The cloud conditions required are cumulous at 2–3,000ft and the visibility from one to four miles according to weather conditions. With these conditions operations can start half-an-hour after sunset at a distance of half-a-mile from the front line, when the letters or images would be projected onto the clouds over the enemy lines the right way up for the enemy troops to read and see.'[4]

Less enthusiastic members of the committee said the beams would immediately reveal the position of the projector to enemy aircraft and gunners, making it a prime target. Two years later, General Wavell employed magician Jasper Maskelyne to confuse the Axis forces with 'tricks, swindles and devices' to camouflage British forces during the desert campaign in North Africa. In his colourful memoir, *Magic: Top Secret,* the magician claimed to have used an array of powerful searchlights as an improvised 'death ray' to dazzle German aircraft attacking the Suez Canal.[5] But the reality was somewhat different. Although a prototype of Maskelyne's 'dazzle light' was tested, there is no evidence of it being used to bring down a single enemy aircraft.

CHAPTER 3

PHANTOMS IN THE ARCHIVES

Ghosts or human apparitions are told of in profusion, but
only one in six are alleged to have been seen by the person
giving the account. The apparition of a recently dead person
is common, and ghosts described usually appear in fairly
normal human form. Instances of the traditional fictional ghost
with head under arms, clanking chains or dripping blood are
exceptional . . .

Extract from a Mass Observation survey of 'Belief in the Supernatural', 1942[1]

Belief in a range of 'paranormal' phenomena is widespread in Britain today, but experiences with ghosts are particularly common. Occasionally evidence of these can be found in records of the police and fire service and has become public when these files have become part of proceedings in the criminal and civil courts. This chapter examines what these exceptional cases can tell us about both belief in and experience of anomalous phenomena in modern society.

Some idea of the numbers of people who have experienced uncanny phenomena can be judged from surveys that began in Victorian times. In 1882 the Society for Psychical Research sent out 17,000 questionnaires that asked whether respondents had ever seen or felt something, or heard a voice, that could not be explained by normal physical causes. Almost ten per cent of those who responded to the SPR's 'Census of Hallucinations in the sane' said they had, with a third saying they had heard disembodied voices.[2]

After the Second World War, when the Mass Observation survey conducted its surveys of supernatural beliefs, historians tended to regard ghosts as something that belonged to the past. For example, in his book *Religion and the Decline of Magic* (1971), Keith Thomas

FIGURE 3.1 A DOUBLE EXPOSURE IMAGE OF A 'GHOST' TAKEN IN 1899 AT THE HEIGHT OF VICTORIAN FASCINATION WITH THE SUPERNATURAL. A SURVEY OF 17,000 PEOPLE BY THE SOCIETY FOR PSYCHICAL RESEARCH FOUND ONE IN TEN HAD EXPERIENCED SOME FORM OF UNCANNY PHENOMENA. (CROWN COPYRIGHT, THE NATIONAL ARCHIVES COPY 1/439)

claimed that 'the social function of the belief in ghosts is obviously much diminished, and so is its extent'.[3] Yet the results recorded in the survey's archives show that large numbers continued to express belief in ghosts and five per cent reported a personal experience.

The Mass Observation surveys suggested that women tended to believe in other-wordly beings more than men, but there appeared to be great differences in what people believed ghosts *were*. More recently there has been a great revival in range of supernatural and extraordinary beliefs. A series of recent opinion polls show belief in, and experience of, ghosts has increased dramatically since the 1940s. A poll carried out in 1998 of 721 adults found 40 per cent believed and almost as many claimed to have had a personal experience.[4] A follow-up survey of 1,005 people in 2007 found belief had grown to 43 per cent and the differences in attitudes towards ghosts between genders remained.[5]

Polls such as these provide a superficial idea of the variety of beliefs and experiences that are common in modern Britain, but in order to understand what people really believe about ghosts it is necessary to interview those who have experienced them. A folklorist, Gillian Bennett, collected supernatural beliefs as part of her doctoral research from a group of women who attended a podiatry clinic in Manchester during the 1980s.[6] She wanted to explore the relationship between stories people told about ghosts and their personal beliefs. Rather than simply asking 'do you believe in ghosts?' as did the national surveys, Bennett gained their trust and simply enquired about their experience of 'the mysterious side of life'.

Of the 87 people she interviewed, two-thirds said they believed contact with the dead was possible and around half of these held that belief with certainty. Of the personal experiences collected in the Manchester survey, none was of the 'clanking chains or dripping blood' variety. Most were accounts of friendly spirits of the family dead who returned to warn or comfort the living. Another category was of 'things in houses' that included poltergeists ('noisy ghosts') and hauntings connected with places and people. Despite the high percentage of women who said they believed in visitations from the dead, omens and ESP, few admitted outright to belief in ghosts, spirits and hauntings. In her conclusions, Dr Bennett said the traditions she found were not what she expected: 'Having been brought up on literary ghost stories, naturally I expected to be told several standard ghost legends [but] the beliefs discussed and the stories told to me were very often far from what I expected,' she wrote. 'But then they were stories told from personal experience – not learned from books!'[7]

PHANTOMS OF EDGEHILL

To understand the origin and function of ghost beliefs in the present day, we need to examine the earliest written records. In medieval England, belief in the existence of ghosts was widespread and sanctioned by the Roman Catholic Church. The doctrine of purgatory, adopted by Rome from the 12th century, introduced the idea of a place where the souls of those who had sinned became trapped after death. It was accepted as natural that some 'revenants' were tormented sinners who were suffering purgatorial punishments. In order to achieve release and progress towards heaven, it was necessary to obtain assistance from the living, by the offering of prayers and masses for their souls. Alongside souls trapped in purgatory, there were undead bodies animated by the devil or demons that had to be 'laid' or exorcised as they were seen as posing a direct threat to the community. Throughout the Middle Ages, the idea that souls survived death and could, in certain circumstances, contact the living for help or be animated by the devil for evil purposes was common.[8] Spectres of many kinds are mentioned in contemporary documents, but the monstrous revenants that plagued medieval society are unlike anything described in the modern day.

Records from the early modern period illustrate the great changes that occurred in ghost beliefs. After the Reformation, Protestants rejected the concept of purgatory and began to regard ghostly manifestations as the work of the devil. In England the destruction of the abbeys and chantry chapels, where masses were once said for the dead, left many communities without the priests that helped them to negotiate their relationship with the supernatural. Ambiguity about the true identity of ghosts was reflected in the literature of the period. In *Hamlet*, for example, much of the narrative in the first half of the play revolves around the question of the ghost's identity.

Monarchs were occasionally drawn into this debate, as can be seen from one of the most famous ghost stories from the English Civil War. The spread and influence of such extraordinary stories had been increased by the invention of the printing press and during the war both sides used broadsides and pamphlets in attempts to discredit their opponents. Many were concerned with 'prodigies' – signs and portents – that appeared at the outbreak of the war. One such pamphlet, in the British Library collection, tells of *A Great Wonder in Heaven* that was witnessed after the battle of Edgehill, in Warwickshire.[9] The phantom army that appeared in the sky two months after the battle became so well known that it was cited in 1915 as a precedent for the visions of angels at Mons in Belgium (see Chapter 1).

The battle was fought near the village of Kineton in October 1642, when forces loyal to King Charles I clashed with the Parliamentarians. The seven-page pamphlet is presented in an altogether different form to the medieval texts that used ghosts to teach social and moral lessons. *A Great Wonder in Heaven* takes the form of a legal document, 'certified under the hands of William Wood esquire, and Justice of the Peace, Samuel Marshall, preacher . . . and other persons of qualitie'. It draws upon eyewitness accounts of those who saw the ghosts of slain soldiers, but unlike medieval ghost stories, it does not provide any clear explanation of their purpose in returning to earth.

The pamphlet describes the appearance of visions just before Christmas , a time of year that became strongly associated with ghosts during the Victorian era. The 17th-century account tells how: 'between twelve and one o'clock of the morning was heard by some shepherds, and other country-men, and travellers, first the sound of Drums a far off, and the noyse of Souldiers, as it were, giving out their last groanes; at which they were much amazed, and amazed stood still, till it seemed, by the neereness of the noyse, to approach them; at which too much affrighted, they sought to withdraw as fast as they could . . .'

Soon the noises were joined by visions in the sky, of 'incorporeall souldiers . . . with Ensignes display'd, Drummes beating, Musquests going off, Cannons discharged, Horses neighing, which also to these men were visible'. As they watched in terror, the observers saw an army carrying the colours of the king make a charge and afterwards these same soldiers were put to flight by the Roundheads. This phantom battle continued in the sky for upwards of three hours, before the visions and the noises faded, allowing the men to escape to Kineton where they woke Mr Wood, the JP, and Mr Marshall, the minister, 'averring it upon their oaths to be true'. These men initially found it difficult to believe this story, suspecting they were 'either mad or drunk'. Their scepticism evaporated on the following night, Christmas Eve, when the two armies appeared again in the sky and were seen by them and other villagers. This was the first of many other phantom re-enactments of the battle that continued into the new year.

When rumours reached King Charles at his camp in Oxford, he sent Col. Lewis Kirke, Captain Dudley, Captain Wainman and three other 'gentlemen of credit, to take the full view and notice of the said business' directly from the eyewitnesses. In what became the first royal inquiry into a ghostly apparition, the minister, Mr Marshall, and others gave their testimony on oath to the king. 'What this does portend,' the pamphlet concluded, 'God only knoweth, and time perhaps will discover', but to many readers the prodigy was a sign of God's displeasure, 'of his wrath against this Land, for these civill wars, which He in his good time will finish'.

Charles I was not the only monarch to concern himself with the supernatural. The Scottish King James VI, who became James I of England in 1603, nurtured a fascination for witchcraft that he shared with many other educated people. In 1597 he published a book, *Daemonologie*, that triggered a period of officially sanctioned witch-hunting that sent many hundreds of Scots to their deaths. James' fear of witches stemmed from his personal involvement in the North Berwick witch trials a decade earlier. Following his marriage to Princess Anne, the sister of the King of Denmark, the royal ship was forced to shelter in Norway after a series of terrific storms in the North Sea. These were blamed in both countries on witchcraft and in 1590, after James' return to Scotland, a plot was uncovered that implicated several Scottish nobles in a conspiracy involving a coven of witches. King James personally interrogated one of the accused, Agnes Sampson, at Holyrood Palace in Edinburgh. She later confessed under torture and was burned as a witch. In the introduction to his book, James refers to 'these detestable slaves of the Devil, the Witches or enchaunters' that had led him to write his justification of witch-hunting 'to resolve the doubting . . . both that such assaults of Satan are more certainly practised, and that the instrument thereof merits most severely to be punished'.[10]

By the 18th century, scepticism about witchcraft and other supernatural beliefs was growing among the educated classes of British society. This was reflected in changes in the laws against witchcraft. During the reign of George II, both the English and Scottish statutes on this issue were rescinded and the Witchcraft Act of 1735 brought an end to the witchcraft craze of earlier centuries (see panel, p.84). The Age of Enlightenment led educated people to reject the reality of witches and their pact with the devil. They began to regard magical beliefs as delusions and Parliament made it an offence for anyone to claim they had such powers or, in the words of one Edwardian commentator, 'turned the witch into a cheat and impostor, and substituted the pillory for the stake'. The penalty for those convicted was a year in prison and the last person executed for witchcraft was a Scottish woman, Janet Horne, in 1727.

THE HAMMERSMITH GHOST

Despite the rejection of magical beliefs as vulgar and superstitious, members of the judiciary – and even monarchs – were occasionally called upon to adjudicate upon court proceedings when cases linked to such matters arose. The most extraordinary example occurred during the reign of George III and led to a change in the law surrounding murder. The story of the conviction of Francis Smith, who shot dead a man he believed to be a ghost in Hammersmith, London, was described by Alan Murdie, a barrister and chair of the Ghost Club, as a case that 'bristles with legal and supernatural interest'.[11] The public fascination with Smith's trial at the Old Bailey is reflected in the account published in *The Newgate Calendar*, a record of trials and executions during the 18th and 19th centuries.

Although Hammersmith today has been swallowed by the bustling modern metropolis of Greater London, at the beginning of the 19th century it was a village surrounded by fields. At night the lanes and roads surrounding the parish churchyard were isolated and unlit and it was from here, before Christmas in 1803, that stories spread describing a terrifying spectre. Dressed in robes of white and sometimes the skin of a calf, the ghost emerged from the graveyard to attack passers-by. The impersonation of ghosts by evildoers would become widespread in Britain during the later Victorian period and panics were frequently generated by the nocturnal activities of bogeymen such as Spring-heeled Jack. In this case earlier beliefs about revenants held sway, in that it was believed the 'Hammersmith Ghost' was the spirit of a local man who had committed suicide by cutting his throat. At this time ghosts frequently appeared in white as it was common for poor people who could not afford a coffin to bury their dead in winding sheets or shrouds. Suicides were singled out for special attention as it was believed those who had suffered a bad death could 'come again' to trouble the living. Until 1823, it was the custom in some areas to bury the bodies of suicides face-down at crossroads with a wooden stake driven through their bodies if a coroner's inquest found they had deliberately taken their own lives whilst of sound mind. This gruesome ritual was to prevent their souls from returning to haunt the community.[12]

According to the *Newgate Calendar's* account of the Hammersmith Ghost, one of its first victims was the pregnant wife of a locksmith who 'when crossing near the churchyard about ten o'clock at night, beheld something, as she described, rise from the tombstones. She attempted to run; but the ghost soon overtook her, and pressed her in his arms, when she fainted; in which situation she remained some hours, till discovered by some neighbours, who kindly led her home, when she took to her bed, from which, alas she never rose'. According to an account published in *The Times*, this woman lay dead from fright and two others were dangerously ill.[13] On another occasion the 'ghost' leapt upon a wagon carrying 16 passengers after the driver fled, so there was no safety in numbers. The

FIGURE 3.2 A DEPICTION OF 'THE HAMMERSMITH GHOST' THAT TERRORISED RESIDENTS IN NORTH LONDON DURING THE EARLY 19TH CENTURY. IN JANUARY 1804 FRANCIS SMITH, AN EXCISE OFFICER, WAS CONVICTED OF THE MURDER OF A BRICKLAYER HE SHOT DEAD WHILST HUNTING THE GHOST. HIS TRIAL AT THE OLD BAILEY EVENTUALLY LED TO A REVIEW OF THE LAW THAT WAS APPLIED WHEN SOMEONE KILLED ANOTHER AS A RESULT OF A GENUINE MISTAKE – IN THIS CASE BELIEVING HE WAS A GHOST. (COURTESY OF THE BRITISH MUSEUM, REF PPA107855)

haunting was the chief topic of conversation in local taverns and anyone wearing white or pale clothes was at risk of attack from vigilantes. This would take a deadly turn. According to a story in *The Times*, Francis Smith, an excise officer, spent the evening of 3 January 1803 drinking in the White Hart Inn when he heard stories of women and children terrorised by the ghost. He was so incensed that he went home and returned with a loaded gun, saying 'he would act this night, go and try to meet the Ghost, and shoot it'.

According to the subsequent indictment, at 11pm Smith took his gun to Black Lion Lane where he saw a man dressed in white, whom he challenged, but received no answer. As the figure approached, Smith fired a shot and it crumpled to the floor. He was horrified to discover he had shot and killed 23-year-old James Milwood (or Milward), who was dressed in a white apron and flannel clothes, his usual outfit for bricklaying. In his witness statement John Lock, a wine merchant, described how he and a watchman met Smith 'who told him he had shot a man who he believed was the pretended ghost of Hammersmith'. The night was very dark and visibility was further impaired by tall hedges on either side of the lane so that 'a person on one side of the road could not distinguish an object on the other'. Lock said he had never seen it '[but] the dress in which the ghost was said to appear corresponded with that worn by the deceased, being white . . . the deceased had on white trousers, down to his shoes; a white apron round him, and a flannel jacket on his body'. Lock said Smith had lost the bravado he displayed earlier at the White Hart Inn. In fact, he was in such an agitated state that he could 'scarcely speak' and, accepting the consequences of his actions, asked to be taken into custody.[14]

On 5 January an inquest was opened at the Black Lion Inn and the jury recorded a verdict of unlawful killing. Smith's trial opened at the Old Bailey just ten days after Milwood's death with three judges attending: Lord Chief Baron Macdonald presided, accompanied by Judges Rooke and Lawrence. Although a full transcript of the proceedings has not survived, Smith's indictment and five witness statements, including that of John Rook, have survived in a folio document at The National Archives.[15] During the trial, the jury heard some extraordinary evidence. A number of witnesses were called by the defence counsel to testify to Smith's good character, including the sister of the victim, Anne Milwood, who said 'she had heard great talk of a ghost stalking up and down the neighbourhood, all in white, with horns and glass eyes'. Milwood's mother-in-law testified that he was obstinate in his nocturnal habits and had earlier scared two women and a man in a churchyard. When the scare broke out in Hammersmith, she warned the bricklayer to wear a greatcoat over his white clothes 'in order that he might not encounter any danger'.

Smith said nothing during the trial, as at that time defendants had no right to give evidence in their own defence, but an unsworn statement in his handwriting was received by the court. In this he admitted the shot was fired at a time when 'he did not know what he was doing' but he bore no malice towards Milwood, 'nor any intention of taking away the life of an individual whatever'. Addressing the jury, the Lord Chief Baron said no matter how they might feel about the 'abominable person guilty of the misdemeanour of terrifying the neighbourhood', Smith had nevertheless committed wilful murder by shooting an innocent man. After retiring for an hour the jury returned a verdict that Smith was guilty of manslaughter. This was not accepted by the judges, who directed them to reconsider, on the grounds that 'the verdict should be "guilty of murder" or "a total acquittal through want of evidence"'. When the verdict of murder was delivered Smith, then aged 29, 'sank into a state of stupefaction exceeding despair'. He now faced a sentence of death by hanging with his body handed over for dissection. Being aware of the sympathy his case had aroused Baron Macdonald told the jury he would immediately report the case to King George. Within a few hours, a message came back from Buckingham Palace and Smith's sentence was commuted to one year's hard labour.[16]

THE WENDIGO

The strange saga of the Hammersmith Ghost did not end with Smith's narrow escape from death. For more than a century his trial was cited in legal textbooks as a test case in discussion of the *mens rea* for murder. As Alan Murdie explains, the mental state of an accused person was rarely examined in 19th-century trials 'and much of the psychological terminology routinely used today had yet to be invented'. Although some allowances were made for mistakes, 'common law could not accept that violent deaths simply happened by accident'. In this case legal opinion was that Smith had used excessive rather than reasonable force when he shot Smith, regardless of his state of mind at the time.

This view was challenged in 1949 by Glanville Williams in an essay published by the *Law Quarterly Review*.[17] Williams argued that a defendant who honestly but mistakenly believed that he was fighting off a supernatural entity should not be convicted of murder. He compared the Hammersmith Ghost with a more recent case from Canada. This involved a member of the Algonquian tribe from the Great Lakes region of Ontario who was arrested after shooting a man he believed was a 'wendigo'. The Algonquian believed that wendigo were shape-shifting evil spirits who could either possess humans or take human form and were associated with cannibalism. But the wendigo could itself be killed by a bullet. When one night in 1894 a wendigo was spotted prowling near a village, guards were posted to keep a look out. Williams said 'the prisoner was one of these and he saw what appeared to be a tall human being running at a distance, which he supposed was a wendigo. He gave chase and after challenging three times and receiving no answer, fired'. The 'wendigo' turned out to be the guard's own foster-father, who died from his injuries. The gunman was arrested and at his trial the jury convicted him not of murder, as in Smith's case, but of manslaughter.[18]

Williams argued that it was 'intolerable that questions as to the reality of psychic phenomena should have to be investigated on a charge of murder', particularly as some jury members might share a belief in ghosts and evil spirits. These arguments led British courts to review the law in cases where someone had killed another person as a result of a genuine mistake. Alan Murdie points out that were the case of Francis Smith to be repeated in the present day, the verdict would almost certainly be not guilty of murder, 'although manslaughter or conviction of a firearms offence would remain a possibility' and a complete acquittal could not be ruled out.[19]

The identity of the real Hammersmith Ghost was never resolved, although one suspect, a shoemaker called James Graham, was arrested late in January 1804, and charged with nuisance and going out at night dressed in a blanket to impersonate a ghost. Questioned by magistrates, Graham accounted for his actions by saying he adopted the disguise to terrify some delinquent apprentices who had terrorised his children.[20]

THE HEADLESS WOMAN

The Hammersmith Ghost scare generated a curious sequel when, soon afterwards, a group of soldiers from the Coldstream Guards came forward to report seeing a 'headless woman' prowling St James's Park, in the heart of London. As *The Times* reported, 'it would appear that the result of the trial of [Francis] Smith, had reached the ears of the headless woman in the Park and that she had, in consequence, bade adieu to her nightly visits in that quarter'.[21] The apparition was seen to enter the park near the Royal Cockpit and glide towards the canal (now a lake), where it vanished or sank into the water. According to Jacob Larwood in *The Story of the London Parks* (1874), the local belief was that 'some twenty years before a Sergeant in the Guards murdered his wife by cutting off her head, and had thrown her body in the canal'. As a result the restless, headless ghost of the victim became a constant theme of conversation among the soldiers in the guard room.[22]

Early in January 1804, the apparition was seen by 'one of the most resolute men in the regiment' who was taken ill immediately on leaving his post and needed hospital treatment. Several days later the headless ghost appeared before another whom *The Times* said had braved cannon-balls but 'was now panic struck at a shadow'. When the ghost appeared, his jaw locked and he found himself unable to utter the customary challenge to intruders. Quitting his post, he ran to the guard room where he collapsed in a fit and soon afterwards joined his comrade in hospital. Several men from the regiment declared on oath that they had seen the apparition and two were summonsed to appear before Sir Richard Ford, one of the magistrates of Westminster. In a statement dated 15 January 1804, Lt Col. George Jones of the Coldstream Guards, declared:

'. . . that whilst on guard at the Recruit House [now Wellington Barracks], on or about the 3rd instant, about half-past one in the morning, I perceived the figure of a woman without a head, rise from the earth at the distance of about two feet before me. I was so alarmed at the circumstances that I had not power to speak to it, which was my wish to have done. But I distinctly observed that the figure was dressed in a red striped gown, with red spots between each stripe, and that part of the dress and figure appeared to me to be enveloped in a cloud. In about the space of two minutes, whilst my eyes were fixed on the object, it vanished from my sight. I was perfectly sober and collected at the time, and being in great trepidation called to the next sentinel, who met me half way, and to whom I communicated the strange sight I had seen.[23]

During the hearing, the Chief Clerk to the court asked Jones 'whether his imagination had received any impressions from reading any dismal story, or if he had . . . suffered the story of the Hammersmith Ghost to dwell on his mind, in order, if possible to ascertain if he had been misled by fancies'. Jones denied this and stated he was 'ready at any time to make oath to what he had stated, and that he firmly believed he had seen a ghost'. Even the sceptical *Times* reporter had to concede it was an undoubted fact that 'two sentinels have been sent [to hospital] from the effects of fright, whatever may have been the real cause of it'.

One week later, the newspaper announced it had solved the mystery: 'The Ghost in St James's Park, we understand, originated in an application of the *Phantasmagoria*, by two unlucky Westminster Scholars, who having got possession of an empty house on the side of the Bird Cage Walk, were enabled to produce the appearance which so greatly alarmed the sentinels on duty in the immediate vicinity of the spot, and has given such an extraordinary subject to the curiosity of the public.'[24]

THE FIERY GHOST OF HACKNEY

The strange case of the Hammersmith Ghost provides an insight into the clash between popular beliefs held by the ordinary folk and educated elite of Georgian society. Although the jury were not obliged to pass judgement on the existence (or otherwise) of the 'ghost' it was evident from the witness testimony that society was divided between those who believed and those who regarded such stories as an example of vulgar superstition. This case was not the first or last where this subject was raised in a British courtroom and, while the judiciary have tended to be sceptical, this has not always been the case.

A slim file at The National Archives, opened by the Ministry of Housing and Local Government in 1968, contains details of one of the most extraordinary cases to come before the civil courts of England.[25] The contents tell the story of a haunted house in the London borough of Hackney that began with a series of poltergeist manifestations. Unlike other hauntings in suburbia, this case led all the way to a judgement at the High Court. According to court documents, a Mr and Mrs Richard McGhee became tenants of the three-storey rented property at 69 Spencer Grove, in 1963. They shared the 150-year-old house with two daughters, one of whom who was unmarried and occupied the ground floor. The second daughter, Sally Strachan, lived on the third floor with her husband and a young daughter. The family appear to have been aware of rumours about the house being haunted, but four years of their tenancy passed without any problems.

In 1967, however, unusual happenings began to occur on a large scale. According to evidence heard by the High Court, 'some of it took the form of what were thought to be poltergeists causing havoc with the furniture, causing noises and the like, and secondly there were said to be manifestations of ghosts . . . [one] that was seen was that of a hunch-backed cobbler who, it was said, had lodged there 90 years ago and who mysteriously caused several fires in the house'. The first apparition was seen by Mrs Strachan's daughter Elaine, then aged three, who called her mother to her bedroom and said she had seen a 'lady in white' emerging from a wardrobe in the corner of the room. Soon afterwards, Mrs Strachan saw the ghost herself. After a series of odd happenings one evening, at midnight she opened her bedroom door to see what looked like a woman in a white dress standing in the middle of the room with one arm crossed in front of her. She wore a long Victorian style dress with buttons fastened by loops, frills at the cuffs and a close-fitting bonnet on her head. The ghost's face was frightening, with enormous black eyes that appeared to radiate hatred.

Petrified by this vision, Mrs Strachan called her sister, June, who saw the ghost from a different angle and was equally disturbed by its menacing black eyes. Their father, Richard McGhee, reached the scene shortly afterwards and noticed what appeared to be a cloud of wispy smoke drifting towards the ceiling. A similar phenomenon was later seen by Mrs Strachan. The smoke emerged from three large wardrobes in the family bedroom, then twisted and formed spiral patterns before dissipating. Soon afterwards, a heavy wardrobe began to dance around the room before coming to rest facing the door.

During the summer, news of the hauntings reached the Society for Psychical Research (SPR) and local newspapers. Visits were made to the house by SPR investigators and clergymen who were interested in spiritualist phenomena, some of whom witnessed unexplained phenomena. On one occasion the SPR's chairman, the late Tom Perrott, accompanied by the author Peter Underwood, arrived for a tour. In his book *Haunted London* (1973), Underwood said Mr McGhee showed them a fixed cupboard from which uncanny rapping noises had been heard. 'As we left the room I suggested that we might try to tempt the entity and I tapped twice on the cupboard shelf, closed the door and we all left the room and began to descend the stairs,' he wrote. 'As we did so two clear and distinct knocks sounded from the direction of the room we had just left, raps that were heard by all four of us, the Rev. John Robbins also being present.'[26]

On another occasion, the Rev. Robbins and another researcher, Ralph Barker, were talking to the family when 'there was a loud explosion outside the room', but nothing could be found to account for it. The 'explosion' and the appearance of 'smoke' in the bedroom was an ominous precedent for the events that were to follow. During October a series of fires broke out in the property, leading the family to spend one uncomfortable night in the garden. Eventually, in fear of the ghosts they believed haunted the old property, the family left to stay with friends and returned only in daytime to secure the doors and windows. During this period, five separate blazes were reported to the London Fire Brigade who produced a report that is included in the case file. In his account, the Chief Fire Officer said the brigade was called to deal with blazes at the house on four separate occasions during October and November 1967. On the first occasion, they found a fire in bedding on the ground floor had already been extinguished by Mr McGhee, but whilst checking the property they discovered a second fire had broken out in the kitchen on the first floor. Their report says there was no obvious connection between them but because the family believed they were 'manifestations of a poltergeist', the officer in charge recorded the cause as 'doubtful'.[27]

Two days later, the brigade were recalled to deal with a 'fairly fierce fire' in a room on the first floor. Richard McGhee told the brigade no one had been in the room before the fire broke out and 'in his opinion the house was haunted and that the fire was the work of a poltergeist'. Two further visits were made to the house and in all cases the cause of the fires was officially recorded as 'doubtful', a phrase used by the brigade, according to the documents, 'in recording the supposed cause when the officer-in-charge considers that the circumstances suggest that a fire be other than accidental origin'. By now the house was badly damaged and Hackney Council recommended that the rent should be reduced to a nominal sum 'representing the value of this to all intents and purposes uninhabited house'.

When the landlord objected to the rent officer's decision, the dispute escalated and the family were called to a hearing of Hackney Council's Rent Assessment Committee. The Rev. John Robbins agreed to represent them and, at the hearing, claimed the fires had been caused by unknown psychic forces. Citing historical precedents, he mentioned the case of Epworth Parsonage, the Lincolnshire home of John Wesley and his family. This was the scene of intense poltergeist activity in 1709, culminating in the destruction of the house by fire. Although he understood members of the committee found it difficult to accept the existence of unexplained phenomena, he said he was personally convinced there was some 'mysterious form of energy' in the house at Spencer Grove. This 'energy' had caused a wardrobe to burst into flames and created the loud explosion that he heard whilst visiting the family. He said there was no one else around at the time and: 'I can voice for this as I was present. I could not find any physical cause.' In his evidence, he pointed out the family were not in arrears for their rent before the fires occurred and the rent book itself had been destroyed in one of the outbreaks. 'No evidence of arson had been discovered and insurance assessors had not found a cause,' he said.[28]

In their written decision, the committee restored the original rent and said: 'the tenant and his family say that these fires were caused by a poltergeist, a psychical phenomenon, sometimes playful and sometimes malicious, which is of a supernatural origin . . . we accept these gentlemen are genuinely and sincerely convinced of their beliefs. Nonetheless, we are unable to accept that the fires were caused by supernatural forces and, as the tenant himself in his evidence ruled out the possibility of outside intruders, we came to the conclusion that the tenant had been negligent in leaving the house uninhabited at night with gas and electricity services still connected.'

GREATER LONDON COUNCIL
Chief Officer of the London Fire Brigade, L. W. T. Leete, CBE, MI Fire E

LONDON FIRE BRIGADE
Headquarters, Albert Embankment, London, SE1
RELiance 3811 ext 363   or ext
    735-3811

your ref 5/SW/885   my ref FB/GL/G/11/1

5 April 1968

Dear Sirs

Fires at 69 Spencer Grove, N.16

With reference to your letter dated 4 April 1968 and to your previous telephone conversation with my assistant, it is confirmed that the Brigade attended four fires at the above address, viz. on 20 October 1967, 22 October 1967, 26 October 1967 and 15 November 1967, and I have pleasure in enclosing copy extracts from the reports of these fires. Additionally, calls were received to the same premises on 24 November 1967, 9 December 1967 and 14 December 1967, but these proved to be false calls of a malicious nature.

On 20 October 1967, when the Brigade arrived, it was found that a small fire in some bedding in the back bedroom on the ground floor had been extinguished by the occupier. During his investigation to endeavour to establish a cause of the fire, the officer-in-charge discovered that another separate small fire had occurred and had burned out in the kitchen on the first floor. In view of the fact that there was no apparent connection between the two fires and the assertions of the occupier that the fires were manifestations of a poltergeist, the officer recorded the supposed cause as "doubtful" and informed the police of the circumstances.

With regard to the attendance on 22 October 1967, a fairly fierce fire was discovered in a corner of the front room on the first floor and was quickly extinguished. On investigation no apparent cause could be discovered but a quantity of wearing apparel was strewn over the floor and the room was in disarray. The occupier informed the officer-in-charge that nobody had been in the room prior to the fire; in his opinion the house was haunted and that the fire was the work of a poltergeist. Having regard to the statements of the occupier and to the previous fire, the supposed cause was recorded as "doubtful" and the police were informed.

Although the fires on 26 October 1967 and 15 November 1967 presented no unusual features no cause could be established and, having regard to the previous incidents at the same address, they have also been recorded as "doubtful".

The term "doubtful" is used in recording the supposed cause when the officer-in-charge considers that the circumstances suggest that a fire could be of other than accidental origin.

A charge of 10s. is made in each instance for the supply of an extract from the report of a fire and I shall be glad if you will remit the sum of £2 to these Headquarters. Cheques or orders should be made payable to the Greater London Council and crossed.

Yours faithfully,

Chief Officer

Messrs. Geo. J. Dowse & Co.
19 Kingsland High Street
London
E.8

FIGURE 3.3 A REPORT ON A SERIES OF UNEXPLAINED FIRES IN A 'HAUNTED HOUSE' AT HACKNEY, BY THE CHIEF OFFICER OF THE LONDON FIRE BRIGADE IN APRIL 1968. (CROWN COPYRIGHT, THE NATIONAL ARCHIVES HLG 121/17)

Afterwards Mr McGhee lodged an appeal against the decision with the Queen's Bench Division of the High Court. On 29 April 1968 the case came before Lord Parker, the Lord Chief Justice of England. In his judgement, Lord Parker appeared more sympathetic to the family's plight and agreed that a number of people 'were fully convinced that this was a haunted house, that there were ghosts that manifested themselves from time to time, and that there were poltergeists . . . [and] so seriously did the tenant and his family take the matter that they began sleeping away from the house and only occupying it during the day'. He said the committee's refusal to accept a supernatural explanation for the fires was 'a view which many of us would take', but said their reasoning was 'difficult to understand'.

Chief Justice Parker said the committee had ruled out supernatural causes, they had ruled out intruders and were not suggesting the tenant or his family 'had deliberately set fire to the house for some purpose of their own, but merely said . . . that he had been negligent in leaving the house uninhabited at night with the gas and electricity still connected'. Overturning their decision, he ruled that if this was a negligent act, then 'I am afraid that many of us would be guilty of negligence'.[29]

The 'haunted house' on Spencer Grove, Stoke Newington, was eventually demolished but the story remains one of the most curious cases in the archives of psychical research. While Chief Justice Parker appears to have been sympathetic towards the ordeal of the McGhee family, a more recent case saw a judge take the opposite view. In 1998 a dispute between two families over a haunted cottage in the Peak District became the subject of a civil case heard before Derby County Court. Andrew Smith and his wife Josie, who had three children, withheld £3,000 on the purchase price on their payment for 300-year-old Lowes Cottage at Upper Mayfield on the Derbyshire/Staffordshire border. The previous owners, two sisters who had lived in the village all their lives, sued the couple for the return of the balance.

When the case came to court, the Smiths had a novel defence to the action. They claimed the women had not warned them that the house was haunted when they agreed to buy. In January 1999 the Smiths and witnesses testified to a host of phenomena they claimed to have endured during their four years in the cottage. These included deep groans, creaking floorboards, footsteps, objects flying through the air, electrical equipment failing, acrid smells and sudden, inexplicable drops in temperature. Josie Smith claimed she had seen apparitions of a bound and naked woman, a little boy with piggy eyes and a woman in 19th-century costume. She also recounted the two occasions in which some invisible entity had gripped her by the neck and pinned her to the bed. As was the case in Spencer Grove, members of a local spiritualist church visited the house and confirmed their belief that the cottage was haunted. Evidence was given in court by a local priest, the Rev. Peter Mockford, who said he had carried out an exorcism at the cottage and was convinced it was haunted.

Nevertheless, the couple's evidence failed to impress the judge, Peter Stratton QC. He said the priest had taken the Smith's story on trust 'after a half-hour conversation – hardly a rigorous examination'. Judge Stretton concluded with a scathing ten-minute summary of the case, saying: 'visitors were in the house, children played there and they were un-troubled. Had there been things of the sort suggested by the defendants taking place then this would have been quite impossible.' He dismissed the stories of supernatural noises, dampness and smell as more likely to have been created by man than by ghosts. In his judgement, he included a statement that summed up the judiciary's attitude towards the supernatural: 'There is no acceptable evidence that the house was ever haunted.'[30]

THE SOLWAY SPACEMAN PHOTOGRAPH

In the cases from Stoke Newington and Upper Mayfield, judges were obliged to rely upon eyewitness testimony. Such testimony is rarely conclusive, but courts have never had the opportunity to examine hard evidence such as photographs or closed circuit television footage of extraordinary phenomena. During the trial of the spiritualist medium Helen Duncan in 1944, the presiding judge famously refused to allow her to demonstrate her powers by holding a séance in the Old Bailey for the benefit of the jury (see panel, p.85).

There is one very unusual case in the British archives that involves photographic evidence of a supernatural entity. This story did not emerge as a result of a court hearing, but it did lead to a police investigation and inquiries by the Ministry of Defence, and its status remains controversial to this day.[31] The mysterious case of the 'Solway Spaceman' began in very ordinary circumstances on a summer evening in 1964. On the afternoon of 23 May Jim Templeton, who was employed by the Cumbrian Fire Service, took his wife and young daughters for a day out at the nearby beauty spot of Solway Marshes. The marshes lie south of the Solway Estuary that separates England from Scotland and, looking north, face the Chapelcross nuclear power station in Dumfriesshire. Templeton was a keen photographer and, using his Zeiss Pentacon SLR camera, he took a series of photographs of his youngest daughter Elizabeth, then aged five, as she sat on the grass holding a bunch of sea pinks. None of the family noticed anything unusual at the time and the film was duly sent to Kodak for processing.

When Jim Templeton collected the prints, the shop assistant told him it was a pity one of the best pictures had been 'spoiled by the man in the background wearing a space suit'. He was baffled until he took a close look at the photographs. On one print, apparently floating just behind his daughter's head, was a large figure dressed in a white outfit that resembled those worn by NASA astronauts. In his own words, Templeton said: 'I thought the girl assistant was joking at first because there was no one else in the vicinity when I took the photograph – but there was the figure. [It] is standing about eight yards behind my little girl and it can be seen fairly clearly on the photograph. The figure appears to be wearing a white space suit of some kind, and he is wearing protective headgear which could be Perspex, because you can see the outer glow of it and the dark outline of the side of his head. He is standing with one hand on his hip and the body is solid.' His first thought was to take further advice from the film's manufacturers, Kodak. In a letter, they concluded 'the object in the background is definitely part of the image and has not been added after exposure . . . what the object is, or who it is, it is not possible to determine due to the background being out of focus'.[32]

FIGURE 3.4 THE MYSTERIOUS SOLWAY SPACEMAN PHOTOGRAPH TAKEN BY AN EMPLOYEE OF THE CUMBRIAN FIRE SERVICE, JIM TEMPLETON, IN MAY 1964. THE IMAGE REMAINS UNEXPLAINED BUT A POLICE INVESTIGATION DECIDED THE 'SPACEMAN' MIGHT HAVE BEEN SOMEONE WHO WALKED INTO THE SHOT OF JIM'S DAUGHTER ELIZABETH, BUT WAS NOT SEEN BY THE PHOTOGRAPHER AT THE TIME. (COURTESY OF THE LATE JIM TEMPLETON)

As Jim Templeton worked for the fire service, it was only natural that he should ask his colleagues in the Carlisle police force to take a look at the photograph. Unfortunately the file on the photograph opened by detectives at Carlisle CID in 1964 has been lost.[33] However, the files of the local newspaper, the *Cumberland News*, provide vital clues. The paper said detectives considered and ruled out various theories including the possibility of a mirage or a double exposure, but were sceptical of the idea it showed a spaceman. Although they were unable to reach a definite conclusion, they decided that the person in the photograph may have been Anne Templeton, Jim's wife, as police asked him if she 'could have stepped into the picture' without him noticing. But Jim Templeton said this was impossible as she was standing behind him at the time, holding their other child's hand. Nevertheless, Supt Tom Oldcorn, head of the CID at Carlisle, said police photographic experts had examined the print and 'the feeling is that someone has got into the picture'.[34]

Soon afterwards, the puzzling photograph appeared in the London tabloids and, to use Internet parlance, news of its existence quickly went viral. Jim and his daughter became media celebrities as the image was flashed round the world, appearing in newspapers as far apart as Australia and Norway. Within days the family were besieged by phone calls and letters from people interested in parapsychology and flying saucers, all putting forward ideas and theories from the mundane to the ridiculous. For example, a woman psychic wrote from Wales to say the 'spaceman' may have been the 'spirit form' of a test pilot killed in an accident at one of the RAF's rocket-testing bases in Cumbria. 'But it is equally possible that you or your little girl is psychic and emanate an invisible power which the sensitive camera negative can pick up and use automatically,' she wrote.[35]

The strange costume of the figure and its appearance in the vicinity of an area that contained nuclear bases and other sensitive military facilities inevitably led the *Cumberland News* to contact the Ministry of Defence. The MoD said they would be pleased to analyse the photograph, but when Jim Templeton was told they required both the original film and camera for analysis, he refused to part with them. Although the photograph is mentioned in letters received by the MoD's UFO desk, S4(Air) there is nothing to suggest they took a deeper interest in what it showed.[36] Whether or not Templeton was just being cautious in refusing to supply the original film and camera for analysis, or whether he had good reason for not letting them out of his hands, is a matter for speculation. In hindsight, a strange event that took place shortly after the photograph came to the attention of the media has led some to believe that a secretive government agency sent secret agents to investigate the mysterious image.

THE MYSTERIOUS MEN IN BLACK

In June 1964, Jim Templeton was quoted as saying that 'perfect strangers passing through Carlisle have come here to see me and discuss the picture'.[37] Two of these were very unusual indeed. They appeared at Carlisle fire station and were dressed entirely in black and drove a brand new black Jaguar car. The men asked to see the place where the photograph was taken. When Jim asked for proof of their identity, he was shown a card bearing an official crest and the word 'Security'. They told him, 'We're from the Ministry, but you don't need to know who we are. We go by numbers'. He noticed the pair referred to each other as 'nine' and 'eleven'. Their obvious lack of knowledge of the area and inability to pronounce local place names led him to conclude they were unfamiliar with the area. Once they reached the marshes the following conversation took place:

'Pull up on here. This is where the photograph was taken' . . . They asked, 'Can you take us to the exact spot?' I said, 'Yes'. So we walked across, and I said, 'This is where the photograph was taken'. One looked at the other, and the other looked at him and said, 'This is where you saw the large man, the alien?' I said, 'No, we didn't see anybody . . . I never saw anybody'. 'Thank you very much,' he said, and he walked away.[38]

In a bizarre conclusion to the journey, the men then drove off in their Jaguar, leaving Jim Templeton on the marshes from where he was obliged to walk a mile to the nearest garage, where he phoned for a taxi. The story of Jim Templeton's 'spaceman' photograph and the visit from the sinister 'Men in Black' (MIB) has become a cause célèbre for UFOlogists. It features in a number of books and television programmes dealing with unexplained phenomena and was recently voted in the 'top ten' of evidential stories by a panel of American UFO experts.

Who were Jim Templeton's mystery 'MIB' visitors? A former incumbent of the British government's UFO desk, Nick Pope, believes there are 'Walter Mitty' types among the civilian population who are prepared to impersonate MoD officials in order to gain access to civilians who have witnessed unusual phenomena for their own reasons.[39] Evidence for the activities of such individuals is well documented in the MoD's UFO files and it is perhaps significant that the two mysterious men turned up, along with many other less eccentric visitors, after the spaceman photograph had received widespread publicity.

When I interviewed Jim Templeton in 2001, he told me he firmly believed the mystery visitors were sent by the British government. However, newspaper archives from 1964 reveal he took a very different view of the matter at that time. In September of that year, his story reached the national media and journalists asked the Carlisle police for confirmation that he had been quizzed by agents of the security services. Detective Chief Inspector Stanley Armstrong told the *Cumberland News*: 'I know nothing whatsoever about this meeting. I don't know who the men were and I have told Mr Templeton that he should have taken the number of the car and reported the incident to the police.' After the police became involved, Jim Templeton moved to play down the significance of the 'meeting'. He told the paper: 'It all looks like a leg-pull to me. I'm sure the men were not security agents and I have no idea why they should want to pass themselves off as such.'[40]

More recently, the visit by the mysterious 'Men in Black' has been linked with the presence of two 'spaceman' on a photograph taken near sensitive military facilities. In 2001, Mr Templeton told me that soon after his photograph was published he was contacted by someone from the Blue Streak missile testing ground at Woomera in South Australia. This person had seen the Cumbrian 'spaceman' photograph in an Australian newspaper and believed it was uncannily similar to two large figures that had appeared on screens at a rocket test just hours before his photograph was taken. According to the letter, this led technicians to call a halt to the countdown and abort the launch. Although the area was searched, no trace of anyone could be found. Blue Streak missiles had been developed for use from 1957 at RAF Spadeadam, near Carlisle, where Jim worked for the fire service. Templeton came to believe it was uncanny that similar 'spacemen' had turned up independently on photographs taken near the missile facilities in England and just hours earlier in Australia, thousands of miles away.

Jim Templeton told this story when interviewed by UFOlogist Jenny Randles for a BBC2 documentary *Tales of the Paranormal*, shown in 1996. He said the Australian technicians had claimed the figures were 'exactly the same type of man: same dress, same figure, same size as in the original photograph'. The mystery appeared to increase when, as part of the research for the programme, Jenny searched UFO files from 1964 held by The National Archives. There she found letters from members of the public referring to both the 'Cumberland spaceman' and to a 'mysterious object' captured on film during the rocket launch.[41] Unfortunately, there was no trace of the 'can of film' mentioned in the archives. The broadcast fascinated a Conservative MP, Christopher Fraser. Soon after watching it, he wrote to the Ministry of Defence asking what had become of the 'missing' film.[42] Files released by The National Archives in 2010 revealed that inquiries by the MoD revealed the film was neither secret nor 'missing'. The footage was part of a British Pathé newsreel that was open to the public at the Imperial War Museum in London.[43] The film shows a rocket test on 5 June 1964 and a 'mysterious object' is indeed visible in the sky beside the launch pad. The phenomenon is a bright diamond shape and according to a note from British Pathé included in the files, 'it is quite clear [it] is nothing more than an internal camera reflection'. Records from the firing range show there were, in fact, two aborted rocket launches at Woomera but none occurred on the day Mr Templeton's photograph was taken. The first, on 25 May, 1964, was halted due to 'bad weather' and the second, on 2 June, was attributed to a systems fault.[44]

No other convincing evidence of any connection between these events, or indeed proof that a similar 'spaceman' was ever seen at Woomera, has emerged, but an aura of mystery still surrounds this story. Analysis of the sparse official records that have survived have not produced any conclusive explanation for the figure on the photograph. What the archives *do* show is a lack of any interest or concern about the incident from the RAF and Ministry of Defence. This does not support the legend that implies the authorities were so worried about the photograph they felt it necessary to send secret agents to investigate who spoke and behaved like characters from a James Bond novel.

There have been claims that the Solway spaceman photo was a hoax, but no one has been able to demonstrate how this was achieved. A detailed photographic analysis carried out in 1997 by Roger Green of Bradford University concluded that the image was '. . . a composite made using some superimposition technique', but the study failed to demonstrate exactly how the composite had been achieved.[45] This conclusion is contradicted by the analysis carried out by Kodak and Carlisle police shortly after the photograph was taken. These both concluded the image was genuine and had not been tampered with. In my view, it seems unlikely that Mr Templeton – who as we know was at that time employed by the fire service – would have taken a photograph he knew to be faked to the police for analysis.

Jim Templeton died in 2011. All those who met him were impressed by his matter-of-fact integrity and it seems likely that, as the police suspected at the time, the 'spaceman' was a real person who 'got into the picture'. Although he was always adamant he could see no one else in the viewfinder when he took the photograph, one theory suggests that was because the type of camera he used revealed only 70 per cent of what the lens actually captured. That being the case, he failed to notice his wife walking briefly into the shot and making her mark in history. Another photograph, taken on the same day, shows Anne Templeton wearing a blue dress which has overexposed to white, the same colour as the 'spaceman'. According to this theory, when the image is manipulated in Photoshop the spaceman begins to resemble a woman in a dress, walking away from the little girl with her back to the photographer.[46]

Even if this simple theory is the correct one, the legend of the 'Solway Spaceman' remains one of the most perplexing stories in the history of anomalous photography.

THE LAST WITCHCRAFT TRIAL?

During the spy scares of the Second World War, anyone suspected of passing on information that might be of use to the enemy could find themselves under investigation by the British security service. In 1940, the Home Office ordered all police forces to compile monthly security bulletins and report any 'matters of security interest' immediately to MI5.

In November 1941, the battleship HMS *Barham* was sunk by a German U-boat in the Mediterranean just a fortnight after the loss of the aircraft carrier HMS *Ark Royal*. Relatives of the *Barham*'s 868-strong crew were not told until January of the following year to avoid giving away secrets to the Axis powers. But shortly after the sinking, it was claimed the spirit of a dead crew member materialised in the presence of his mother at a spiritualist seance in Portsmouth, the ship's home port. When his anxious mother called the Admiralty for confirmation she was visited by two naval intelligence officers who wanted to know the source of her information.[1]

The leak was traced back to a Scots-born spiritualist medium, Helen Duncan, who had been prosecuted by Edinburgh police for fraud in 1933.[2] Although it is suspected that Duncan may have heard gossip about the loss of the *Barham* in the busy port, the authorities were concerned that she might reveal other, more damaging, secret information gleaned from her many clients, some of whom were members of the armed forces.

In the build-up to the D-Day landings, any careless leak about the date or location of the imminent invasion of France could have had disastrous consequences. Late in December 1943 a young naval officer, Lt Stanley Worth, began attending seances at a seedy flat belonging to a couple called the Homers in Portsmouth. What he and a colleague saw convinced them that Duncan was making money out of the gullible and bereaved who regularly attended the spiritualist demonstrations. The 'spirits' summonsed by the overweight mother-of-six were, they told their commanding officer, crude fakes made from cheesecloth and the 'revelations' allegedly passed from the spirit world to the audience appeared to be bogus.

Early in January 1944, Worth returned to a further demonstration at the flat and this time he was joined by plain-clothed detectives. As Duncan slipped into a trance, an apparition floated from behind the curtains, and a policeman tried to grab it. Lt Worth stood up and blew a whistle. Police rushed in and placed Duncan, her assistant Frances Brown and the Homers under arrest.[3]

In what became one of the most sensational wartime trials, in March 1944, Helen

Duncan was tried under the 1735 Witchcraft Act at the Old Bailey. She was prosecuted not for sorcery as such, but for making money out of fraudulent seances. The trial lasted for seven days, during which the Crown presented a strong case based on the testimony of Worth and others who had attended her seances. Her defence barrister, Charles Loseby, called 46 people from hundreds of potential witnesses who were prepared to swear to Duncan's psychic abilities. But despite his efforts Loseby, who was himself a believer in spiritualism, failed to persuade the judge to allow Duncan to demonstrate her skills by holding a seance in the courtroom.

The jury found her guilty and she was sentenced to nine months in Holloway prison. Frances Brown was given a four-month sentence for aiding and abetting the fraud, while the Homers escaped jail as they had no previous convictions. The precise role played by MI5 in Duncan's prosecution has never been revealed, but in his evidence to the Old Bailey the Chief Constable of Portsmouth, Arthur West, referred to the earlier incident in which she was reported for 'having transgressed the security laws, again in a naval connection, when she forecast the loss of one of His Majesty's ships long before the fact was made public'.[4]

PANEL FIGURE 3.1 A TYPICAL NEWSPAPER HEADLINE PUBLISHED DURING THE SENSATIONAL TRIAL OF SCOTS-BORN HELEN DUNCAN FOR MAKING MONEY OUT OF FRAUDULENT SÉANCES IN WARTIME ENGLAND. (CROWN COPYRIGHT, THE NATIONAL ARCHIVES HO 144/221727)

The historian Malcolm Gaskill, in his book *Hellish Nell* (2001), says the unusual way in which Duncan's case was dealt with by the wartime authorities suggests a decision was taken to silence her. 'Perhaps the security services did not have to believe that Helen Duncan was a genuine medium in order to be concerned,' he wrote. 'Information flowed from her at a time when victory depended on secrecy, and MI5 were unlikely to have ignored such a woman, however strong the hunch that she was harmless.'[5]

Helen Duncan is often wrongly described as the last person to be prosecuted under the Witchcraft Act. Over a number of years, and during both world wars, a number of other mediums and fortune-tellers had been warned by police and convicted under the act. A 72-year-old spiritualist, Jane Yorke, was the last person convicted under the 1735 act in September 1944.[6] Since the 19th century, most prosecutions for fortune-telling, astrology and spiritualism had been made under Section 4 of the Vagrancy Act of 1824. But the Home Office insisted that Duncan was indicted for fraud not for sorcery, which had been abolished under the Witchcraft Act of 1735. This made it an offence to pretend to use such arts or powers 'whereby ignorant people are frequently deluded and defrauded'. In March 1945, after Duncan's release from prison, a confidential memo was circulated to chief constables, advising that police should prosecute bogus mediums only if three conditions were met. There must have been a complaint by members of the public, evidence 'that the person is an imposter and is pretending to have powers which he or she is conscious of not having', and a suspicion the medium was making money out of the fraud.[7]

Several legends have grown up around Helen Duncan's trial, including the claim that both Winston Churchill and King George VI were among her clients. The Prime Minister's interest in her plight can be traced to a note he wrote to Home Secretary Herbert Morrison on 3 April 1944. This demanded to know the cost of the trial, 'observing that witnesses were brought from Portsmouth and maintained here in this crowded London for a fortnight, and the Recorder kept busy with all this obsolete tomfoolery'.[8] Morrison responded that police had been advised to prosecute spiritualist mediums only if there were complaints from the public about alleged fraudulent practices. 'Such frauds are especially prevalent in wartime when relatives of men killed or missing are easy victims,' he told the Prime Minister.

After her conviction, both Churchill and Morrison received letters from Duncan's relatives pleading for them to intervene. One example from the Home Office file on her case, written by a Mrs Burfield of York, reads: 'I am deeply grieved to read of . . . Mrs Duncan's ordeal. I have attended three of her seances and was convinced that she has the power to bring the spirit people back. I saw, kissed and spoke to my only sister. The evidence she gave me was known to only my husband and myself. My husband is the most sceptical man and nobody could fool him, but he believed all he saw . . . I could relate dozens of happenings at those sittings, that could not possibly have been faked. I examined Mrs Duncan's clothing before the sittings for any possible white stuff and found nothing . . . so it is impossible for Mrs Duncan to be a fake, I will never believe it.'[9]

Despite Churchill's distaste for the 'obsolete tomfoolery' of the trial, Duncan's appeal against her conviction was subsequently upheld by the Court of Appeal in June 1945. Responding on the campaign to free her, Home Office official Francis Graham-Harrison wrote in the file: 'On the face of it, it is pity that Duncan was convicted under the Witchcraft Act and not simply for conspiring to obtain money under false pretences. It is already clear that Spiritualists will make the most of the fact that she was convicted under an Act 200 years old, which they can represent with some show of reason to be archaic and out of harmony with modern feeling.'[10]

PRIME MINISTER'S
10, Downing Street,
Whitehall

PERSONAL MINUTE

HOME SECRETARY.

SERIAL No. M.362/4

[Let me have a report on why the Witchcraft Act, 1735, was used in a modern Court of Justice.

What was the cost of this trial to the State, observing that witnesses were brought from Portsmouth and maintained here in this crowded London for a fortnight, and the Recorder kept busy with all this obsolete tomfoolery, to the detriment of necessary work in the Courts.]

3.4.44

PANEL FIGURE 3.2
WINSTON
CHURCHILL'S MEMO
ON THE DUNCAN
TRIAL. (CROWN
COPYRIGHT, THE
NATIONAL
ARCHIVES
HO 144/22172)

In 2007 a fresh campaign was launched by spiritualist groups, supported by Duncan's granddaughter, Mary Martin, to clear her name. A petition was sent to the then Home Secretary John Reid, calling upon him to grant her a posthumous pardon.[11] The campaign is just the latest in a long series of letters and petitions that can be followed at The National Archives. Home Office files contain letters from spiritualists who called upon successive Prime Ministers and Home Secretaries to repeal the Witchcraft Act. They saw the legislation as a form of religious persecution of those who sincerely believed in the existence of the spirit world. Arthur Conan Doyle and the scientist Oliver Lodge were just two of the celebrities of the day who put their names on a royal petition against the act in 1921 that was kept secret for 80 years.[12] Duncan's conviction did have one positive outcome in that it paved the way for the repeal of the act under which she was convicted. Campaigners had to wait until 1951 when Parliament finally repealed the Georgian legislation and replaced it with the Fraudulent Mediums Act. At the time of writing, Helen Duncan's conviction still stands.

CHAPTER 4

SPECIAL POWERS

CORPSE DIVINING

In the early hours of Saturday 17 May 1941, a Luftwaffe crew, returning to Germany from a raid on the West Midlands, dropped their surplus bombs over the Warwickshire countryside. Minutes earlier, two reservists had left their late shift at an aircraft factory in Warwick to return home. James Hiatt and his friend Harry Marston, aged 50, who had survived the horrors of the Battle of the Somme in 1916, died instantly when the bombs exploded near a footpath on St Mary's Common. Their bodies were buried under debris thrown up from two 20ft craters.

When the men failed to return home, their foreman alerted the police and the grim task of shifting tonnes of earth and rubble in search of their remains began. It was a dirty, exhausting task that was all too familiar for those who had been caught up in the air raids on nearby Coventry that had killed hundreds, and left many thousands homeless, in the previous December.

What made the Warwick bombing more than just another tragic statistic was the unusual manner in which the men's bodies were found. Many victims of the Blitz were never formally identified and others were left entombed in the debris. With resources stretched to their limit, the Ministry of Home Security, responsible for civil defence, were naturally keen to explore any new method that would help speed up the process of locating bombing victims. Enter PC Philip Terry. He was one of the policemen called to the bomb site in Warwick. After spending hours fruitlessly digging for the missing men, Terry decided to try a very unconventional method: 'corpse divining'.

In his type-written report to his Chief Constable, dated 19 May 1941, Terry said that before joining the police he was employed by a district council in his home town of Shipston-on-Stour to help locate water supplies by divination. Although he admitted to not having 'much experience . . . [in] divining human bodies', he suggested to a colleague that it might work if he could obtain some items of the men's clothing. PC Terry cut a forked stick out of a privet bush. When it was done he held the stick and a cap, belonging to Harry Marston, in his hands.

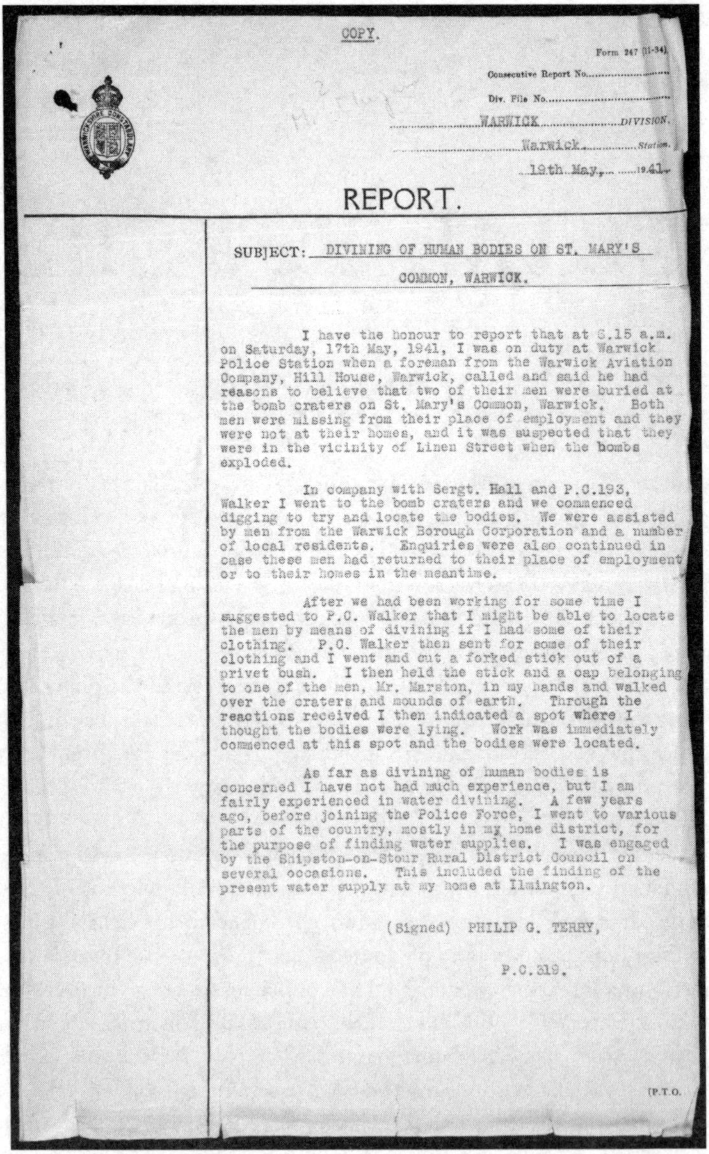

COPY.

Form 247 (11-34)

Consecutive Report No............................

Div. File No............................

WARWICK........................DIVISION.

Warwick...................Station.

19th May, ...19 41.

REPORT.

SUBJECT: DIVINING OF HUMAN BODIES ON ST. MARY'S

COMMON, WARWICK.

    I have the honour to report that at 6.15 a.m. on Saturday, 17th May, 1941, I was on duty at Warwick Police Station when a foreman from the Warwick Aviation Company, Hill House, Warwick, called and said he had reasons to believe that two of their men were buried at the bomb craters on St. Mary's Common, Warwick. Both men were missing from their place of employment and they were not at their homes, and it was suspected that they were in the vicinity of Linen Street when the bombs exploded.

    In company with Sergt. Hall and P.C.193, Walker I went to the bomb craters and we commenced digging to try and locate the bodies. We were assisted by men from the Warwick Borough Corporation and a number of local residents. Enquiries were also continued in case these men had returned to their place of employment or to their homes in the meantime.

    After we had been working for some time I suggested to P.C. Walker that I might be able to locate the men by means of divining if I had some of their clothing. P.C. Walker then sent for some of their clothing and I went and cut a forked stick out of a privet bush. I then held the stick and a cap belonging to one of the men, Mr. Marston, in my hands and walked over the craters and mounds of earth. Through the reactions received I then indicated a spot where I thought the bodies were lying. Work was immediately commenced at this spot and the bodies were located.

    As far as divining of human bodies is concerned I have not had much experience, but I am fairly experienced in water divining. A few years ago, before joining the Police Force, I went to various parts of the country, mostly in my home district, for the purpose of finding water supplies. I was engaged by the Shipston-on-Stour Rural District Council on several occasions. This included the finding of the present water supply at my home at Ilmington.

        (Signed) PHILIP G. TERRY,

           P.C.319.

[P.T.O.

FIGURE 4.1 A REPORT PREPARED BY PC PHILIP TERRY OF THE WARWICKSHIRE POLICE ON HIS ROLE IN THE RECOVERY OF THE BODIES OF TWO MEN KILLED IN AN AIR RAID IN MAY 1941. PC TERRY USED A FORKED TWIG CUT FROM A PRIVET TO DIVINE THE PRECISE LOCATION OF THE BODIES UNDER TONS OF EARTH AND RUBBLE. (CROWN COPYRIGHT, THE NATIONAL ARCHIVES HO 199/480)

In his report, police sergeant John Hall wrote: 'Knowing that PC Terry had previous experience of divining I kept him under observation. Wrapping what appeared to me to be a [sic] handkerchief round one of the forks, PC Terry commenced to walk over the bomb craters. About 30 seconds later he came to a standstill and I noticed that the forked stick which he was folding had commenced to wriggle very violently and from my observations I could see that he had great difficulty holding it. PC Terry eventually released his hold on the stick and I could see that he was suffering from a severe nervous strain. He pointed to a particular portion of heaped soil near to one of the craters and said: "They are under there." Digging operations were immediately commenced and a quarter of an hour later the bodies of both men were discovered.'[1]

Sensing the potential importance of Terry's powers for the war effort, his chief constable forwarded a dossier on the incident for the attention of Herbert Morrison's Ministry of Home Security in London. The cover note mentioned police were aware of two other incidents 'of a somewhat similar nature' in the Warwickshire area before the war. The extraordinary contents of the police file landed on the desk of a physicist, Professor William Curtis, who in peace time taught astronomy at Newcastle University. On the outbreak of war, Curtis began work as an advisor to the Research and Experiments Branch of the ministry working for the Chief Scientist, Dr Reginald E. Stradling.

On 12 June Professor Curtis visited the bomb craters with PC Terry and Sergeant Hall. On examining them, he found a line joining the centres was roughly perpendicular to a footpath along which the two victims would have followed on their journey home. The path partly overlapped the outer lip of one. Curtis knew the rising moon was three-quarters full during the raid and, as there was no other light or shelter on the common, the two men would likely have followed the path and thrown themselves to ground when the bombs dropped. In his report to Stradling, Curtis said that even before he asked the officers where the bodies were found, he had guessed it would be close to a section of the footpath that was buried under the lip of the crater. 'The bodies were in fact found within a few feet of [that] spot,' he reported. 'This cannot be regarded as a very convincing case of "dowsing", since there are several other factors present, any or all of which may have influenced PC Terry subconsciously.'

Nevertheless, Professor Curtis remained open-minded about the possibility of a 'supernormal' explanation. He suggested that 'if an opportunity should occur for a further test of PC Terry's alleged powers, it should certainly be taken', adding: 'PC Terry himself, I gathered, is a little scared of these manifestations, and is certainly not out to turn them to his advantage. He has only once previously tried to locate a body (in a river), but failed, although another dowser succeeded, using a copper wire and a handkerchief belonging to the deceased. The latter is what gave him the idea of sending for a cap belonging to one of the men, although he frankly admits he has no idea whether it did any good.'[2]

Just days after Professor Curtis completed his report, another strange incident occurred that once again put PC Terry's special powers to the test. On 1 July police were called to the banks of the River Avon near Warwick to search for the body of a 45-year-old wood cutter, Lewis Bluck. Friends feared Bluck had drowned after he disappeared whilst swimming in the river. In a report submitted to the chief constable, Inspector W. Drakeley said he went to the scene with PC Terry and found items of the missing man's clothing on the river bank. They also noticed clear track to the point where he entered the river. PC Terry cut a strong hazel fork from a bush and wrapped it with a vest belonging to the missing man. Then the two men crossed the river in a punt.

'I was standing immediately behind him,' wrote Inspector Drakeley. 'When the hazel fork was pointing about 15 feet to the south of the clothing on the opposite bank, it commenced to quiver violently and twisted round PC Terry's hand with such force that he was compelled to release it and it shot out of his hands towards the river.' The inspector drove a stake into the ground at this point and noticed the bearing pointed towards a willow tree on the riverbank opposite. The constable then walked forward 25ft and repeated the experiment, experiencing in the process an even more violent reaction from the fork. He then made a third attempt and received a less violent reaction. All three points were marked by the inspector who said 'the direction was exactly the same and cross bearings pointed directly to the tree'.[3]

The pair then climbed into the punt and went upstream past the stakes, as PC Terry clutched the hazel fork. Nothing unusual happened until the punt passed the willow tree, whereupon the fork 'twisted so violently that it snapped in half and so tightly wound itself round the under vest that it was several minutes before he could get it free'. PC Terry was now convinced the body lay directly under the tree near the riverbank. Insp. Drakeley ordered his men to drag the river. Branches, buckets, weeds and even an old pram emerged from the mud but no body. PC Terry remained convinced Bluck's body was there. At daybreak a second drag of the riverbank turned up a piece of human flesh exactly under the spot indicated by the hazel fork. After six hours, the body of the drowned man was found.

In his report, the inspector said PC Terry 'had nothing else to help and no one had any idea where the body lay. He was, however, so convinced with the result of his divining that he told me it was useless dragging anywhere else other than the spot he had indicated'. He added that PC Terry's powers had 'saved many hours, and probably days, of dragging operations and the accuracy of the information he is able to give unquestionably proves that his methods have so far withstood all tests he had undertaken'.[4]

Despite the police endorsement, Professor Curtis remained sceptical. He visited the river and noted that it was logical for the body to be found downstream from the point where the clothes were found on the bank. He thought it probable the constable had 'formed some expectation, subconsciously, it may be, of the probable position of the body', before he began to search for it. The only other alternative was to accept 'this is a genuine case of divining'. Unsure which option was correct, he decided there was justification for a more detailed investigation 'by an experienced worker in this field'.

After taking advice from Solly Zuckerman of the University of Birmingham, who advised the government on scientific matters, Dr Stradling visited Eric Dingwall in Cambridge, who had a reputation as 'a debunker of so-called spiritualist phenomena'. Dingwall was an officer for the Society for Psychic Research who had spent several years travelling in North America investigating mediums. Dingwall said it was necessary to exclude 'all normal sources of information' before the ministry could justify explaining the phenomenon 'supernormally'. He did not want to rule out using PC Terry in further experiments but felt wartime was not the best time for them. In his report Dr Stradling said Dingwall agreed with him 'in strongly deprecating any official support to matters which could in any way be connected with spiritualism and although in the mind of the average person water divining is not usually connected in this way . . . if the mysterious comes into it, it does give a certain amount of support to the more extreme claims and in war time this is particularly dangerous'.[5]

Closing the file on this curious and unique case, the Inspector General, Wing Commander Eric Horsfall, said he was unconvinced they had 'found anything abnormal . . . there is certainly a quick appreciation of certain signs, but nothing more, as far as we can detect'. Nevertheless he asked Professor Curtis to keep in touch with the Warwickshire force to ensure that he was present as and when PC Terry's powers were called upon again.

There is no indication in the Ministry of Security files that Terry's powers were called upon by the authorities during the war, but there are hints that such techniques were informally used by other police forces. A report by Superintendent R. Read from the Buckinghamshire constabulary, in a Metropolitan Police file, describes a case in 1948 where police dragged a river in search of the body of a small child who had been missing for several days. After failing to make any discoveries, the police called for help from a retired tobacconist, George Adams, who practised water divining. 'Mr Adams offered his services which I accepted,' Supt Read wrote, 'and with his divining rod and an article of the child's clothing he indicated a spot in the river where the child was found within a very short time'.[6]

WARTIME DOWSING EXPERIMENTS

Police officers and tobacconists were not the only individuals who offered their special powers in support of the war effort. Some skilled dowsers were serving members of the armed forces. One of these, Major Charles Pogson of the British Army in India, presented a paper on water divining to the Bombay Engineering Congress in 1923. In retirement Major Pogson used his powers to locate underground water sources in the countryside around Bombay at times of drought. He learned the skill from his father as a child in south-west England and, after many experiments, began to trace the history of dowsing from books and manuscripts at the British Library in London.

Major Pogson said he found an image of 'the forked twig or *virgule divina*' in a German textbook published in 1500: 'In this work there is a quaint picture of a diviner striding over the hills with a forked rod prospecting for minerals for which the rod at that time was only used,' he told the conference. 'The miners of Saxony appear to have been the first to use the forked rod. This probably arose from the belief, once universal, that metallic ores attracted certain trees which thereupon drooped over the place where these ores were to be found.' The first stage for the novice dowser was to fashion a divining rod from the tree itself, but 'later a branch was grasped in each hand and the extremities fashioned together . . . from this it was an easy transition to the use of a forked or Y-shaped twig'.

At the British Library, Major Pogson found references to an English delegation that visited Saxony during the reign of Elizabeth I in order to investigate methods of finding ore in the Cornish mines. Soon afterwards divining rods were adopted in England as a reliable method of locating not just ores but also water. He said that he was given to understand, 'notwithstanding beliefs and disbeliefs, that [this method] was used certainly up to quite recent times', in English villages, to locate hidden treasure and even missing persons. In effect, 'corpse divining' of the type practised by PC Terry:

> Fortunately or unfortunately there are some who require a scientific explanation of all the mysteries of our surroundings and will even go so far as to be short of water in consequence . . . The refusal of its acceptance by some is because scientists have not yet been able to explain fully its marvels, or apparent marvels, as if an occurrence that has not been explained by scientific methods must necessarily be a fraud.[7]

The retired soldier tried to explain his own powers by offering his opinion that all metals, minerals, water and oils 'emit certain radiations' similar to radioactive elements. He believed gifted individuals acted as 'human galvanometers' when working with a Y-shaped fork. Yet despite Major Pogson's conviction that dowsing worked in practice, specially constructed experiments to test its efficacy in the field have failed to produce convincing results. Just eight months before the remarkable case of PC Philip Terry came to the attention of the wartime authorities, the Ministry of Supply worked with an experienced army dowser on a secret experiment using a soldier's dowsing powers to locate unexploded bombs.

The experiments were carried out in the grounds of the National Physical Laboratory at Teddington, as the Battle of Britain raged in the skies above London. Major Kenneth Merrylees served as a bomb disposal expert for the British Army. During his wartime career, he claimed to have discovered an unexploded bomb under a swimming pool at Buckingham Palace. For the experiment, he offered to detect and mark the locations of buried objects such as gas mains in the grounds of the former royal residence at Bushy House. Four locations were marked out by officials and the soldier set to work with his dowsing rods.

The brief conclusion of the War Office report summarises the results: 'Since Major Merrylees agreed that the conditions of all these tests were fair . . . and the gas mains [used as conductors] were of a reasonable size and at a reasonable depth and not near any "disturbing matter", the only proper scientific deduction to be made from these experiments is that the "dowsing" method is completely unreliable in indicating the presence of a conductor underground.'[8]

POST–WAR DOWSING EXPERIMENTS

Despite the lack of success in wartime, the army did not entirely close its mind to the potential for dowsing to be used in future military operations. During the Cold War, the threat to personnel grew worse as new enemies developed deadly non-metallic mines in theatres of conflict such as the Middle East. On the road between Radfan and Aden, for example, magnetism in the rocks where mines were scattered made them doubly elusive to conventional methods used by bomb-disposal teams. The problem had become so serious by 1968 that the army's Chief Scientist asked the Military Engineering Experimental Establishment (MEXE) to investigate unconventional methods of mine detection.[9] Scientists from MEXE devised a series of experiments to test dowsers' powers in the field. The project aimed to test not only what MEXE called 'in situ dowsing', but also claims that buried objects could be located remotely by dowsing on a map. The trials were planned meticulously to reassure dowsers, some of whom were members of the armed forces, that they would be treated fairly and the results were scientifically valid.

In preparation for the experiment, Royal Engineers buried 20 British-made light metallic inert mines in roads and tracks across a 384-acre site on Barnsfield Heath, between Hurn Forest and Foxbury Hill in Dorset. The locations were carefully chosen to make the 'minefield' more realistic. Maps were sent to three dowsers who were invited to find the buried ordnance and one, who worked for the Army, was sent a mine to examine, 'it being a fair assumption that the Army dowser would know what type of mine he was looking for'. Unfortunately, all his attempts to dowse using a map failed miserably. The nearest 'hit' was 80ft away from the correct location. The results from the other participants were no better. One sent a bottle of homeopathic medicine to be buried in one of the named roads, but the mark he made on the map was nowhere near where the bottle was actually buried.

Ten dowsers took part in the 'in situ' experiments. They used a mixture of divining rods, including both the V-shaped forked twig-type held by both hands and the L-shaped wires held one in each hand. The dowsers said they were confident of their ability to distinguish between mines and other types of buried objects, such as large stones and tree roots. So the Army took them at their word and buried both metallic and plastic mines alongside wooden and concrete blocks in the improvised 'minefield'. These were hidden within 200 marked squares on cleared, raked sandy soil and in a similar number of squares on rough, cleared natural heathland. Five groups of 40 objects were hidden inside each square. Teams of soldiers buried the objects and a single location plan was kept under lock and key under conditions of 'maximum security' during the experiment.

FIG 7 DOWSING WITH V SHAPED ROD

FIG 8 DOWSING WITH TWO L SHAPED RODS

FIGURE 4.2 BRITISH ARMY DOWSERS AT WORK IN DORSET DURING A GOVERNMENT EXPERIMENT ORGANISED IN 1968 TO TEST THE POWERS OF WATER DIVINERS TO DISCOVER BURIED OBJECTS IN A MINEFIELD. (CROWN COPYRIGHT, THE NATIONAL ARCHIVES WO 195/166)

The Army report said dowsers were told only that metallic and plastic mines had been buried in the area, and samples of these mines were made available for them to examine. The experimenters were not told to search for the mines. They were simply asked to dowse just in front of a small wooden peg at the centre of each square and 'say "yes" if they thought a mine was present and "nothing" if they thought there was no mine and all volunteered to distinguish between metallic and non-metallic mines in their responses'.[10]

Results from the trials were collected on score cards. Only three of the dowsers produced results that were different from what would be expected by chance. The better results clustered on the raked ground and the Army suspected, just as Professor Curtis had during his visit to the Warwick bomb site, that 'there [were] visual signs on the raked ground which are helping the dowsers'. On the natural heathland, the dowsers failed to locate any buried objects.

In conclusion, R.A. Foulkes of MEXE said the results obtained by dowsing were 'no more reliable than a series of guesses'. As far as the British Army was concerned, dowsers were of no use in hazardous war zones. Foulkes also believed he had found an explanation for what he called 'a large part of the mystery surrounding the practice of divining'. This was based on the way that dowsers held their rods. He noted that: 'we have an uncanny ability to focus our attention on the tips of the rods and to be almost unconscious of what is happening at the other ends. This is not surprising [as] a golfer has to keep an eye on the ball, not on his hands, in order to hit it effectively.' Foulkes added that despite repeated failures in trials, dowsers continued to defend their claims and remained unconvinced by the negative results. 'It is a common complaint amongst dowsers that scientists dismiss their powers almost out of prejudice,' he wrote. 'Actually, it is more a case of "not proven".'[11]

The MEXE trials of 1968 did not put an end to the enduring belief in dowsing that continues in some members of the armed forces, emergency services and other public bodies, however. For example, on retiring from his customer advisor job at Yorkshire Water in 2001, Dougie Scriven told journalists that he had been using divining rods to find underground leaks and old mains since he began working for the company in the 1970s. To locate a leak or a main, he walked slowly along the ground, holding a metal rod or wire in each hand until he felt 'tension' or until the rods crossed. Mr Scriven said he was taught divination by senior staff when he first joined Yorkshire Water and added: 'I have used them for 24 years now and they have come up trumps when everything else has failed.'[12]

Others continue to believe that similar methods can be used successfully to locate mines and booby traps in war zones. The potentially dangerous nature of this type of belief was brought home in 2013 when two men were jailed after selling thousands of useless 'bomb detectors' to security forces. The Old Bailey heard evidence that the 'detectors' were nothing more than empty boxes with plastic handles and aerials. Thousands of these 'devices' were sold to military forces in Iraq, Mexico and other places and they continued to be used even after they were exposed in a damning Home Office report produced in 2001.[13]

Writing in the *Huffington Post*, psychologist Bruce Hood compared the bogus 'bomb detectors' with dowsing rods. Hood went further than Foulkes and pointed to a psychological phenomenon known as the 'ideomotor effect' that he said explained any remaining mystery. He summarised this as follows: '. . . when you are aware of the location of a potential target, you make imperceptible body movements that make finely balanced rods or pendulums point in the same direction. There is no evidence that these devices or the user can detect sources through supernatural powers'.[14]

PSYCHIC DETECTIVES

Despite an abundance of anecdotal evidence, the ability of dowsers to locate water and hidden objects underground has never been replicated under the conditions demanded by scientists. Equally unproved are claims that some gifted individuals have successfully used extra-sensory perception (ESP) or clairvoyance for crime fighting purposes. Ever since organised police forces came into existence, claims have been made that psychic mediums have provided information that has helped detectives to resolve notorious crimes, including murder. While publicly police forces in the British Isles have always denied that such information has been used as part of their inquiries, psychics continue to claim information they have provided is used informally by individual officers and forces.

Until recently it has been difficult to establish the truth behind these claims as the public have no automatic right of access to police records on criminal investigations. The introduction of the Freedom of Information Act in 2005 and the opening of a number of historical case files at The National Archives in Kew allow a partial insight into the facts behind these persistent stories.

Possibly the earliest rumour about the role of psychics in police work occurred during the Jack the Ripper murders in Victorian London and was discussed in the Introduction (see p.5). In 1895 a story published by the *Chicago Herald* claimed a famous clairvoyant, Robert James Lees, had led police to the murderer after he was troubled by horrible visions of the killings. Lees had a colourful life as a spiritualist medium, preacher, writer and healer. Among his many stories was a claim that he helped a bereaved Queen Victoria communicate with her beloved Prince Albert. No convincing evidence for either his royal connections or his assistance to the Ripper inquiry has ever come to light, but the latter was such a good story that it refused to die.

In 1931 it was resurrected by the London *Daily Express* who claimed Lees had identified the murderer as a member of the aristocracy.[15] The story became so firmly embedded in the Ripper legend that Lees was used as a key character in the 1979 Sherlock Holmes film adventure, *Murder by Decree*. Investigations by journalist Melvin Harris found the only evidence for Lees' contact with the police were the psychic's own diary entries from October 1888. Three days after the murders of Elizabeth Stride and Catherine Eddowes in Whitechapel, Lees visited the City of London police but was turned away and 'called a fool and a lunatic'. He tried twice more, including a visit to Scotland Yard on 4 October, with the same result but he was promised a written reply. As Harris remarks: 'these are not the words of someone already involved with the police. Neither are they the words of someone who has already forecast two murders.'[16]

THE MYSTERIOUS STONE OF DESTINY

While the story of Lees' involvement in the Ripper investigation appears to be entirely anecdotal, the archives of the Metropolitan Police contain documentary evidence that clairvoyants were involved in two more recent high-profile criminal investigations. The first concerns Scotland Yard's investigation of the removal of the Stone of Scone from Westminster Abbey by Scottish Nationalists in 1950. What the Attorney General, Sir Hartley Shawcross, described as a 'vulgar act of vandalism' shocked post-war Britain and triggered an inquiry that lasted four months. The Stone of Scone, also known as the Stone of Destiny or the Coronation Stone, is an oblong block of red sandstone that was used during the Middle Ages in the coronation rituals of 34 successive Scottish kings at the monastery in Scone, near Perth. In 1296 it was captured by the English King Edward I and taken to London as one of the spoils of war. On arrival it was built into a specially constructed chair that was kept in St Edward's Chapel, Westminster Abbey. There it remained for 650 years during which it was used in the coronation ceremonies of all English (and subsequently British) sovereigns.[17]

The actual origins of the stone are obscured by layers of legend and folklore, much of it manufactured during the medieval period. One story links it to the Biblical story of 'Jacob's Pillow', the stone on which Jacob rested when he had his dream of angels at Bethel. Others claim it was a pagan altar brought from Ireland when the Dál Riata Celts first settled in western Scotland, or that it began life as a Roman building stone. More recently conspiracy theorists have suggested the stone, currently residing in Edinburgh Castle, is a fake. What can be said for certain is that it was one of many ancient sacred stones that were used in inauguration ceremonies for medieval kings across the British Isles, and as such it retained mystical and symbolic power for those who adopted it.

Wherever it originally came from, by the end of the Second World War this block of stone became a symbol for those Scots who yearned for devolution from English rule. Its

FIGURE 4.3 THE CORONATION STONE OR STONE OF DESTINY THAT WAS STOLEN FROM WESTMINSTER ABBEY IN 1950 BY SCOTTISH NATIONALISTS. A NUMBER OF 'TELEPATHISTS' WERE CONSULTED BY SCOTLAND YARD DETECTIVES DURING THEIR HUNT FOR THE ANCIENT STONE. IT WAS RETURNED TO EDINBURGH CASTLE IN 1996 WHERE IT IS NOW ON DISPLAY. (COURTESY OF EDINBURGH CASTLE)

removal from London and return to Scotland caught the British authorities off-guard and brought the nationalist movement briefly back to the attention of the British public. The stone was removed from the Abbey on Christmas Eve 1950, by four students from Glasgow. Among the group were three men – Ian Hamilton, Gavin Vernon and Alan Stuart – and a woman, Kay Matheson. Late that night the men forced their way through a door at Poet's Corner. After the stone was freed from the chair with a jemmy, it fell to the floor and broke into two pieces. They were dragged across the floor to separate cars and driven off into the night. At one stage during the operation Matheson spotted a policeman standing outside the Abbey but she and Ian Hamilton evaded suspicion by falling into a lovers' clinch. After leaving London by car, the two pieces were hidden at locations in Kent and the Midlands before the group separately made their way back to Glasgow, evading police roadblocks.[18]

When the loss of the stone was discovered, police closed the border between England and Scotland for the first time in 400 years. Police initially had few leads and came under intense pressure to solve the crime. For a while they were willing to accept help from anyone who could provide assistance, including from those described as 'telepathists'. A report in the *Daily Telegraph* on 22 January 1951 revealed that 'though this is the first time Scotland Yard has given facilities to a telepathist it is not the first time people claiming special powers have assisted in investigations'. In what may have been a reference to wartime experiments, the paper claimed 'water diviners have helped in searching for bodies in rivers and for hidden loot . . . [and] it is Scotland Yard policy to accept genuine offers of help if there is a possible chance of success'.

It is a measure of the sensitivity that surrounded information provided by dowsers and psychics that the Metropolitan Police file on the Stone of Destiny was withheld from release at The National Archives for half a century. The contents of the file, opened in 2011, suggests the outcome of the case set a precedent for British police forces in their dealings with people claiming to have special powers. It contains a nine-page report prepared for Chief Superintendent Tom Barratt of Scotland Yard in January 1951 that was used to brief Geoffrey de Freitas of the Home Office. The report says publicity generated by the removal of the stone from the Abbey had resulted in a large number of people offering information to help police.

> Included in these persons have been a number of water diviners, clairvoyants, persons who claim a second sight and other similar believers who have offered their services to Police in the full belief that they could tell us where the stone is hidden. In practically every case these persons have, when writing to us, done so on the strict understanding that there should be no publicity as far as they are concerned and that any expenses incurred should be defrayed by them.[19]

In order to make progress, these unconventional helpers wanted access to Westminster Abbey and to what they called 'witnesses'. By this they meant articles left at the scene of the crime by the intruders. These included a watch, a jemmy and the plaque attached to the stone. Among the messages received were several from psychics providing definite locations where the stone could be found. A report in the police file describes how a dowser, Paul de Garis, was convinced the stone was hidden near Newark and travelled from his home on the island of Guernsey, at his own expense, to offer his services to Nottinghamshire police. He arrived at Newark police station on 6 January and immediately began using a hazel twig to dowse a large scale map of the area, where '. . . after a few minutes he said the reactions were strong over the centre of the town in the vicinity of the Great North Road'.

A fruitless trip along the road commenced, following the route that de Garis believed the stone had been taken. The search resumed the following morning when police went to a storehouse used by a firm of heating engineers. After a thorough search of the property, no trace of any stone was found and, eventually, '[de Garis] admitted his diagnosis was wrong'. The crestfallen dowser returned to Guernsey the following morning, offering no explanation as to why his powers had failed him.[20]

Fortunately for Newark police, de Garis was genuine in his offer of help and did not seek publicity for his own personal gain. Colleagues in the Metropolitan Police were soon to have a completely different experience at the hands of a man who has been described as 'one of the most famous psychic detectives of modern times'. On 11 January Chief Supt Barratt was approached by John Jackson, who was the manager of the Comedy Theatre in Leicester Square. Jackson had contacted a 39-year-old Dutch psychic, Peter Hurkos, to inform him about the loss of the stone. Hurkos was described by Scotland Yard as 'a well known telepathist' who had built up a reputation for solving crimes – including several murders – in the Low Countries. Chief Supt Barratt said Jackson appeared to have complete faith in the ability of Hurkos to use his powers to locate the stone and his letter of invitation, included in the file, said it 'presents itself a wonderful opportunity and if you feel yourself that you may be able to throw some light on this mystery and so help in the recovery of the stone, then you would be made – not only in England, but throughout the world'.

Police said they would provide Hurkos with 'similar facilities' to those offered to others who had offered their psychic powers, but nothing more. This included access to the crime scene in the Abbey, on 'the strict understanding that no publicity should be given to the matter and that any expenses incurred would have to be met by Hurkos himself'. But Chief Supt Barratt was soon to discover that Jackson and Hurkos had no intention of keeping their side of the bargain. Secretly, the pair had already made moves to sell their story to a Sunday newspaper. Hurkos arrived at London airport on 16 January accompanied by his manager and two young female companions described as 'secretaries'. From the moment he left the plane his 'confidential' visit turned into a media scrum. As he stepped onto the tarmac, he was surrounded by press reporters and photographers who had been tipped off in advance. Evading their questions, the six-foot tall Dutchman climbed into a police car driven by a detective sergeant from Scotland Yard and departed for the sanctuary of Jackson's flat in central London.

The following morning the detective met the two men at the abbey where they were given access to the damaged Coronation Chair. They also examined objects recovered from the crime scene including the jemmy used to remove the stone from the chair. After dictating notes to Jackson, Hurkos said he wanted to visit the Round Pond in Kensington Gardens, but on arrival he realised the pond was too shallow to hide the stone. In the afternoon the trio returned to Jackson's flat and Hurkos began to write further notes drawn from the mental impressions he claimed to have received. The next day, Hurkos and

Jackson set out with their police driver to begin a magical mystery tour of London. Firstly they visited the grounds of the bombed churchyard at St Dunstan's in the East End. From there they drove to a café in Fashion Street where Hurkos believed a man named 'Brooks', connected to the mystery, lived. After failing to identify anyone of that name, Hurkos took them next to a hardware shop on Brick Lane where he believed the jemmy, manufactured in Sheffield, had been bought. The shopkeeper explained that the manufacturers had more than 3,000 customers, 200 of whom lived in Scotland.

After this inauspicious start, Hurkos handed his notes to the police. The Scotland Yard report said these contained references to a prominent Scottish Nationalist and a series of car registration numbers. Detectives described them as 'almost unintelligible' and said Hurkos gave them no indication of how they were relevant to the removal of the stone. Soon afterwards Hurkos left for his home in Antwerp. He returned to London on Friday 23 January, to begin a second attempt to solve the mystery. Again he was met by a detective and during the course of the next three days he travelled 75 miles around the capital in a police car, re-tracing the route he believed the stone had travelled after its removal from the abbey. During the weekend Hurkos paid a second visit to the Coronation Chair and searched a series of wharves along the Thames at Rotherhithe. Then he turned his attention to a bomb site in Westminster where a plaque attached to the chair had been discarded. After further deliberations at Jackson's flat, he produced a detailed map showing the route taken by those who removed the stone. He was now sure the stone had never left the capital.[21]

Meanwhile *The Sunday Express*, in a story headlined 'Coronation Stone Surprise – the astonishing story of the detective and the Flying Dutchman', set out in astonishing detail Hurkos' supposedly confidential dealings with the police. The paper revealed how on his first visit to the abbey 'all other visitors were cleared from the Sanctuary . . . and gates locked as Hurkos knelt at the Coronation Chair for 30 minutes . . .'. Reporter E.V. Tullet revealed the Dutch psychic had told police five men were involved in the removal of the stone: 'Three broke in and two waited outside with a lorry. Seconds later he gave two sets of letters and numbers. One of these sets of figures, he said, was the registration number of a vehicle involved in the theft.'[22]

Inside the paper, reporter Gwyn Lewis, in a dispatch from Antwerp, reported on an interview with police officials who cast doubt on Hurkos' claims to have solved a number of crimes in Belgium and Holland. Lewis found that Hurkos had been born Pieter van der Hurk in Dordrecht in 1911 and attributed his psychic powers to a fall from a ladder whilst working as a housepainter during the Second World War. Since then he had developed a flourishing career as a clairvoyant and was consulted by about 1,500 clients a year. His technique involved asking for some article linked to the person about whom information was desired, usually items of clothing. By this method he claimed to have assisted detectives solve numerous murders, including that of a priest in Antwerp. According to a confidential Metropolitan Police report, on arrival at London airport the Dutchman's luggage was examined and found to contain 'a personal letter from the Pope, thanking him for the help he gave in solving the murder of a priest'. Despite this endorsement from the Vatican, according to the Belgian Ministry of Justice, Hurkos had never at any time assisted the police but 'now and again he passes on his ideas to detectives'.[23]

Shortly before Hurkos returned to London, the police commissioner in Apeldoorn wrote privately to Scotland Yard stating that: 'it had never been proved that Hurkos had solved any crimes in Holland and that he had been given official notice by Police there to abstain from giving any information on missing persons to their relatives who had consulted him. This was considered necessary because of the frequent suggestions that [they] were still alive and the hopes of the relatives were thereby quite unnecessarily revived.'[24]

The day after the *Sunday Express* published their story, Chief Supt Barratt told Jackson the police no longer required Hurkos' services. Undeterred, the latter's agent continued to offer information obtained by his client through psychic means and claimed the pair intended to raise £1,000 to allow them to continue their investigation privately. In his communications with Scotland Yard, Jackson again tried to implicate a well-known member of The Scottish National Party in the removal of the stone. Police were sceptical of this suggestion and believed Hurkos could have easily obtained the name from newspaper stories. Summarising the situation in a note to the Home Office on 6 February, Chief Supt Barratt said there was 'little doubt that Hurkos has certain abilities from an entertainment point of view' but so far all the information he had provided 'has been vague and, so far, of no material value'. He also revealed 'a very reliable informant' had told them the psychic's main desire was 'to get away from the Continent and work in some other country'. He believed this explained the Dutchman's desire to put himself to so much trouble, and personal expense, to help the police inquiry.[25]

On 11 April 1951 police were led to the missing stone, which had been left on the altar at Arbroath Abbey in Scotland. It was returned to Westminster Abbey in the following year when it was used in the coronation of Queen Elizabeth II and there it remained until 1996. The four students who removed and damaged the stone were interviewed by police and all confessed to their role. None faced prosecution as the British authorities decided the event was so politicised there was 'no public interest' in initiating criminal proceedings. Two weeks after its discovery, Chief Supt Barratt received a report from CID that summarised the Met's bittersweet experience working with psychics. Basing their conclusions mainly on their dealings with Peter Hurkos it concluded: '. . . the evidence which has been obtained regarding the removal of the stone and its subsequent recovery shows that Hurkos did not at any time say anything which could now be regarded as a possible or likely clue in this case. It is quite true therefore to say that he was of no assistance at all in the inquiry.'[26]

THE 'GINGER' MARKS
MYSTERY

What emerges from the Metropolitan Police file is that Scotland Yard had their fingers burned in their dealings with Hurkos and were determined not to be drawn into further public work with psychic detectives. The only exception to this rule came in 1965 when the Yard were drawn into the investigation of a gangland murder in the East End of London. The case of Tommy 'Ginger' Marks, a small-time criminal and car dealer from Stepney, officially remains an unsolved mystery. On the night of 2 January 1965 Marks, then 37, told his pregnant wife Anne that he was just 'popping out' but never returned. His friend George Evans, who was with him, later testified how they were followed by four men in a car along Cheshire Street in Bethnal Green, just a mile from Marks' home. Marks was called over, three shots rang out, and Evans fled the scene, diving under a van for safety. He then saw the car drive past with Marks' legs dangling from the rear passenger door.[27]

Since that night, no trace has ever been found of Marks' body. Apart from a spent .22 cartridge, a bullet mark on a wall, a bloodstain on the pavement and the dead man's glasses and trilby hat, police had little evidence to work on and no one with knowledge of the murder would talk to them. Three suspects were arrested but at their trial in 1975 all were acquitted by a judge at the Old Bailey. This left detectives without any firm leads in what *The Guardian* described as a murder that had 'become something of a Cockney legend'. Rumours spread that the body had been dumped, using a method favoured by Chicago gangsters, in a 'cement overcoat' in the River Thames or had been set into concrete pylons supporting London's Western Avenue flyover. Others suspected he had been killed for welshing in some way on the hidden loot from the Great Train Robbery. Given the lack of police success in solving the mystery by conventional methods, it was perhaps inevitable that his family and friends would seek answers from the spirit world. [28]

The Metropolitan Police files on the Marks case contain anonymous letters offering information, tip-offs and, in some cases, the names of those responsible for his murder. One letter sent to police one month after the disappearance by a man in Hampshire suggested 'a good psychic medium who does psychometry – the handling of something belonging to the person concerned – could give a vital clue to your hard-working officers'. He suggested Marks' glasses case, found at the scene in Bethnal Green, would be ideal for that purpose. It added: 'I have known cases of psychometry being absolutely correct . . . [and] there may be in your Division an officer interested in psychic work.'[29]

There is no evidence in the files that Det Supt Ron Townsend, who led the investigation, followed up this and other offers of help from psychics. The police records do, however, contain a curious tape recording of an interview with a Dutch clairvoyant and Marks' wife

Anne, recorded three months after his disappearance. Mrs Marks was determined to discover what had happened to her husband and in March 1965 she armed herself with a map of London and aerial photographs of the docks. Accompanied by a reporter and photographer from the *Daily Express*, she took a plane to the Dutch university town of Utrecht. Here she met Gerald Croiset who, much like Peter Hurkos, had built up a formidable reputation as a powerful psychic. Newspapers had dubbed Croiset 'the Wizard of Utrecht' and 'the man with the X-ray mind' as a result of his healing powers and clairvoyance that, it was claimed, was often used to help Dutch police investigate serious crimes. [30]

FIGURE 4.4 THE DUTCH CLAIRVOYANT GERALD CROISET, SHOWN HERE WORKING IN HIS HOME IN UTRECHT IN 1963. IN 1965 HIS CRIME-BUSTING POWERS WERE CALLED UPON BY THE *DAILY EXPRESS* TO LOCATE GANGLAND VICTIM THOMAS 'GINGER' MARKS. CROISET TOLD MARKS'S WIDOW HIS BODY HAD BEEN DUMPED IN WATER. (COURTESY OF THE MARY EVANS PICTURE LIBRARY)

A tape-recording of the meeting with Croiset was transferred from Metropolitan Police files at The National Archives to the British Library Sound Archive in 2011. Much of the 66-minute interview consists of Croiset answering questions in his native language, with his responses translated into English by a second Dutch speaker.[31] On the recording, Croiset is questioned by Anne Marks and Robert Girling, a press photographer. The Sound Archive description says 'it is not clear from the tape whether the police themselves were involved in the interview or the recording' but a report in the *Express*, published on the following day, reveals that Mrs Marks phoned Det Supt Townsend on return to London to brief him.[32] The tape was later added to the police file on the case.

On the recording, Croiset says Marks was followed out of a pub by a gang member and shot twice before he was pushed into an old model car containing two other men. He described one as 'a small man with an ugly face about 34 who is constantly smoking marijuana or something like that'. In the later stages of the interview, Croiset refers to a map and an aerial photograph of London. He then points to a spot on the Thames foreshore at Woolwich where he believed his body was taken. According to the *Daily Express*, Croiset told Mrs Marks: 'I am afraid he is dead. In fact, I am sure he is dead. Your husband is under water.'[33] In the recorded version Croiset says he believes the body was 'heavy with stones or something – in water'. On their return to London, Mrs Marks and the *Express* team searched the stretch of the Thames at Woolwich identified by Croiset for clues. They were hampered by the age of the aerial photograph they had relied upon and when they arrived at the suggested location, they found the terraced houses visible in the photo had been replaced by a new 13-storey block of flats.

There the trail appeared to go cold, but the words used by Croiset to describe Marks' final resting place resurfaced in an uncanny admission made 35 years after his disappearance. Although the murder of Tommy Marks remains officially unsolved, in 2000 Freddie Foreman, who claims he worked as a hitman for the notorious Kray brothers, confessed both to the killing of Marks and that of another gangster, Fred 'Mad Axeman' Mitchell. The confession was doubly significant because Foreman was one of the three suspects who were acquitted of Marks' murder in 1975. In a frank interview recorded by Carlton TV, he admitted both killings and claimed that Marks' body had been buried at sea. Although he was questioned by police after the confession, no action followed because the 'double jeopardy' law, as it was, did not allow people to stand trial on similar charges following a legitimate acquittal in a British court.[34]

The Marks case remains a fascinating footnote among the archive references to police dealings with psychics. In 2007 Portuguese police revealed they were checking leads offered by local psychics as part of their hunt for the missing three-year-old Madeleine McCann, who vanished from a holiday apartment in Praia da Luz, a resort in the Algarve. Chief Inspector Olegario Sousa spoke for many other police officers when he said all information received had to be checked in case it turned out to be significant. Over the years since Scotland Yard's dealings with Peter Hurkos, similar tip-offs have been received by British police working on many high-profile murder inquiries, including the hunt for the Yorkshire Ripper, Peter Sutcliffe, who was arrested in Sheffield in 1981.[35]

It is well known that police departments in the United States have, at least informally, made much more frequent use of information provided by clairvoyants. Occasionally these are revealed when tip-offs turn out to be false leads or public money is spent following them up. For example, in 2011 police surrounded a farmhouse in rural Texas after a woman psychic called to report a vision that led her to believe 30 dismembered bodies, including those of children, were buried there. Police said they took the calls seriously because of the detailed description she gave them of the interior of the house. When the search revealed nothing, she called back to say they were looking at the wrong address. This led to a fresh search that drew the attention of both the FBI and the world's media. After several hours, the police called off the search and announced there was 'no crime scene'.[36]

A similar case in 2009 reignited the debate on whether British police forces should ever act on unsolicited evidence offered by psychics. In November of that year it was revealed at an inquest that Dyfed-Powys Police had investigated an alleged 'murder' based upon evidence supplied by a group of psychics consulted by the relatives of the deceased. The story emerged during proceedings of an inquest into the death of a 32-year-old fitness enthusiast, Carlos Asaf, who was found hanged in his flat at Lampeter in south-west Wales. Although police suspected Asaf had taken his own life, a new line of inquiry opened when they were told he had been killed after being forced to drink petrol and bleach. Detectives interviewed the mediums and visited locations they had identified on the basis of psychic visions. These included 'a lion, a horse and the name Tony Fox'. As in earlier cases, they found the information supplied was 'far from conclusive'. The Ceredigion coroner, Peter Brunton, recording a verdict of suicide, said 'a great deal of effort' had been invested by police on the case. Afterwards the Dyfed–Powys force announced the investigation was conducted to reassure the family that 'the full circumstances of the death were as they appeared [and] police have a responsibility to the deceased, their family and the public to investigate all deaths thoroughly'.[37]

Following these revelations, a BBC investigation led reporter Hannah Barnes to conclude that there was 'no denying that some individual officers are pursuing leads that have arisen from someone professing to have paranormal powers'. Unfortunately, inquiries with individual police forces named by psychics as having acted on their information produced only ambiguous responses.[38] In 2005, after a television programme featured psychics who claimed their powers were regularly used by police, Home Secretary Hazel Blears was questioned in the Commons. She said the 'use of psychics by police forces is an operational matter for individual chief officers [and] information on their use is not collected centrally'.[39]

Eddie Silence of UK Skeptics tried a more systematic approach to the question in 2006. He submitted Freedom of Information Act requests to every police force, asking them to provide details of 'where, when and at what cost such psychics have been used' and 'if psychics have been used . . . whether their input was useful'. Of the 28 responses received, none admitted to using psychics. A typical reply came from Det Supt Ken Lawrence of Warwickshire Police, who said to his knowledge, no psychic had been used to assist any serious crime investigation in the county:

We do get correspondence or telephone calls from people claiming to be mediums or psychic and offering their views or assistance in relation to specific investigations that have appeared in the media. 'But I would not advocate using them. The police deal in factual evidence admissible in a court of law and all such evidence must be credible and tangible.[40]

In 2013 the Association of Chief Police Officers (ACPO), in response to a Freedom of Information Act request, denied providing any advice to individual forces on the use of psychics.[41] Nevertheless, documents released by the Ministry of Defence have revealed that both chief constables and Special Branch have been used to contact individuals with special powers for use in 'remote viewing' experiments (see p.117). A Defence Intelligence document from 2001 says one candidate 'was traced via a contact in the local Special Branch' and senior officers had suggested others. The document, marked 'Secret – UK Eyes Only', reveals: 'The general guidelines for Police Forces in the UK is that such unorthodox means [sic] be used "with appropriate discretion".'[42]

REMOTE VIEWERS

Remote viewing (or RV) is the phrase used to describe the ability to see events, places and people at distances by psychic means. This special power appears to be a modern development of 'travelling clairvoyance' (from the French *clair voyance* or 'clear vision'). The Mass Observation survey of supernatural belief in Britain conducted during the Second World War collected several accounts of 'knowledge of distant events' experienced in dreams and via the 'astral body transported in space'. Their report implies this was a 'ritual' that was learned and invoked as follows: '. . . wait until one has a vivid dream in which the sensation of knowing one is dreaming yet still not awake occurs. At this point one wishes to be in a certain place and the "astral" body accordingly separates itself from the actual body and travels to the appointed spot.'[1]

In some societies, gifted individuals who communicate with spirits and make predictions about the future are known as 'shamen'. During the early modern period in Europe, accounts of what would be today described as 'remote viewing' were reported by assorted mystics and visionaries. For example following a mystical experience in 1745, the Swedish scientist and polymath Emmanuel Swedenborg (1688–1772) claimed to have regularly travelled to other worlds. During his visits to heaven and hell, he communicated with spirits including angels and demons and returned to make predictions about future events. His most accurate prediction through clairvoyance was a description of a great fire that raged in Stockholm on 16 July 1759. This disaster was 'seen' by Swedenborg as he dined with friends 250 miles (400km) away in the city of Gothenburg. At that time, news of the fire took three days to reach Gothenburg by courier.[2]

Naturally if such remote viewing techniques could be shown to work in the modern world, the potential benefits for crime-fighting and the war against terrorism would be huge. Due to the secrecy that surrounds all aspects of intelligence work, documentary evidence of remote viewing projects has emerged into the public domain only in the past two decades. What we know about this government-funded work is partly a result of revelations made by former members of the CIA's 'remote viewing' project that operated under a number of code names such as Grill Flame, Sun Streak and Star Gate. Since the introduction of Freedom of Information legislation, thousands of pages of declassified documents have surfaced about these projects, not only from the US but also from the UK.[3]

Although the scientific establishment never accepted ESP and remote viewing as subjects worthy of a funded investigation, the shadowy world of espionage was more open-minded. The primary task of the intelligence community is to collect information, from any source, that might prove useful for the defence of the realm. Sources that provided information for intelligence operations during the Second World War were, in many cases, a motley collection of eccentric individuals, much like the remote viewers. In the United States, the CIA and US Army actively recruited members of the armed forces who were skilled in photographic analysis techniques for work on their RV projects. They were also interested in those with a history of psychic experiences and who claimed to have seen UFOs. At various times the experiments involved not only talented military personnel but also civilians, including psychic mediums, who claimed to be able to use their powers to penetrate some of the most sensitive targets, such as nuclear facilities and military installations.

The impetus behind these experiments was the ongoing Cold War. Information reached the CIA during the 1960s that scientists in the Soviet Union were studying parapsychology and had reached an advanced stage in their plans to develop a 'psychic weapon'. Much of the Soviet RV research was deeply flawed, but fear of the Russians gaining a lead in the psychic Cold War led the US intelligence agencies to set up their own psychic warfare units. Initially these drew on early experiments with ESP in laboratories across the US. The best known were conducted by two physicists, Russell Targ and Harold Puthoff, at the Stanford Research Institute (SRI) at Menlo Park in California. This work included pilot studies with the famous spoon-bending Israeli psychic Uri Geller. Publishing their results in *Nature* during 1974, Targ and Puthoff claimed 'a channel exists whereby information about a remote location can be obtained by means of an as yet unidentified perceptual modality'. The scientists suspected that what they called 'remote perceptual ability' was common in the general population but was often repressed or ignored. They concluded that experiments in the area of 'so-called paranormal phenomena can be scientifically conducted' and encouraged other laboratories to test their findings.[4]

The apparent success of the Stanford experiments brought both interest and funding from the CIA. Later, the project was taken over by the Defence Intelligence Agency (DIA) and simultaneously, US Army intelligence began work on their own RV project at Fort Meade in Maryland. This employed a talented psychic, Ingo Swann, to recruit and train novice remote viewers. From the early 1980s the United States was operating two top secret military remote viewing units, often referred to collectively as 'Star Gate'. These culminated in a series of operations that attempted to channel the powers of the most promising remote viewers to collect information on a variety of foreign enemies. From 'viewing rooms' in the military installation participants, who lay on couches, were encouraged to leave their bodies behind and travel to distant 'targets' in the Soviet Union, Middle East and elsewhere. Their mission was to collect intelligence and, on return, describe what they 'saw'. Among the successes claimed was the discovery of a missing

Soviet Tu-95 bomber in Africa, accurate descriptions of several nuclear testing facilities and, during the first Gulf War, reporting on the whereabouts of Saddam Hussein's secret underground facilities.[5]

Some very senior military personnel, including former CIA Director Admiral Stansfield Turner, have vouched for the usefulness of the intelligence gathered by remote viewers. Interviewed in 1993 by journalist Jim Schnabel, Turner acknowledged there were problems but said 'no intelligence officer would ever turn his or her back totally on what could be a valuable source of information'.[6] Although the claims sound impressive, almost every 'hit' claimed by the remote viewers has been questioned. Psychologist David F. Marks dismissed remote viewing as 'nothing more than a self-fulfilling subjective delusion' in his book *The Psychology of the Psychic* (2000). Marks also rejected the significance of the results obtained by Targ and Puthoff at SRI, arguing that clues in the transcripts indicated these were 'spurious'.[7]

The controversial $22 million project ran until 1995 when the CIA, who had resumed responsibility, ordered a review by the American Institutes for Research (AIR). Despite claims that RV experiments had produced statistically significant results, a blue riband panel of scientists were unimpressed. The AIR panel decided there was 'a compelling argument against the continuation of the program, even though laboratory testing had produced 'a statistically significant effect'. Their report concluded:

> The laboratory studies do not provide evidence regarding the origins or nature of the phenomenon, assuming it exists . . . further, even if it could be demonstrated unequivocally that a paranormal phenomenon occurs under the conditions present in the laboratory paradigm, these conditions have limited applicability and utility for intelligence-gathering operations . . . Most importantly, the information provided by remote viewing is vague and ambiguous, making it difficult, if not impossible, for the technique to yield information of sufficient quality and accuracy of information for actionable intelligence. [8]

The existence of the Star Gate project was not officially acknowledged until 1995, when the CIA acted on the recommendations of the AIR panel and closed it down. Revelations about the US Army's attempts to develop psychic powers as a wartime weapon then became the subject of investigations by journalists Jon Ronson, Jim Schnabel and film-maker John Sergeant. Ronson's 2004 book, *The Men Who Stare at Goats*, was subsequently adapted into a 2009 movie of the same name starring George Clooney.[9]

BRITAIN'S REMOTE VIEWERS

Given the existence of the 'special relationship' between the US and UK and the routine sharing of intelligence by agencies on both sides of the Atlantic, it was inevitable that at some stage the British military would want to experiment with 'remote viewing' too. Unfortunately, the records of the UK's three secret intelligence agencies, MI5, MI6 and GCHQ, are not covered by the Freedom of Information Act and as a result it has proved difficult to trace the history of British experiments with ESP. Since the mid-1990s some hints have emerged in records that have been proactively released by the security service, MI5, to The National Archives. These reveal that during the Second World War, intelligence officers drew on the talents of an eccentric collection of witches, psychics and astrologers in attempts to manipulate the occult beliefs of prominent Nazis, including Adolf Hitler.[10] In 1976 Clifford Lindecker's book, *Psychic Spy*, claimed that MI5 recruited a Jamaican-born clairvoyant and faith-healer, Ernesto Montgomery, to work for them before the D-Day landings. The book claimed Montgomery was part of a secret unit that used psychic spies to travel in astral form behind German lines to gather vital information of use to the Allied invasion. While much of Montgomery's claims appeared fanciful at the time, they are not far removed from those that emerged from the US Star Gate project.[11]

Files at The National Archives show that privately, some British officials were interested in the potential of developing clairvoyance and other forms of ESP for military purposes. During the 1960s, research by Dr Celia Green into 'out of the body experiences' at the Psychophysical Research Unit at Oxford University attracted attention from the Department of Scientific and Industrial Research. In 1964, a DSIR official asked the Medical Research Council whether they supported or funded any work on psychic abilities as the subject was one that interested politicians. He was briefed by a psychologist from the University of Cambridge that 'the probability of achieving any spectacular result . . . seems sufficiently low to justify only a relatively low investment by the [scientific] community in work on ESP'.[12]

Further clues to the involvement of British intelligence in psychic spying have emerged from the contents of formerly secret files released by the Ministry of Defence under the Freedom of Information Act. Hidden among the thousands of pages reporting encounters with strange flying objects and alien abductions, there are occasional references to a range of other strange phenomena, some of them reported on military installations. As UFO desk officer Kerry Philpott put it: '[as] we are the MoD focal point for "UFO" enquiries we tend to get saddled with answering questions about strange or out of the ordinary incidents and (reluctantly) accept this.'[13]

In 1995 the UFO desk received a letter from a journalist, Rob Irving, who asked for confirmation that a well-known British psychic, Chris Robinson, had alerted the RAF administration depot in Stanmore on the outskirts of London to a potential IRA bomb attack. Despite her initial scepticism, Philpott's inquiries discovered that Robinson did indeed visit the base, two months before a device exploded there in the spring of 1990. MoD Security records showed that '[Mr Robinson] informed the RAF Police that he had had a dream that in the near future a bomb would explode in the London area, but he thought that the target might be a London-based naval unit. He believed the Ministry of Defence ought to be made aware of his dream and decided to notify RAF Stanmore's military police'.[14] Robinson claims to have provided many other accurate predictions to both police and security forces. But when Irving tried to obtain confirmation from the Metropolitan Police, he was given evasive and contradictory responses. While officially the force said it could 'categorically state that we have never used psychics during any investigations', police officers told him unofficially that 'when Chris comes to the police with his dreams, he is taken seriously and the information is acted upon'.[15]

Elsewhere in Whitehall, more shadowy branches of the Ministry of Defence were developing their own version of the Star Gate project. While the records of MI5, MI6 and GCHQ are exempt from disclosure, the Defence Intelligence Staff (DIS) – part of the Ministry of Defence – is subject to the Freedom of Information Act. Papers released in response to my own FOI requests have revealed that MoD branches who provided technical advice to the UFO desk were drawn into a range of unconventional research projects during the Cold War. But as one senior DIS officer told me in 2006, 'there are many misconceptions about the involvement of the DIS in unexplained phenomena'. He added: 'Our primary concern was to discover what new techniques potential enemies were working on that we didn't know about. It was our duty to keep an eye on all the crazy things the Russians were up to. They had some ideas for unconventional weapons that we did not understand, such as plasma technology and other types of "blue sky" technologies. And the remote viewing project was just another example of the topics our people looked at.'[16]

The powers of British remote viewers for use in espionage were one of the 'novel phenomena' investigated by DIS during the 1990s. Although the DIS did not have access to the same level of funding available to the CIA from the US Department of Defense budget for 'black projects', MoD officials were prepared to allow desk officers to create a pilot RV project. In 1994, personnel from the US Star Gate project met scientists from a British defence intelligence agency to discuss their work and officers collected material from 'open sources' on experiments in Russia and other foreign countries as they developed their own ideas.[17]

Seven years passed before the British project was approved and once again the impetus came from a desire to harness intelligence sources in the face of a new and unpredictable enemy. Although the Cold War was over, the attacks by al-Qaeda on New York and Washington on 11 September 2011 suddenly placed psychic spying back on the intelligence agenda. The desire to capture Osama bin Laden and the leaders of the 9/11 plot led to rumours of renewed interest in remote viewing by American intelligence agencies. By 2001 some of those who had served in the original Star Gate project had established their own commercial RV training companies, while others had turned their talents to the world of entertainment.

It can be no coincidence that the British intelligence remote viewing trial began just weeks after 9/11. A document dated 10 October 2001 said the 'existence and results of [the trial] will be classified Secret UK Eyes Only' and stipulated that 'no indication of MoD involvement in this trial must be given'. A DIS branch, DI51, planned to 'evaluate the effectiveness of the technique generally known as Remote Viewing' in order to locate terrorist targets. The tone of the memo implied that DI officers were confident that the technique had been proven as effective:

'Remote Viewing *is* [my emphasis] used to locate defined targets or to find information about specific locations . . . There is considerable literature on this technique and it is claimed that the US Government and the former Soviet Union invested significantly in its use in the 1970s.[18]

Qualifying this optimistic assessment, DI51 admitted there 'continues to be considerable speculation about the effectiveness of remote viewing for intelligence purposes. The full results of the study were revealed in a response to a Freedom of Information request and a heavily redacted version of its 168pp final report was published on the MoD website in 2006.[19] The distribution list reveals that only three copies were ever produced. The ministry revealed a mere £18,000 had been spent 'to assess claims made in some academic circles and to validate research carried out by other nations on psychic ability'.

The report further reveals that unlike their counterparts in the CIA, the British team struggled to recruit 'experienced' remote viewers. One working memo admits that DIS officers had some difficulty in locating anyone suitable in the UK as: 'they are either "flaky" or those of any interest want to know details of why the enquirer is interested, together with a biography.' Intelligence officers posted messages on websites used by 'known Viewers' who advertised their powers on the Internet. For various reasons, 'of those that replied, none showed any interest in participating'.

D/DI51/5/03/10

3

10 October 2001

DI54

OPERATION ▬▬▬ - REMOTE VIEWING TRIAL

It is intended to evaluate the effectiveness of the technique generally known as Remote Viewing, with particular reference to location of targets required for Operation ▬▬▬.

Remote Viewing is used to locate defined targets or to find information about specific locations. There is considerable literature on this technique and it is claimed that the US Government and the former Soviet Union invested significantly in its use in the 1970s. There continues to be considerable speculation about the effectiveness of the technique.

▬▬ will be tasked to set up the trial. Test targets will be specified and an experimental protocol developed. Facilities that are consistent with the requirements for Remote Viewing and suitable test subjects will be identified by ▬▬ and the MOD.

The existence and results of this trial will be classified SECRET UK EYES ONLY. **No indication of MOD involvement in this trial must be given.**

The trial will take place in stages. The first stage will assess 10 subjects and is estimated to cost a maximum of £10k. At the end of the first stage, the results will be reviewed before any follow-on action is considered. If necessary, additional contract amendment action will be requested at that stage.

Please raise an appropriate amendment to Contract ▬▬▬ as soon as possible.

▬▬ DI51

IN 78 - 742

Page 1 of 1

PANEL FIGURE 4.1 A DECLASSIFIED MINISTRY OF DEFENCE DOCUMENT THAT MARKS THE OPENING OF THE SECRET BRITISH 'REMOTE VIEWING' PROJECT THAT AIMED TO HARNESS PSYCHIC POWERS FOR USE BY THE INTELLIGENCE AGENCIES. THE PROJECT WAS APPROVED JUST ONE MONTH AFTER THE TERRORIST ATTACKS ON NEW YORK AND WASHINGTON ON 11 SEPTEMBER 2001. (CROWN COPYRIGHT/AUTHOR'S COLLECTION)

Frustrated in their attempts to recruit openly, DI51 asked Special Branch if they could recommend any reliable psychics who assisted police with criminal investigations (see p.109). A desk officer also admitted that contact had been made with several American remote viewers who had participated in the defunct Star Gate project.

After this setback the project decided to use a group of untrained volunteers for 'phase one': this aimed to establish a baseline 'which would demonstrate any capability of novices in the field'. Following protocols established by the CIA, the project manager was keen to ensure the surroundings were 'likely to create a sympathetic environment' with 'minimal distraction'. A property in London was rented through a commercial company that acted as a 'front'. The MoD was keen to hide the fact this house was being used by the government for secret research on psychic warfare. Two psychologists were invited to participate in overseeing the work. They took part in one session, but they were unhappy about the ethical aspects of the experiments and refused to continue. The issue of liability if anything went wrong was mentioned in a memo dated 6 November 2001:

> What happens in case of injury or death during an experiment? An inquest would inevitably reveal the true nature of the experiments. Should medical facilities be at hand?[20]

Volunteers were taken to a specially prepared room where they completed a questionnaire that included questions such as 'at what age did you have your first psychic experience?' and 'what accuracy do you think you have when viewing targets?'. They were asked to identify photographs of six 'targets' hidden inside sealed brown envelopes. Their responses, including facial expressions and eye movements, were recorded by hidden cameras as the subjects recorded their impressions on paper. DI51's expertise was in the field of ELINT (electronic intelligence) and that may explain their use of sophisticated equipment during the experiment to monitor ELF and VLF radiation. This was to assess whether there was any link between background electromagnetic fields, electrical activity in the brain and 'the mechanism (undefined) that enables RV to take place'.

The officer monitoring the experiment had access to photographs of people, places and objects that formed the targets for remote viewing. These were all hidden inside the sealed envelopes. Written beneath each photograph was a question such as 'what is this place?' and 'who is this person?' The 'targets' selected included photographs of a wine glass, a knife, a petrol station and Mother Teresa. Images of other more sensitive 'targets' have been redacted from the sanitised version of the report, but the context suggests some were photographs of living individuals. One caption below a photograph reads: 'Asian inhabitant. What colour is he wearing?'[21]

By the completion of the project in June 2002, 18 remote viewing sessions had taken place in the safe house and the results, collated by the report, are a mixture of the banal and the bizarre. One volunteer wrote the word 'rats' in capital letters and another appeared to fall asleep as he meditated upon the contents of a sealed envelope. Afterwards, the results were assessed under three categories: 'the subject did not access the target, the subject may have accessed the target and the subject accessed the target beyond reasonable doubt.'

Overall, in 28 per cent of the sessions there was some evidence that the subject 'may have accessed some feature of the target' but overall the results were disappointing. In reaching this conclusion, the remote viewing study repeated the failure of earlier attempts by the military to demonstrate that special powers could be used for operational or intelligence purposes. As was the case with the dowsers, the uncanny powers of talented remote viewers were unpredictable when tested in controlled laboratory conditions. The MoD's RV report concluded that 'it is clear that as untrained Remote Viewers the subjects were almost completely unsuccessful'. Even so, officials remained confident the results might be useful in providing a baseline for any future trials involving more experienced psychics. The author admitted that the 'key issue in pursuit of scientific understanding of RV activity is getting talented subjects who will co-operate with testing regimes'.

This failure meant the second phase of the study, that would have involved the selection of remote viewers whom the intelligence services felt could be 'trusted to be used for the sensitive targets', never went ahead. Or did it?

The true identity of these 'sensitive targets' is hinted at by a line that refers to follow-up work 'including the search for [redacted]'. This reference has led some to conclude the missing word/s refer either to Osama bin Laden or the fabled Weapons of Mass Destruction that preoccupied Tony Blair's government during the second Iraq War of 2003. According to the Ministry of Defence, after the completion of the study, no further work was carried out into the use of special powers for defence or intelligence purposes: 'The study concluded that remote viewing theories had little value to the MoD and was taken no further.'

CHAPTER 5

THE INEXPLICABLE SKY

. . . I have seen the beauty and I have seen the horror of the heights — and greater beauty and greater horror than that is not within the ken of man.

Arthur Conan Doyle, 1913[1]

Until the mid-20th century, human knowledge of the zone between our atmosphere and the edge of space was limited to the observations of aerial explorers who risked their lives in hot air balloons. What we did not know about the 'inexplicable sky' was replaced by the vivid imaginations of writers such as Jules Verne, whose stories told of trips to the moon and beyond. Verne wrote of giant airships that carried passengers across continents while H.G. Wells predicted future wars in the air and invasions by hostile Martians who wished to conquer the Earth and plunder its natural resources. Today we know that the moon and our nearest planetary neighbours are uninhabited. Decades of space exploration have allowed astronauts to gaze down upon our planet both from orbit around the Earth and from the surface of the moon. From this vantage point we can now fully appreciate how much all life on our planet depends upon the thin layer of atmosphere that surrounds us.

The troposphere is the lowest portion of the Earth's atmosphere and ends somewhere between 30–56,000ft, where the stratosphere begins. It is estimated that this lowest layer contains about 80 per cent of the planet's atmospheric mass and much of its weather. The area above the tropopause, where the temperature drops to -76F on the edge of space, was as remote and mysterious to the early aeronauts as the remotest depths of the world's oceans remain today.

A decade after the Wright brothers became airborne in a heavier-than-air flying machine, Arthur Conan Doyle wrote of the perils that he imagined might be faced by future explorers in the upper atmosphere. A short story, *The Horror of the Heights*, was published in 1913 at a time when powered flight was very much in its infancy. Pilots risked their lives daily to stay aloft in rickety biplanes and many believed future wars in the air would be fought by airships. At that time, the world height record was held by two pioneering English aeronauts, Henry Coxwell, the son of a naval officer, and Dr James Glaisher. In 1862 they ascended in a hot air balloon from a gasworks in Wolverhampton in what was to become one of the greatest feats of Victorian exploration. Although they reached a height of 37,000ft (seven miles) above the earth's surface, their expedition almost ended in disaster. On reaching a height of five miles, they began to struggle to keep awake and both suffered paralysis caused by cold and lack of oxygen. Coxwell later claimed they escaped death only because he was able to grip the balloon's ripcord with his teeth.[2] This allowed them to release sufficient gas from the balloon to allow them to descend before it exploded.

The physical dangers faced by Coxwell and Glaisher were nothing compared to the horrors that in Conan Doyle's imagination lay beyond the seven-mile barrier. *The Horror of the Heights* told the 'extraordinary narrative' of an Army airman, Joyce-Armstrong, through the fragments of his blood-soaked notebook. This was recovered from the wreckage of his biplane that crashed into fields in south-east England. When the notebook was examined at the Aero Club in London, it revealed how he had become obsessed by the fate of a series of airmen who had disappeared without trace after pushing their machines beyond 30,000ft. In another case, a pilot appeared to have died from fright on his return to earth. His biplane was found covered in a slimy, grease-like substance. Before he expired, he uttered just one word, 'monsters!'.

As the story unfolds, Joyce-Armstrong says he is convinced 'there are jungles in the upper air' inhabited by squadrons of ghost-like living creatures in the stratosphere. These he compares to the strange life forms that inhabit the depths of the oceans. His research pinpoints one of these 'air jungles' as lying directly above the Army flying school on Salisbury Plain in Wiltshire. The intrepid explorer sets out in his biplane to break all previous altitude records. Rising above seven miles, he narrowly avoids being struck by a meteor shower. Then he encounters beautiful balloon- and bell-like creatures floating on the edge of the troposphere. Some are small with 'a delicacy of texture and colouring which reminded me of the finest Venetian glass', while others appear coiled, like serpents, of 20 or 30ft in length. Soon, however, the 'monsters' who prey upon the smaller creatures begin to appear:

Conceive a jelly-fish such as sails in our summer seas, bell-shaped and of enormous size – far larger, I should judge, than the dome of St Paul's. It was of a light pink colour veined with a delicate green, but the whole huge fabric so tenuous that it was but a fairy outline against the dark blue sky. It pulsated with a delicate and regular rhythm . . .'[3]

Suddenly the biplane is attacked by a hideous purple creature that hovers above him like a bird of prey and propels itself along by drawing on long, glutinous streamers. Joyce-Armstrong escapes from the tentacles of this beaked monster by firing both barrels of his shotgun directly into its gas-filled body. As the beast writhes in agony, the biplane drops like a stone towards the earth. Like Coxwell and Glaisher before him, Joyce-Armstrong battles to regain control and lands safely in a meadow near Devizes.

In the final pages of the recovered manuscript, Joyce-Armstrong writes of his plan to venture once more into the air jungle to capture one of the smaller aerial creatures. He wants to secure proof of his remarkable discovery before he announces the existence of this secret world. But the final page of his manuscript is missing. Written on the next page in large, straggly letters is a final, chilling message: 'Forty-three thousand feet. I shall never see earth again. They are beneath me, three of them. God help me; it is a dreadful death to die!'

STRATOSPHERIC GREMLINS

Conan Doyle's fantasy appeared just before the outbreak of the First World War, when the life expectancy of fighter pilots was just 11 days. In 1915 the first air raids on civilian targets in England were launched by Germany's high-flying Zeppelin airships. Both aeroplanes and airships were extremely vulnerable to sudden changes in weather conditions and relied upon the most basic techniques to help them navigate. It was inevitable that mishaps to aircraft that could not be easily explained by limited knowledge of the laws of aerodynamics would be attributed to supernatural forces. For Allied pilots and aircrew, these took the form of mischievous sprites they called 'gremlins'.

FIGURE 5.2 THE CREATOR OF SHERLOCK HOLMES, ARTHUR CONAN DOYLE (1859–1930), THE AUTHOR OF A NUMBER OF FICTIONAL STORIES THAT BECAME LEGENDS. DOYLE'S WRITINGS PLAYED A PIVOTAL ROLE IN THE *MARY CELESTE* LEGEND AND HIS STORIES ABOUT PREHISTORIC MONSTERS AND CREATURES THAT LIVED IN THE SKY REMAIN HUGELY INFLUENTIAL IN POPULAR BELIEF. (CROWN COPYRIGHT, THE NATIONAL ARCHIVES COPY 1/425)

Gremlins were diminutive in stature and rarely seen. They were the aerial cousins of the fairy folk that appear in British folklore. In a book on military slang written in 1943, Squadron Leader C.H. Ward-Jackson said gremlins were invented during the First World War by pilots who flew with Royal Naval Air Service, before the creation of the RAF as a separate branch of the armed forces. A rival theory traces them to an incident during the 1920s where they had become the *genii loci* of RAF messes in India and the Middle East. Bottles of Fremlins Ale were a treat in the mess and one officer, on opening a bottle, was taken unawares when the over-heated gas shot the cork out. 'He, desiring to say "a goblin has jumped out of my Fremlins" spoonerised and said, "a gremlin has jumped out of my Foblins"', and the word entered RAF folklore.[4]

Whatever the truth may have been, the gremlins gradually become the embodiment of all mischance. They were blamed for anything that went wrong on the ground or in the air. Eventually the term became so familiar it was applied to almost anything that inexplicably went wrong in human affairs. 'There are different sorts of gremlin skilled in different sorts and grades of evil,' Ward-Jackson explained. 'Thus, the orderly room gremlins remove all paper clips and drawing pins when they are most wanted, the watch office gremlin shoots flares off at the wrong times and the flying gremlin drinks your last gallon of fuel.' In the folklore of the RAF, officers and airmen who knew how to get on the right side of the gremlins were highly thought of by the Station Commander but were objects of suspicion among their fellows.

Gremlins were just one of the aerial anomalies that plagued aircrew during the early 20th century. Another was St Elmo's Fire. This was a weak, luminous electrical discharge that flared from gun-muzzles and wing-tips of aircraft, commonly during bad weather. St Elmo was a corruption of St Erasmus, the patron saint of sailors in the Mediterranean. This electrical phenomenon was also familiar to naval crews and was believed to precede storms and low temperatures. When seen by aircrew, it sometimes appeared as a ball of flame or fire and some believed this was the origin of the American phrase *foo fighter* from the French word *feu* or fire. Foo fighters were sometimes, but not always, reported as balls of fire that pursued Allied bombers in both the European and Pacific theatres of war.[5]

Stories and rumours about various types of poorly understood aerial anomalies, fuelled by fiction and folklore, inspired writers such as Charles Fort who collected stories about mysterious lights in the sky and the disappearance of ships and aircraft long before the arrival of flying saucers and UFOs. Transforming Conan Doyle's fiction into potential fact, in *New Lands* (1923) Fort wrote that 'it seems no more incredible that up in the seemingly unoccupied sky there should be hosts of living things than that the seemingly blank of the ocean should swarm with life'.[6] Fort also speculated about the existence of a 'super-Sargasso sea', a kind of fourth dimension from where people and objects might sometimes disappear and other things, like fishes and out-of-place objects, might fall. Fortean ideas even reached the US Air Force who, in a 1949 press release on flying saucers, referred to the idea they could be 'sky animals' rather than men from Mars.[7]

Fort's often playful speculations about the existence of other dimensions in time and space were reflected in early pulp science-fiction . In Jack Williamson's short story *Through the Purple Cloud* (1931), a character called George Cleland is returning home on a small passenger plane when a purple cloud appears from nowhere. On entering the 'cloud', the crew and passengers are teleported through a 'portal' into the fourth dimension. Here they find themselves trapped in a strange, inhospitable alien world where they struggle to survive.[8] Williamson's story introduced the intriguing idea that humans – and planes – could be swallowed forever by forces that lurked in certain hazardous zones around the globe, often above the oceans. Journalist Vincent Gaddis was the first to collect examples of missing ships and planes and link them to the concept of a geographical 'triangle'. Writing in the American adventure magazine *Argosy* in 1964, Gaddis created a modern legend with his article 'The Deadly Bermuda Triangle'.[9]

THE TRIANGLE OF DEATH

Gaddis developed and refined his ideas for a chapter in his 1965 book *Invisible Horizons*. In the book he defined the geographical focus of what he called 'the triangle of death' as follows: '. . . draw a line from Florida to Bermuda, another from Bermuda to Puerto Rico, and a third line back to Florida, through the Bahamas.'[10] Within this roughly triangular area, covering 400,000 square miles of ocean, Gaddis then went on to list case after case where people had disappeared without trace, primarily in ships and planes. More recently claims have been made that hundreds of aircraft, a similar number of ships and up to 5,000 crew and passengers have been swallowed by this limbo of the lost. The best known example cited by Gaddis is the disappearance of a flight of five US Navy Avenger torpedo bombers, known as Flight 19, during a routine training flight from Fort Lauderdale over the Florida Keys on the afternoon of 5 December 1945. This case is often referred to as 'the *Mary Celeste* of aviation'. What happened to the aircraft and their crews remains an unsolved mystery, but a US Navy investigation blamed human error as the last radio message from the planes indicated they were uncertain of their true position or the location of the Florida coast. The US Navy's summary of the mystery says: '. . . it is assumed that they made force landings at sea, in darkness somewhere east of the Florida peninsula, possibly after running out of gas.' Although there was no evidence of freak storms in the area at the time, 'it is . . . possible that some unexpected and unforeseen development of weather conditions may have intervened'.[11]

The disappearance of Flight 19 became a foundation stone of the Bermuda Triangle legend and continues to provide fuel for speculation about time warps and UFO abductions. Soon after the appearance of the article in *Argosy*, Gaddis received letters from readers suggesting explanations that 'included all manner of wild things from interference by "flying saucers" or "something from outer space", to space-warps that caused the planes and ships to enter another dimension'.[12] These stories had such an impact upon the collective imagination they inspired a scene in Steven Spielberg's science fiction epic *Close Encounters of the Third Kind* (1977). The movie opens with the discovery of the five Avengers, perfectly preserved but missing their crews, in the Mexican desert following a UFO landing. It emerges these have been left by visiting extra-terrestrials as part of a build-up to open contact with the governments of the world. As the plot unfolds more missing planes, boats and people turn up in unlikely locations around the world. At the climax of the film some of the missing aircrew from Flight 19 are glimpsed disembarking from the alien mothership, to be debriefed by US government officials about their journey into space. None appears to have aged a day since their disappearance in 1945.

A number of British planes and ships are listed by Gaddis as having fallen victim to the curse of the Bermuda Triangle. Two of the most puzzling losses were of giant four-engined Tudor IV airliners operated by British South American Airways (BSAA). They disappeared without trace almost within 12 months of each other in 1948–49, triggering massive air–sea searches. In the aftermath of the tragedies, the British government opened courts of inquiry into the losses, the first since the crash of the airship R101 in 1930. The *Star Tiger* vanished over the Atlantic Ocean on a 2,000 mile flight from London to Bermuda via the Azores in the early hours of 30 January 1948. The plane was on the second leg of its journey via Lisbon and had a crew of six and 23 passengers on board. The last message received by the control tower at Kindley Field in Bermuda was timed at shortly after 3am. The message requested a radio bearing and this was acknowledged by the radio operator, Cyril Ellison, at 3.17am.[13]

Despite a five-day search by ten US Navy ships and 25 aircraft, including a Fortress equipped with a radar scanner, no traces of the *Star Tiger* were ever found. The inquiry into the loss by the Ministry of Civil Aviation, held in London, concluded that 'it may truly be said that no more baffling problem' had been presented to the court. The complete absence of any reliable evidence meant the inquiry was unable to do more than list 'causes that cannot be eliminated'. The inquiry heard the *Star Tiger* was flying at the low altitude of 2,000ft when it vanished. Any loss of control as a result of a fire or engine failure, if it coincided with strong winds, could have caused the disaster, according to air accident investigators. Although conditions were described as stable on departure from the Azores, the report highlighted the 'unreliability of forecasts on the crucial portion of this route'. The weather deteriorated rapidly during the search operation and the low altitude flight would have burned fuel more quickly. Despite these factors, the inquiry decided that 'what happened in this case will never be known and the plane's fate must forever remain an unsolved mystery'.[14]

One notorious line in the report referred to the possibility that 'some external cause' may have led to the loss. These three words of conjecture provided fuel for what a BBC investigation called 'conspiracy theories, hack journalists and mischief makers' in the decades that followed. The mystery was compounded in the following year when the aircraft's sister ship, *Star Ariel*, vanished on a four-hour daylight flight from Bermuda to

Jamaica. The 1,000 mile route was the shortest hop on the plane's route from London to Santiago, Chile. By all accounts the weather conditions were stable when its experienced captain, John McPhee, left Kindley Field, Bermuda with his crew of six and 13 passengers at 8.41am on the morning of 17 January 1949. One hour later, the captain announced he was switching frequencies to Kingston. But more than four hours passed before air traffic controllers in Jamaica called Bermuda to say they had not made any contact with the *Star Ariel*. This was just 18 minutes before its arrival time. Unfortunately the long delay meant a full air–sea search did not commence until dawn the following day, by which time no sign of the missing plane could be found. Given the conditions at sea, the chances of rescuers finding any wreckage after this length of time were limited. The Ministry of Civil Aviation report admitted 'lack of evidence due to no wreckage having been found' meant 'the cause of the accident is unknown'.[15]

Unlike its sister aircraft, the *Star Tiger* vanished within the borders of the area originally defined by Vincent Gaddis as forming the Bermuda Triangle. But as the legend grew, so did the boundaries of the area included within what some referred to as the 'vile vortice'. Some accounts incorporate vast adjacent areas of ocean to the north and east of Bermuda, parts of the Caribbean, and the Gulf of Mexico. Even the disappearance of the crew and passengers of the *Mary Celeste* (described in Chapter 6) have become incorporated into the 'triangle' legend, although this derelict ship was found adrift 500 miles east of the Azores.

In 1972, librarian Lawrence Kusche of Arizona State University conducted a thorough investigation of all the most important Bermuda Triangle mysteries in order to compile a bibliography of the legend. His research found many were presented as unexplained only because the primary evidence, such as that published in accident investigation reports, had been misquoted, distorted and even suppressed by writers who preferred to work up the idea of an unsolved mystery. In some cases he found examples of missing ships listed in the legend 'as it is usually told' that were entirely fictional. He concluded that the number of planes and ships lost in the 'triangle' was, proportionately, no greater than any other area of the Atlantic ocean.[16]

Kusche shares the opinion of the US Navy who regard the Bermuda Triangle as a manufactured mystery kept alive by sensational and inaccurate reporting. According to its factsheet, the majority of disappearances there can be explained by human error combined with the area's unique environmental characteristics. The Gulf Stream 'is extremely swift and turbulent and can quickly erase any evidence of a disaster' and unpredictable weather patterns can play a role in erasing any trace of wreckage or oil slicks. 'The Coast Guard is not impressed with supernatural explanations of disasters at sea,' it concludes. 'It has been their experience that the combined forces of nature and unpredictability of mankind outdo even the most far fetched science fiction many times each year.'[17]

The lack of any wreckage from the two British Tudor airliners confounded the Court of Inquiry, but given the circumstances, that should not be regarded as unduly mysterious.

Both aircraft were operating at the far limit of their range over a vast ocean when they were lost, long before black box recorders began to be carried by civil aircraft. Although Tudors were used successfully during the Berlin airlifts, they were never used for passenger transport after the loss of the *Star Aerial*. During this period, the state-owned BSAA fleet had a poor safety record. In three years it suffered eleven serious accidents, losing five planes with 73 passengers and 22 crew members killed. These losses led one of its directors, Don Bennett, to claim some of its aircraft had been sabotaged. Bennett was fired in 1948 after he objected to the judicial investigation into the loss of the *Star Tiger* and a year later the company merged with the British Overseas Airways Corporation (BOAC).

THE FATE OF THE *STAR DUST*

The truth about the fate of a third BSAA airliner that disappeared on a flight above the Andes in 1947 took half a century to emerge. During this period the mystery that surrounded the loss of the *Star Dust* inspired conspiracy theories and claims about UFO abductions. The plane, a civilian version of the wartime Lancaster bomber, vanished in August 1947, a time when newspapers across the world reported sightings of 'flying saucers' in the skies of North America. The very first UFO flap soon spread to Europe and South America, where sightings of fast-moving saucer-shaped objects were made during the summer of 1947. The disappearance of the *Star Dust* was compounded by an enigmatic transmission in Morse code sent by the wireless operator, Denis Harmer, shortly before contact was lost with the plane en route from Buenos Aires to Santiago. Five years later one of Mr Harmer's relatives, Captain Edgar Plunkett, founded the British Flying Saucer Bureau and until recently, some members of his family continued to believe Denis' disappearance was an early example of abduction by aliens.[18]

In *Invisible Horizons* Vincent Gaddis described the loss of the *Star Dust* as 'a classic enigma of the skyways'.[19] The plane left Buenos Aires at 1.46pm on the afternoon of 2 August 1947 and its flight plan took it on the most direct route at 24,000ft across the high Andes. The last transmission from Harmer, sent in Morse code at 5.41pm, was received by air traffic control at Santiago and confirmed arrival time as: 'ETA SANTIAGO 17.45 HRS STENDEC.' The accident investigation report says: 'The Chilean Air Force operator states that the reception of the signal was loud and clear but that it was given out very fast. Not understanding the word STENDEC he queried it and had the word repeated by the aircraft twice in succession. A solution to the word STENDEC has not been found [and] from this time onwards nothing further was heard from the aircraft and no further contact was made with the control tower at Santiago.'[20]

Intensive searches by Argentinian and Chilean search teams, including aircraft and ski troops, found no trace of the plane. The British investigation, led by Air Commodore Vernon Brown of the Ministry of Civil Aviation, concluded the cause of the accident was 'obscure' as no wreckage had been discovered, 'although the possibility of severe icing cannot be ignored'. The chief inspector's report was in no doubt, however, that the remains of the aircraft and its crew would eventually be found 'in the Andes Mountains, probably within 40 miles eastward of Santiago-de-Chile'.[21] Files on the accident refer to wreckage believed to be of an Avro-Lancastrian that was spotted on a glacier in 1957, but investigations discovered this was the remains of an American aircraft that had vanished in a flight over the Andes in 1932.

In 1998 two mountaineers spotted wreckage at the foot of the 22,000ft Tupungato glacier, 50 miles east of Santiago. Search teams found fragments of clothing and human remains that had been preserved by the freezing conditions. Five of the eight British passengers from *Star Dust* were subsequently identified by DNA testing. An Argentine Air Force investigation cleared Captain Roger Cook of any blame for the accident. It concluded the crew had probably become lost or disorientated in cloud, possibly after flying through the jet stream, which was not fully understood at the time. Wrongly believing they had cleared the tops of the Andes, the crew began their descent to Santiago and flew straight into the vertical glacier. Investigation of the wreckage found the aircraft was cruising at the time with its undercarriage retracted when it struck the vertical face of the glacier.[22] The meaning of the enigmatic final transmission, 'STENDEC', was never satisfactorily explained but one suggestion is the word is an anagram of 'descent'.

THE COMET DISASTERS

One of the first British writers to link the disappearance of aircraft with extra-terrestrials was the prolific journalist and author Harold T. Wilkins (1891–1950). His book *Flying Saucers on the Attack* was published in 1954, the same year that a series of disasters befell the world's first commercial jet airliner, the de Havilland Comet. Comets were powered by four powerful turbo-jet engines buried in their wings. Turbo-jets had been invented during the Second World War and allowed the jet-airliner to cruise seven miles above the earth at a speed of 450mph. At the time, the Comet was proclaimed as a triumph of British engineering. It could fly higher and faster than any other passenger aircraft in service and promised to dramatically reduce flight times across the world.

These dreams came to an end on 10 January 1954 when Flight 781 exploded at 31,000ft above the Mediterranean close to the Italian island of Elba. All 35 passengers and crew including Captain Alan Gibson, an experienced wartime pilot, died in the tragedy. Fishermen who saw the disaster reported hearing loud explosions and saw a ball of fire in

FIGURE 5.3 A PHOTOGRAPH SHOWING A BOAC COMET AIRLINER FROM THE CIVIL AVIATION AUTHORITY ACCIDENT INVESTIGATION REPORT ON THE LOSS OF TWO AIRCRAFT OVER THE MEDITERRANEAN IN 1954. THE INVESTIGATION CONCLUDED THE AIRCRAFT CABINS HAD EXPLODED AFTER SUFFERING CATASTROPHIC METAL FATIGUE. (CROWN COPYRIGHT, THE NATIONAL ARCHIVES DR 11/112)

the sky. Unlike the disasters that befell the BSAA fleet, this time bodies were found and part of the fuselage was later recovered from the seabed following an intensive search by the Royal Navy. Whilst the investigation was ongoing, on 8 April a second Comet crashed into the sea off Naples, killing all 21 passengers and crew and the entire fleet was grounded.

For a time the cause of the crashes remained a complete mystery, but the sudden explosion that destroyed Flight 781 led to speculation about sabotage or a bomb planted on board by terrorists. The accident investigation into the first Comet crash was led by an experienced scientist, Sir Arnold Hall, director of the Royal Aircraft Establishment (RAE). During his meticulous investigation, Hall decided to reconstruct the entire aircraft in a giant hangar at Farnborough, Hampshire. His team examined every tiny scrap of evidence from the wreckage recovered from the sea in search of a clue that might explain the mystery. The investigation ruled out the possibility of sabotage but did find evidence from the remains of the fuselage that pointed to metal fatigue as the cause of the explosion that had ripped open the pressurised cabin.

As the investigation progressed, letters poured into Farnborough from people who believed they could help solve the mystery. A collection of these have been preserved in a Ministry of Aviation file at The National Archives. Some revived the idea of gremlins and other supernatural explanations for the explosions that destroyed the Comets. One dated 2 October 1954 from John J. Graham says: 'I know you will play down and deny the possibility of attack by hostile spaceships but the evidence strongly suggests this unpleasant possibility. Space travel developments open up the possibility of a gigantic and fateful struggle between the inhabitants of this and some other world.'[23]

Flying saucers were first reported by an American pilot, Kenneth Arnold, shortly before the loss of the *Star Dust* in 1947. A fresh wave of sightings occurred across Europe in 1954 and stories about the latest sightings frequently made headlines in newspapers. In June, newspapers and TV reported a sighting by the crew and passengers of a BOAC Stratocruiser of a formation of strange objects in the sky above the North Atlantic. These UFOs were arranged around a large 'jellyfish-shaped' object that appeared to hover at 19,000ft above Newfoundland during the flight from New York to London.[24] At the time those who were prepared to declare their belief in the reality of visiting spacecraft included some of the top names in British society, including Lord Mountbatten and Sir Hugh Dowding, the hero of the Battle of Britain. Dowding was a spiritualist and believed the pilots of flying saucers had friendly intentions. In London, the Air Ministry followed the US Air Force in setting up its own investigation unit that was kept busy investigating reports of flying objects sighted by RAF pilots.[25]

Given the popularity of the subject with the press and public, it was inevitable questions about flying saucers would be raised at the public inquiry into the loss of Flight 781 when it opened in October. On the fourth day Sir Lionel Heald, counsel for the Crown, asked Sir Arnold Hall if he could confirm that he had received, both directly and indirectly, a number of suggestions from the general public about the cause of the crash. Hall responded: 'Yes, we have received certainly many hundreds, and possibly thousands, of suggestions . . . we made an arrangement at Farnborough that every letter received from the public went through a particular administrative channel, was examined and passed to an appropriate expert for a comment.' Heald then went on to give 'an example of one which has caused a good deal of interest and certainly occurred in my correspondence on one or two occasions' as follows: 'That is that this Comet might have come into contact with something like either a flying saucer or a meteorite, or something of that kind, or a stratospheric gremlin is another one that was suggested. Would you mind explaining why it is we can write off those things?'

Sir Arnold responded: 'I suppose the most useful answer is that we at Farnborough and our colleagues in all other aeronautical laboratories quite frequently fly in the skies in these regions, and we have yet to meet up with a stratospheric gremlin or flying saucer. So the probability of a foreign body of some kind striking an aircraft is extremely remote, and certainly there is no recorded case where the evidence is such that one can take real notice of the existence of such objects.'[26]

From his examination of the wreckage at Farnborough, Sir Arnold Hall was confident the Comet 'did not come into contact with any large foreign body which caused it any damage which could be detected in the wreckage'. But Sir Lionel continued the line of questioning, asking 'if, for example, it was shot down by some plane from Mars, or something of that kind, there be some signs on it?' The chief investigator responded that 'unless their ammunition is very different from ours, certainly I would expect to find it'.

The idea that some unexplained losses of both civilian and military aircraft might be caused by encounters or collisions with some unknown atmospheric phenomenon, either of natural origin or craft from elsewhere, has persisted even among defence officials. In a 2006 book, British author Timothy Good says he expects many of his readers will be 'shocked to learn that early military actions against UFOs led to an unprecedented number of military and civilian aircraft crashes worldwide'.[27] Good believes that hundreds of military pilots have lost their lives 'or simply disappeared during interceptions of UFOs' and that governments are concealing a secret war with 'some extraterrestrial species'. While accepting there have been far fewer cases in the UK, Good continues the tradition established by Gaddis and Wilkins by declaring he is convinced the disappearance of 'hundreds of planes and ships in the Bermuda Triangle' and other vile vortices around the world, are the result of hostile alien activity.

How seriously such claims should be taken can be judged by the conclusions of a secret British government-sponsored study that examined both UFO sightings and unexplained aircraft losses. By the late 20th century, phenomena that were once labelled as 'stratospheric gremlins' or 'flying saucers' were referred to as UAPs (unidentified aerial phenomena) by scientists working for the Ministry of Defence. In 1996 the MoD commissioned a retired RAF intelligence officer to compile a report based on records of unusual sightings reported by members of the British public. This concluded there was no doubt UAPs existed but they were not structured craft built by terrestrial enemies or spaceships from other worlds. According to the report, released by the MoD following a request I made under the Freedom of Information Act in 2006, UAPs are a type of atmospheric plasma 'almost certainly attributable to physical, electrical and magnetic phenomena in the atmosphere, mesosphere and ionosphere'.[28] The conclusions reached by the anonymous author of the study are intriguing given the rumours about 'stratospheric gremlins' that inspired Arthur Conan Doyle to write his story *The Horror of the Heights* almost 90 years earlier.

The author of the Condign report, as it has become known, gathered data on 100 fatal accidents involving military aircraft from the RAF's Inspectorate of Flight Safety for the section of his report that dealt with 'potential UAP hazards to aircraft'. He also examined records of unexplained 'air miss' investigations involving civil aircraft, where the conflicting aircraft was never identified. Only those fatal accidents since 1976 'where there were no survivors and where the cause was not absolutely determined' were examined in detail.

No firm correlations between accidents and UAP sightings in the MoD database were identified by the study. Despite numerous stories about military encounters with flying saucers, it also stated there was 'no firm evidence in the available reports that an RAF

crew has ever encountered or evaded a low altitude UAP event'. While the risk of a collision between an aircraft and a UAP remained 'extremely remote', the report boldly
stated 'the possibility exists that a fatal accident might have occurred in the past'. This
could have been the result of aircrew losing control as a result of taking evasive action to
avoid a UAP whilst flying low and fast. As a result, the report recommended that military
pilots should be advised that 'no attempt should be made to out-manoeuvre a UAP
during interception'. The author's advice to civilian aircrew was: '. . . although UAP
appear benign . . . pilots should be advised not to manoeuvre, other than to place astern,
if possible.'[29]

After the report was released, I tried to discover if these recommendations had been
passed to the Civil Aviation Authority or RAF for training purposes. I was informed there
was no record they had been.

THE MISSING PILOT

One dark September night at the height of the Cold War, Captain William Schaffner, a US
Air Force pilot on exchange duties with the RAF, was scrambled from an airfield in
Lincolnshire to intercept a mysterious blip on radar. This was to be his last mission and the
beginning of a mystery that would endure long after the stand-off between superpowers
had ended.

The 28-year-old father was an experienced pilot who had seen action in Vietnam. But
in the early hours of 9 September 1970, his wife and young family were told the RAF
Lightning he had been flying had crashed into the North Sea. Lifeboats and coastguard
rescue units spent two days searching the choppy seas but could find no trace of his body.
Although the wreckage of the plane was eventually recovered from the sea largely intact,
Captain Schaffner's body was never found. These mysterious circumstances transformed a
tragic accident into a modern legend.

Official secrecy was endemic at the time and the findings of the RAF Board of Inquiry
into the crash were withheld for 30 years.[30] During the intervening period, rumours spread
about what had happened to Captain Schaffner. One of the most bizarre claimed he had
been spirited from the cockpit of his aircraft as he closed on a UFO above the North Sea.

To the pilots and ground crew on duty at RAF Binbrook that night, the intruder that
triggered the 'alert' was, by definition, unidentified. Was it a Russian intruder or something much stranger? For a long time, the fact that Schaffner died in tragic circumstances
was the only definite fact that could be ascertained from publicly available material. As the
years passed, it became the lynchpin around rumours and gossip that suggested Schaffner
lost his life whilst pursuing an alien craft.

The UFO connection was born in 1992 when a journalist on the *Evening News* in Grimsby, near the Lincolnshire air base, received a call from a man claiming to be a member of the original RAF crash investigation team that examined the remains of the Lightning.[31] The source, who wished to remain anonymous, claimed Schaffner's squadron was involved in a secret operation to intercept UFOs over the North Atlantic that had been tracked moving at incredible speed on NATO radars.

According to the newspaper's source, Schaffner took off in Lightning XS-894 not long after he had returned from a training mission. A UFO was being tracked on radar about 90 miles east of Whitby and Schaffner was quickly vectored onto it. The information about what happened next was taken from a transcript provided by the source that purported to be describing the actual interchange between Schaffner and the radar controller at RAF Patrington in East Yorkshire. According to the transcript, Schaffner saw a bluish conical object that was so bright he could hardly look at it. As he closed in he exclaims: 'Wait a second, it's turning . . . coming straight for me . . . am taking evasive action . . .'[32]

At that point the controller lost contact and Schaffner's radar plot merged with that of the UFO for a while before losing altitude and disappearing from the scope. His Lightning was later recovered from the sea with the cockpit closed. There was no sign of the pilot's body inside.

Captain Schaffner's wife was never told the full findings of the inquiry and afterwards she remarried and settled in Chicago. Two of his children, Glenn and Mike, now adults, were shocked when they read the account of their father's last moments on the Internet. Prompted to help them discover the truth, in 2002, BBC North's *Inside Out* TV programme obtained access to the RAF Board of Inquiry report on the crash.[33] This included photographs of the Lightning jet after its recovery from the water, and the transcript of Captain Schaffner's final conversation with ground controllers. It was obvious that critical passages from the transcript differed drastically from the version published by the Grimsby *Evening Telegraph* in 1992 by the mysterious 'crash investigator'. The inquiry report gave a very different account of the circumstances in which Captain Schaffner died to that circulating online.[34]

The records of the RAF inquiry, released in 2008, contained more than one thousand pages of testimony and other contemporary evidence including photographs and charts. The file comprehensively debunked any link between his death and UFOs. These stories, it emerged, were the product of rumour and wishful thinking rather than hard fact.

Although Schaffner and his colleagues in 5 Squadron may not have known the *true* identity of their target, that was the whole purpose of the exercise. The proceedings of the RAF Board of Inquiry in June 1972 reveal that Schaffner was taking part in a TACEVAL (Tactical Evaluation) exercise on the night he died. This was just one of many dry-runs set up by the RAF to test the readiness of its front-line pilots. Aircrew were deliberately kept in the dark as to whether their target was friend or foe and the aim was initially to locate

FIGURE 5.4 A PHOTOGRAPH FROM THE RAF BOARD OF INQUIRY FILE INTO THE DEATH OF CAPTAIN WILLIAM SCHAFFNER IN 1970. THE USAF PILOT DIED DURING A TRAINING EXERCISE WHILST SHADOWING AN RAF SHACKLETON OVER THE NORTH SEA. THE IMAGE SHOWS THE WRECKAGE OF HIS LIGHTNING INTERCEPTOR AS IT WAS LIFTED FROM THE SEA-BED NEAR FLAMBOROUGH HEAD. (CROWN COPYRIGHT, THE NATIONAL ARCHIVES DEFE 71/95)

and intercept an unknown. The report reveals the 'UFO' was an RAF Shackleton that 'entered the UK airspace during daylight and remained on station through dusk and into darkness'.[35]

During the night, Lightning pilots from Binbrook were scrambled one by one to identify, intercept and shadow the intruder. Schaffner's initial orders were cancelled as he taxied down the runway and he was ordered back to dispersal. RAF regulations stipulated the aircraft should have been given a full service before he rejoined the exercise but despite his combat experience, and while under pressure, he broke the rules and called off his ground crew. When a fresh scramble order arrived minutes later, he failed to sign his aircraft's servicing certificate. Keen to join the action, he left it behind as his Lightning zoomed skywards.

These unfortunate circumstances now conspired to seal his fate. The RAF had changed their scenario from the straightforward interception he was expecting. It now required pilots to shadow and shepherd the slow-moving, low-flying Shackleton transport out of UK airspace. Although Captain Schaffner had much experience at interceptions, he had little training to prepare him for this potentially hazardous exercise in darkness low above the North Sea. After he located the target, his last contact with ground control at RAF Patrington was timed at 8.45pm GMT. The accident file contains the *actual* transcript of his conversation with ground controllers that mentions visual 'contact with a set of lights'.[36] He then says he is closing upon them.

He explains he will have to 'do some manoeuvring to slow her down a little bit' and controllers warn him to 'keep a sharp look out'. Suddenly contact is lost and the final moments contain the Fighter Controller's desperate calls: 'Do you read – over. Do you read – over.'[37]

In their testimony, the crew of the Shackleton said they saw his Lightning flying low below them in a port turn. Immediately afterwards visual contact was lost. This is the moment the RAF concluded his aircraft struck the sea.

Two months after the accident, Schaffner's Lightning was discovered lying on the sea bed five miles off Flamborough Head. It appeared the aircraft had struck the sea at low speed and planed along the surface before sinking. The evidence confirmed one part of the legend. When the aircraft was recovered and examined at Farnborough, aircrash investigators found the canopy was closed but there was no trace of the pilot inside the cockpit.

The clues that helped to explain the mystery were found by a careful examination of the cockpit. This discovered the Lightning's ejector seat mechanism had not been properly serviced and had failed to fire when Schaffner activated it. He then tried to open the canopy manually to escape from the sinking aircraft and succeeded in doing so, but as he entered the water lost his emergency life-support equipment. With no life raft, he had no chance of surviving alone for more than a few minutes in the freezing water. As the aircraft sank, the cockpit closed under hydraulic pressure, leaving it empty.

The story of Captain Schaffner's 'abduction' by a UFO over the North Sea resembles that of the 'vanishing battalion' at Gallipoli in the way the legendary version, spread by newspapers and the Internet, radically diverged from the true facts about his death. It would have been an extraordinary tale if any part of it had been true. Not only did it raise uncomfortable political and diplomatic questions about Cold War secrets, it also resonated with other disturbing stories surrounding the unexplained disappearance of aircraft and their crews that have become part of the UFO literature.

PHANTOM HELICOPTERS

In one classic scene from Francis Ford Coppola's film *Apocalypse Now* (1979), set in the Vietnam war, a formation of US Navy attack helicopters reduces a Vietcong village to ashes as Wagner's *Ride of the Valkyries* plays through their loudspeakers. The ability of modern helicopter gunships to strike terror into the enemy and deliver death and destruction from the air has been further enhanced during the wars in Iraq and Afghanistan. In American folklore, 'black helicopters' have developed a sinister reputation as agents of conspiracies linking government agencies with crashed UFOs and mysterious cattle mutilations. Latent fears about the use of helicopters for nefarious purposes emerge in many films and TV programmes. For example, unmarked helicopters disrupt an outdoor gathering of UFO spotters in a scene from *Close Encounters of the Third Kind*.

The link between helicopters, UFOs and conspiracy theories emerged between 1973 and 1977 when more than 700 cases of animal mutilations, primarily of cattle, were reported from 15 western states, triggering investigations by the police and FBI. The 'mutes' often took place at night with cattle killed without a struggle, their blood drained and organs removed with surgical precision. In some cases it appeared the animals had been mutilated elsewhere and then dropped from the air. Unmarked helicopters, often equipped with searchlights, were often seen and heard flying by night in the areas where clusters of mutilations occurred and their elusive behaviour mirrored that of UFOs. Explanations ranged from the activities of mysterious occult groups to secret experiments on livestock as part of a programme to monitor radioactivity from underground nuclear experiments. The FBI investigation attributed the majority of mutilations to attacks by predators rather than extra-terrestrials, but the link between sinister unmarked helicopters and strange phenomena continued to grow in the UFO mythology.[1]

In Britain, similar fears surfaced during the early 1970s when rumours spread linking phantom helicopters with Irish terrorists and illegal immigrants. In 1976, Peter Rogerson summarised the stories circulating at the time: 'Helicopters fly the night sky, what do they carry – terrorists who will blow up our cities, foreigners who will take away "our way of life", Russian agents who stir up trouble, or Satanists who will drink the blood of our cattle. Whatever, it bodes no good, fear is contagious.'[2] Rogerson was writing in the aftermath of an Irish republican bombing campaign on mainland Britain. This began with the 1972 car bomb attack on the headquarters of the Parachute Brigade in Aldershot that was claimed as a revenge attack for Bloody Sunday. During the campaign that followed, rumours spread that a low-flying helicopter had been seen hedge-hopping in parts of northern England late at night.

Was this sinister machine being used by Irish terrorist groups to steal explosives or for attempting to free members held in English prisons? Or was the entire panic a product of a collective delusion?

Despite their fantastic nature, rumours about the helicopter's movements were widely spread by the media and had to be taken seriously by police and Special Branch detectives. In 1973–74, British police and security personnel were over-stretched as they investigated a string of bomb blasts and other terrorist outrages across the country. In February 1973, the imposition of direct rule in Ulster led to a renewed campaign of terrorism by Irish republicans on mainland Britain. The attacks culminated in the bombing of the Tower of London and public houses in Guildford, Woolwich and Birmingham in October 1974. At the height of the carnage, some senior police officers suspected Irish republican groups planned to use unregistered helicopters and even light aircraft to smuggle guns, explosives and terrorists across the Irish Sea to feed the cells operating on the mainland. Although helicopters were noisy and difficult to conceal, there were precedents for their use by terrorists in Ireland. On one occasion a hijacked private helicopter was used to free a republican prisoner from a compound in Northern Ireland and another was used to attack a police station from the air. The existence of a regular ferry service between Northern Ireland and Liverpool placed northwest England, particularly Manchester and the industrial Mersey valley, on a list of potential targets. This area became the focus of the phantom helicopter sightings during the winter of 1973–74.

The sighting that triggered off the panic occurred in a complex of quarries and mines near the spa town of Buxton in Derbyshire. Late one September night in 1973, security guard Simon Crowe was alerted by an urgent phone call. Crowe guarded high explosives stored in a quarry high on the Peak District moors near Buxton. Nearby residents had seen what they thought was a helicopter about to land inside the quarry and called police. Crowe raced towards the site in his Land Rover™. This was the second time in a week he had been called out in the middle of the night and this time he was determined to get to the bottom of the mystery.

'But I had no luck,' he told me. 'On the first occasion it hovered at about 50 feet from the ground with the spotlights shining downwards into the main quarry floor. When I approached in the Land Rover with my headlights on, it rose slowly and flew away. On this occasion it rose out of the quarry and I was not aware of it until I saw the lights. It quickly disappeared in the same direction as before. But it was odd, because at no time could I positively identify it as a helicopter – apart from its ability to hover and the sound from the rotor-blades.'[3]

Crowe reported the sighting to Derbyshire Police and soon afterwards he was questioned by detectives from the Metropolitan Police's Special Branch. Shortly thereafter, police appealed through local media for information 'from anyone who saw an unidentified aircraft or helicopter in the Buxton area'. The mystery remained unsolved one month later when further sightings were reported on the border between Derbyshire and Cheshire. By November, detectives had received 12 reliable reports of helicopters 'apparently practising landings in the vicinity of quarries and explosive stores in the Derbyshire countryside'. One of the most detailed was made by two police officers who saw the copter at close range. They were able to identify the exact type of machine involved as a two-seater Augusta-Bell 206A Jet Ranger. This was a medium-sized helicopter, capable of carrying five people, with a range of 250 miles. Derbyshire Police contacted the Metropolitan Police Special Branch unit at Gatwick Airport for help in identifying the owner. They were sent a list of 37 individuals and companies who owned Augusta-Bells in the UK.

On 22 November both the Home Office and MI5 were briefed on the mystery by Special Branch. Their report says Derbyshire CID officers had made detailed inquiries to discover the owner and reasons for the flights without success. It said: '[They] have contacted an experienced RAF helicopter pilot with night flying experience who explained that night flying in the Derbyshire area would be extremely dangerous due to the nature of the terrain and to the number of overhead pylons in that area. There is therefore a strong possibility of these flights being of an illegal nature.'[4]

The involvement of anti-terrorist detectives in the investigation was first revealed by press reports. But the actual reason for their interest remained a mystery until 2005 when I obtained a copy of a formerly secret Metropolitan Police file under the Freedom of Information Act. Even today, the full content of the file is being withheld from public viewing at The National Archives due to the 'sensitive nature of the contents'.[5] The papers reveal how news of the mystery reached the newspapers early in January 1974 when fresh sightings poured into police stations in Derbyshire and Cheshire. After midnight on Monday, 14 January, police patrols spotted a helicopter flying in the Cat and Fiddle area of Cheshire (not too far from Buxton) and contacted colleagues in the neighbouring force. They gave chase and said the pilot appeared to veer off towards Sheffield to avoid identification. The same night, police nearby in Macclesfield mounted a fruitless search of fields near the Jodrell Bank radio telescope after reports were made that the machine had landed in a field nearby. A spokesman said: 'Our officers spotted the helicopter and then lost it. They managed to spot it again and it gave the impression that it had landed, but the helicopter took off before the officers could get to it.'[6] According to the police, the helicopter was active only in the early hours and swooped as low as 100ft, sometimes without lights. On other occasions the crew used a searchlight to pick their way through the darkness.

SA

S.B. No. 1 (Plain)

Special Report }

SPECIAL BRANCH

.....22nd..day of.....November.....................19.73..

SUBJECT................

Unidentified

helecopter/sighted

in Derbyshire.

Reference to Papers

....

....

1.   With reference to a report dated 15th November 1973
from D.S. Taylor at Gatwick Airport, London, which includes
a list of owners of Augusta Bell 206A Jet Ranger helicopters
in the U.K, a type of machine recently seen flying at night
in the Derbyshire area; I have made enquiries to ascertain
the validity of the circumstances surrounding these incidents.

2.   On Wednesday 21st November 1973 I contacted D.C. Harvey
of Derby County and Borough Constabulary who stated that
a positive identification of an Augusta Bell 206A Jet Ranger
helicopter has been made by a number of individual witnesses
including two police officers. The machine was observed on
a number of occasions over a period of two weeks to be
apparently practicing landings in the vicinity of the sites
of quarries and explosives stores in the Derbyshire
countryside. The helecopter was last seen on the 3rd
September 1973.

3.   D.C. Harvey has made numerous enquiries to discover
the ownership and reasons for the flights from various
sources but has asyet failed to establish any positive facts.
He has contacted an experienced R.A.F. helicopter pilot with
night flying experience who explained that night flying in
the Derbyshire area would be extremely dangerous due to the
nature of the terrain and to the number of overhead pylons in
that area. There is therefore a strong possibility of these
flights being of an illegal nature.

4.   I have been requested by D.C. Harvey that the list of
owners of the Bell Augusta helecopters be forwarded to Derby
County and Borough Constabulary in order that they may make
further enquiries regarding this matter.

David H. Sisterson
Constable

Submitted:

Chief Inspector

CHIEF SUPERINTENDENT

AB. 698.

M.P.-73-87728/20M (2)

PANEL FIGURE 5.1 A PAGE FROM THE SPECIAL BRANCH REPORT ON
'UNAUTHORISED HELICOPTER FLIGHTS' IN DERBYSHIRE AND CHESHIRE DURING
THE WINTER OF 1973-74. THE PILOT OF THE PHANTOM FLYING MACHINE WAS
NEVER IDENTIFIED. (CROWN COPYRIGHT/AUTHOR'S COLLECTION)

For weeks tabloid headlines were dominated by news of the unfolding drama. Rumours spread that linked the midnight flights with terrorists, spies, drug smugglers and even cattle rustlers operating from the air. Most bizarre of all was one theory reported by the *Daily Telegraph* that 'it might be a "home-made" helicopter which the owner, unable to obtain an air-worthiness certificate, is flying dangerously at night, or . . . it might be a modern – and wealthy – lover who finds it the most convenient way to reach his mistress or girlfriend'. The espionage theme was a favourite of the *Daily Mirror*, who described the flier as 'a devil-may-care pilot' and said the helicopter mystery had 'all the drama of a James Bond spy spectacular'. The *Mirror* sent a reporter, Edward Macauley, to join an ex-Army pilot, Alex Parker, on a flight above the Peak District moors following in the footsteps of the phantom. The pair flew in daylight at an altitude of 500ft. In comparison, the phantom flew at night between 50 and 100ft from the ground. This led Alex to observe that: '. . . to try to get through these hills at such a low level makes this guy a madman – or a great pilot. Whichever he is, I still feel he has been lucky to get away without having an accident.'[7]

N. Staffs. and South Cheshire patrols alerted, but . . .

PHANTOM 'COPTER MYSTERY HAS POLICE BAFFLED

POLICE HUNTING A MYSTERY LOW-FLIGHT HELICOPTER SWOOPED TWICE IN QUIET PARTS OF SOUTH CHESHIRE EARLY TODAY.

They moved in after a 'copter was reported to have landed near Jodrell Bank radio telescope, at Goostrey, and close to Arclid traffic lights.

A helicopter was also seen by a person in the North Staffordshire village of Audley at about the same time.

"But we do not know whether it landed," said a police spokesman. "There were several sightings near the border and we are checking them out."

Joined hunt

Special branch detectives in the Midlands have joined in the hunt for the night-flight helicopter which is baffling police in four counties. It has been seen many times flying over rural parts of Staffordshire, Cheshire, Derbyshire and Lancashire in the past six months.

Some of its trips have taken

"If the helicopter is not on legitimate business there are many forms of illegal practices it could be involved in."

Meanwhile, police in the four counties are still appealing for any information about night-time helicopter flights.

Co-operation

"We have had a number of reports from the public—some were perfectly legitimate aircraft—and we are checking them out. We appreciate the co-operation," said the senior policeman.

At the weekend, a helicopter was seen at Goostrey and it gave the impression that it landed. But it took off before police could get to it.

A Derbyshire police spokesman said: "We have pretty

PANEL FIGURE 5.2 A TYPICAL NEWSPAPER HEADLINE FROM THE TIME OF THE PHANTOM HELICOPTER SCARE IN NORTHERN ENGLAND. THE SIGHTINGS COINCIDED WITH AN IRISH REPUBLICAN BOMBING CAMPAIGN IN ENGLAND AND DETECTIVES SUSPECTED THE NOCTURNAL FLIGHTS WERE CONNECTED WITH TERRORISM. (AUTHOR'S COLLECTION)

His views were echoed by Lt Col. Bob Smith, a former Army helicopter pilot, who said: 'It's quite likely this man received his training in the services. To fly safely, the way he does, he would need at least £30,000 worth of extra equipment including radios, blind flying instruments, a very wide range of navigational aids, homing devices and a moving map display. It is possible to fly without all these aids but he could never find his way from A to B. This man must be an extremely competent pilot, because flying at night in the sort of country he is in you can meet all sorts of hazards.'[8]

By this point police in Derbyshire and Cheshire were exchanging information with five other neighbouring forces where helicopter sightings had been made, including Lancashire and West Yorkshire. According to the Metropolitan Police file, Detective Supt George Oldfield of Wakefield CID claimed to have intelligence that certain members of the Provisional IRA had trained in the Derbyshire hills using a helicopter. Oldfield led the investigation of the coach bomb that killed nine soldiers and three civilians on the M62 in February 1974. He feared the machine was being prepared to free IRA prisoners and wanted Special Branch to draw up a list of the owners of all privately owned helicopters in the UK so that they could be investigated for links to republican terrorists.[9]

The scare reached its height in March 1974 when the Home Office convened a conference in London to allow northern police forces to review a dossier on 'unauthorised helicopter flights' with Special Branch detectives. The conference was attended by representatives from the Derbyshire and Cheshire forces along with officials from the Ministry of Defence. A summary of the proceedings included in the file records how: 'In the event there were found to be only three "hard" sightings and no useful pattern of timing or positioning was discernible . . . no crimes were reported at the times of the alleged flights [and] Special Branch had no hard information to place potential subversive activities in the area. However, it was agreed that the sightings could not be ignored and the Ministry of Defence was asked what facilities they could provide to assist with identifying the helicopter. The use of searchlights, radar, MoD helicopters and the Harrier Jump Jet were discussed but considered either impractical or too expensive.'[10]

The head of Special Branch's anti-terrorism force, Supt John Warwicker, attended the meeting and was asked to comment on the police request for the Harrier to be used to intercept the phantom copter. He had direct knowledge of the night-flying hazards highlighted by Lt Col. Smith as he had experienced both as an observer and navigator in police helicopters during service as Chief Flying Instructor for the Metropolitan Police's flying club at Biggin Hill. His feelings were that if a real helicopter were involved, it should have been easily identified as there were so few specialist aircraft and pilots capable of operating in the Peak District. In his briefing for the meeting, Warwicker said: 'Helicopter flights at night are a highly specialised undertaking, requiring a fully equipped aircraft and an expert pilot. Blind landings at night are a risky undertaking and this point is well taken by the MoD who are reluctant to place even one of their fully equipped aircraft in such a night-flying situation.'[11]

Recalling his contribution to the meeting in 2013, Warwicker told me his intervention was greeted with 'tangible sighs of relief' from the MoD officials. 'There were clearly logistical problems of secrecy and security and the massive expense involved would probably finish up with the Cheshire constabulary. Thus was the abandonment of the project mutually agreed and there was never a repeat of the local threat assessment.'[12]

By June 1974, when the Home Office asked Warwicker to prepare a more detailed report on the helicopter mystery, doubts about the credibility of the sightings were beginning to surface.[13] Police also realised the publicity their investigation received had been counter-productive. Hundreds of reports had poured in, many describing perfectly normal helicopters on legitimate flights. Throughout the world an oil crisis was causing widespread fuel shortages and the cost of keeping a helicopter airborne were huge, yet the phantom seemed to be untroubled by this problem. Doubts were increased when a psychologist put forward the theory that the sightings were a rumour-fuelled panic encouraged by the media and the police themselves. Professor John Cohen of Manchester University said the initial reports by police and security guards might have triggered off the flap. 'It is contagious,' he said. 'Plant an idea and you get a kind of visual epidemic.'[14] With no resolution found and no evidence of IRA involvement established, the scare ended almost as quickly as it began. The Special Branch file was closed in October 1974 with the comment 'the helicopter and pilot were never identified'.

In hindsight John Warwicker, who retired from Special Branch in 1979, recognised that the border separating the helicopter sightings and the equally nebulous UFO reports received by the authorities on a daily basis was very thin. In the Special Branch file, he noted the fact that the helicopter sightings 'seem to be only loosely connected and may in fact simply be a random amalgam of the frequent [UFO] sighting reports which are made to one authority or another on a daily basis'. From the point of view of the security forces, as soon as the existence of a *real* helicopter was eliminated, police interest came to an end. As Jenny Randles remarks in *The Pennine UFO Mystery*: 'Since, as far as officialdom is concerned, UFOs do not exist, the object must be a helicopter, even if no one knows where it comes from, or goes to, or why its pilot is insane enough to fly over such dangerous terrain in such a foolhardy fashion.'[15]

CHAPTER 6

MYSTERIES OF THE SEA

PHANTOM SHIPS

Fast gliding along, a gloomy bark
Her sails are full, though the wind is still,
And there blows not a breath her sails to filll

Thomas Moore (1806)[1]

Around 70 per cent of the Earth's surface is covered by water and the oceans are the source of many puzzling and hitherto unrecognised phenomena. The *Mary Celeste*, found drifting without its crew in the Atlantic in 1872, is a classic example of a 'derelict' ghost ship (see p.164). However, there is another type of ghost ship that is less substantial but no less ominous in terms of its impact upon nautical folklore. The lines above, from a poem by Thomas Moore (1779–1852), was written 'on passing Dead-man's Island in the Gulf of St Lawrence, late in the evening, September, 1804'. It refers to a belief once common among sailors in the North Atlantic who feared an apparition known as 'the flying Dutch-man'. By the 19th century, this legend was so widespread that it became the generic label for all 'phantom ships' encountered by seafarers. Writing in 1924, British author J.G. Lockhart said that within living memory the story of a spectral vessel, doomed to sail the oceans with its crew of damned spirits, 'was still an article of faith among mariners' across the world.[2] For the superstitious, the appearance of this vessel was regarded as a portent of doom.

The legend first appears in narrative form during the 18th century but its roots can be traced to the Middle Ages when the Netherlands produced many skilled sailors. The phantom became so familiar to mariners during the age of exploration that it was said every ship had at least one member of its crew 'who pretends to have seen the apparition'. George Barrington, in *A Voyage to Botany Bay*, published in 1795, says that he heard the story direct from sailors who told him of a Dutch man-of-war lost off the Cape of Good Hope with its entire crew:

> . . . her consort weathered the gale, and arrived soon after at the Cape. Having refitted, and returning to Europe, they were assailed by a violent tempest nearly at the same latitude. In the night watch some of the people saw, or imagined they saw, a vessel standing for them under a press of sail, as though she would run them down: one in particular affirmed it was the ship that had foundered in the former gale, and that it must certainly be her, or the apparition of her; but on clearing up, the object, a dark thick cloud, disappeared . . . nothing could do away the idea of this phenomenon on the minds of the sailors; and, on their relating the circumstances when they arrived in port, the story spread like wild-fire, and the supposed phantom was called the Flying Dutchman.[3]

The ghostly vessel was immortalised in art, theatre and literature. A novel, *The Phantom Ship*, was published in 1839 and Richard Wagner used it as the theme for an opera set on the North Sea. A ghost ship also appears in the poem *The Rime of the Ancient Mariner* by Samuel Taylor Coleridge and more recently, the ship and one of its fictional captains, Davy Jones, appears in Disney's *Dead Man's Chest* (2006) that formed part of the *Pirates of the Caribbean* movie franchise. Jones is a relatively recent model for its captain. Some versions of the legend identify him as Bernard Fokke, a Dutch captain from the 18th century, who made a pact with the Devil that allowed him to perform incredible feats at sea. According to Lockhart, 'he was, for instance, reported to have sailed to the East Indies in ninety days, an anticipation, perhaps, of Jules Verne'. During one of these trips he vanished and it was believed the Devil had taken his soul: '. . . thereafter his spectral ship may be seen between the Cape of Good Hope and the Horn, beating eternally the waters of the Southern Seas, manned by none save Fokke, his boatswain, his pilot and his cook.'[4]

An elaborate version of the legend was published by *Blackwood's Edinburgh Magazine* in 1821. This gave the captain's name as Hendrick Vanderdecken and refers to the ship as 'an Amsterdam vessel [that] sailed from port seventy years ago'.[5] It introduced the idea that if hailed by the crew of a real ship, the ghostly crew would try to send messages to land or to people long dead. If these were accepted, bad luck would inevitably follow. Vanderdecken swears to round the Cape of Good Hope even if it takes him until the Day of Judgement to complete the task. Versions of this legend are found in North America and elsewhere and all talk about a cursed ship that, if sighted, was a bad omen.

There are frequent accounts of strange glowing lights reported by crews during the 19th and 20th centuries and attempts have been made to explain some of these as optical illusions caused by unusual meteorological conditions. For example, a first-hand account of a phantom ship seen in Chaleur Bay, Canada, in 1861, describes it as: 'a light far out in the bay that appeared as if the hull of some little craft was on fire, and the devouring element was sweeping through the rigging and consuming everything within its reach. Such, of course, were the first efforts of the imagination in endeavouring to give outline or shape to an indefinite something that was far beyond the power of closer investigation.' The observer, a newspaper editor, said the appearance of the 'ghost ship' always preceded a northerly storm 'and is a sure forerunner of it . . . it is not confined to one locality, but is seen from time to time at different places'. When it appeared during the summer, boats went out to approach the burning light, 'but as they approach it it disappeared, and after they have passed the place where it had been to some distance, it reappears behind them, giving the curious but little chance of a close investigation'.[6]

Robert de la Croix made a study of unusual sightings recorded in the logbooks of merchant ships between 1831 and 1885 for his book *Mysteries of the Sea* (1956). He found accounts of 'three hundred apparitions for which there seems to be no logical explanation'.[7] Peter Underwood says that sightings are recorded in the logbooks of ships that ply the South Atlantic and in particular around the Cape of Good Hope. One of those who personally assured him of having seen a 'phantom ship in full sail in those wind-swept seas' was the author and broadcaster Commander Archibald Bruce Campbell. Commander Campbell served on HMS *Otranto*, an armed merchant cruiser, in the South Atlantic during the First World War and survived its sinking in 1918 when it collided with a troop ship.[8]

One of the best documented sightings of the 'Flying Dutchman' was made by Prince George of Wales, who became King George V and was the grandfather of Queen Elizabeth II. At the age of 16 he joined his elder brother Prince Albert Victor on a three-year voyage around the world as a naval cadet on the 4,000-tonne corvette HMS *Bacchante*. The young princes were accompanied by their tutor John Dalton, who wrote a detailed account of the journey. In July 1881 the two princes transferred to HMS *Inconstant* whilst repairs were carried out on the rudder of their ship. At the time, a number of British warships were in Hobson Bay off the south coast of Australia, accompanying the *Inconstant* en route from Melbourne to Sydney.

It was during this cruise, in the early hours of 11 July, that a sailor on lookout duty in the forecastle called out that 'a phantom ship all aglow' was visible close to the port bow. A crowd of people gathered to watch the apparition. There are many versions of what happened next, including stories that Prince George recorded the experience in his personal diary or that it was mentioned in the ship's log that Peter Haining said 'was preserved by the Admiralty in London'.[9] The most authoritative account appears in Dalton's book, *The Cruise of Her Majesty's Ship The Bacchante*, published in 1886. The prince's tutor describes how, at 4 am:

FIGURE 6.1 A PHOTOGRAPH OF THE FUTURE KING GEORGE V IN 1903. IN 1881 PRINCE GEORGE AND HIS OLDER BROTHER WERE AMONG A GROUP OF NAVAL OFFICERS WHO SAW A PHANTOM SHIP, THE FLYING DUTCHMAN, PASS THE HMS *INCONSTANT*, WHILST IN HOBSON BAY, AUSTRALIA. (CROWN COPYRIGHT, THE NATIONAL ARCHIVES COPY 1/466)

. . . the Flying Dutchman crossed our bows. A strange red light as of a phantom ship all aglow, in the midst of which light the masts, spars, and sails of a brig 200 yards distant stood out in strong relief as she came up on the port bow. The look-out man on the forecastle reported her as close on the port bow, where also the officer of the watch from the bridge clearly saw her, as did also the quarterdeck midshipman, who was sent forward at once to the forecastle; but on arriving there no vestige nor any sign whatever of any material ship was to be seen either near or right away to the horizon, the night being clear and the sea calm.[10]

Dalton says that in all 13 people saw the phantom ship. He does not specify whether this group included the two princes but adds 'whether it was Van Diemen or the Flying Dutchman or who else must remain unknown'. Their sighting was corroborated by the crewmembers of two other ships, the *Tourmaline* and *Cleopatra*, who were sailing on the starboard bow. Shortly afterwards both flashed signals to HMS *Inconstant* asking whether they had seen 'the strange red light'.

Two hours later, the lookout sighted land to the north-east. Then the old superstitions about portents of doom were confirmed as he 'fell from the fore topmast crosstrees on to the topgallant forecastle and was smashed to atoms'. According to Dalton's account the lookout, Henry Youle, 'was a smart royal yardman, and one of the most promising young hands in the ship, and everyone feels quite sad at his loss'. He was not the only casualty. When the *Inconstant* reached Sydney, ' the Admiral also was smitten down'. There is no reference to the 'Flying Dutchman' in the logbook of HMS *Inconstant* held by The National Archives, but a note dated 11 July 1881 confirms: '10.45 . . . Henry Youle, 20 years, killed by a fall from the mast aloft. Buried at sea.'[11] The matter-of-fact way in which the log deals with Youle's death is consistent with Dalton's account. Despite the appearance of this ancient prodigy of doom, the royal princes did not appear to be unduly concerned and, soon afterwards, they began preparations to sit an algebra exam.

SUBMARINE LIGHTWHEELS

The Flying Dutchman is often dismissed as a wild story told by superstitious sailors, but evidence from the archives suggests it may be based on actual observations of some rare and poorly understood natural phenomena. An indication of the type of anomalies that have been recorded in ships' logs is provided by accounts of another persistent mystery of the ocean. Unlike the Flying Dutchman, there can be no doubt that submarine 'light-wheels' really do exist. Sightings of these dazzling and beautiful phenomena have been made by crews of warships on patrol in the Persian Gulf as recently as 2009. Accounts of earlier sightings have been found in written records dating back to the 18th century.

Sightings of lightwheels have been carefully recorded in the publications of the British Meteorological Office and the US Navy but at present they remain unexplained. Although marine bioluminescence is widely suspected as their source, no detailed scientific study – or expedition – has investigated the mechanism which creates the complex geometric forms that have amazed observers. An American study says that although there are dozens of reliable first-hand accounts of lightwheels, they defy classification because of the many and varied forms in which they appear.[12]

Those who have observed the phenomena from ships report pulsing or flashing lights and moving, parallel bands of light before spoke-like bands of the wheels appear in the water, much like aquatic Catherine wheels. Lightwheels often approach and cross the paths of ships from beneath the surface of the water. Many different forms have been reported and the spokes of the rimless wheels can be straight, curved or even S-shaped. Some take the form of concentric circles that pulsate from the brilliant glowing hub as if they are sending a signal to some unknown source. In some cases multiple wheels have been sighted rotating clockwise or anti-clockwise at varying speeds. They can be a few feet in diameter or so enormous they appear to fill the entire ocean with luminescence. The displays can be short in duration but some have gone on for several hours. In the majority of cases, the source of light appears just below the water, but some reports describe wheels of phosphorescent mist spinning just above the surface. Light produced by the wheels is usually white (or occasionally green) in colour and occasionally it has been bright enough to read by.

FIGURE 6.2 A DISPLAY OF PHOSPHORESCENT LIGHT ON THE SURFACE OF THE SEA, REPORTED BY CAPTAIN GABE OF THE STEAMER *BINTANG*, AS IT PASSED THROUGH THE STRAIT OF MALACCA IN JUNE 1909. (COURTESY OF FORTEAN PICTURE LIBRARY)

In whatever form they have appeared, lightwheels have inspired awe and sometimes terror in those who have seen them. For example, Captain E.E. Harris of the British merchant ship SS *Shahjehan* said the lightwheel he saw in the Indian Ocean one night in April 1875 was 'the most remarkable phenomenon that I have ever seen at sea'.[13] In earlier centuries, such marvels may have been interpreted as ominous ghost ships. More recently, lightwheels have appeared in the UFO literature where they have been interpreted as giant revolving machines operating from underwater alien bases or as Unidentified Submarine Objects (USOs). One American researcher, Kris Sherwood, believes that 'at least some of the physics involved' in their creation are similar to those that create crop circles on land.[14]

Another researcher, Michael Shoemaker, collected 129 accounts of lightwheels and related phenomena from scientific publications dating back to the 18th century.[15] He also found references to their appearance in ancient Indian literature. One of the earliest modern observations was made by the French naturalist Michel Adanson (1727–1806) and appeared in *The Naval Chronicle*, a publication of the British Admiralty, in 1799. Adanson described how one night, off the coast of West Africa, his ship sailed into what he described as 'a luminous enclosure which surrounded us like a large circle of rays, from whence darted in the wake of the ship a long stream of like'.[16] Adanson may have witnessed natural bioluminescence that is common in warm, shallow waters in parts of the Indian Ocean, the Persian Gulf and the South China Sea, where lightwheels have been reported most frequently. However, his reference to a 'large circle of rays' suggests this was no ordinary display.

Bioluminescence is caused by millions of tiny microorganisms and marine plankton (*Noctiluca miliaris*) that drift near the surface of the oceans. They emit light when shocked or disturbed by passing ships, lighting up the wakes and bow waves and forming milky white blankets beneath the water. In other cases they are stimulated by radar and sonar, or the movement of larger animals such as whales and shoals of fish. Luminous displays of this type were observed by Thor Heyerdahl during his voyage across the Pacific on the *Kon-Tiki* in 1947. Although witnesses have suspected a link with bioluminescence, they have noticed the odd fact that the ship's wake is not luminous whilst the spinning wheels are present.

During his research, Shoemaker found that references to lightwheels as a distinct phenomenon, separate from ordinary bioluminescence, began in 1879 when a detailed account by a naval officer was published by the scientific journal *Nature*. This was based upon an official report 'of an unusual phenomenon observed at sea' submitted to the British Admiralty by J. Elliot Pringle, who commanded a British gunboat, HMS *Vulture*. Although Pringle's original report is not at The National Archives, a copy was, fortunately, forwarded to *Nature* by Captain Evans, the Hydrographer of the Navy.

HMS *VULTURE'S* CLOSE ENCOUNTER

Commander Pringle also made a note in HMS *Vulture's* logbook where he records, on the evening of 15 May 1879, ' luminous waves or pulsations' seen in the water beneath the ship whilst en route to Bahrain in the Persian Gulf. The lights first appeared from the south-west and were followed by 'successive rays of light, revolving apparently on a centre (radius about one mile)'.[17] In his report to the Admiralty, Commander Pringle added: 'On looking towards the east, the appearance was that of a revolving wheel with its centre on that bearing, and whose spokes were illuminated, and looking towards the west a similar wheel appeared to be revolving, but in the opposite direction.' Commander Pringle and his first lieutenant then went to the mizzen top, situated 50ft above the water, where they noticed 'the luminous waves or pulsations were really travelling parallel to each other, and that their apparent rotary motion, as seen from the deck, was caused by their high speed and the greater angular motion of the nearer than the more remote part of the waves'. Pringle estimated the rays of light to be 25ft broad, with dark intervals of around 75ft between them. He timed their movement as about 75 per minute, 'giving a speed roughly of 84 English miles an hour'. He described the phenomenon, which began at 9.40pm local time and lasted 35 minutes as both 'beautiful and striking'.[18]

The appearance of first-hand accounts from credible observers encouraged others to submit details of their own sightings to the journal. One of the most detailed came from Captain Harris, commander of the SS *Shahjehan*. One evening in January 1880 the ship was steaming south along the Malabar coast in the Indian Ocean when a strange 'bank of light' crossed its path. Harris reported: 'The whole thing appeared so foreign to anything I had ever seen, and so wonderful, that I stopped the ship just on its outskirts, so that I might try to form a true and just conception of what it really was.' By this time all the officers and engineers had assembled on deck to witness the spectacle 'and were all equally astonished and interested'. Captain Harris, using his binoculars, saw 'a huge mass of nebulous matter [and] I distinctly saw spaces between what appeared to be waves of light of great lustre. These came rolling on with ever-increasing rapidity until they reached the ship'. Unlike Pringle, who described parallel bands of light, Captain Harris' ship was 'completely surrounded with one great body of undulating light, which soon extended to the horizon on all sides'.[19]

On peering into the water, Captain Harris saw patches of luminous matter, but these were faint compared to the great waves of light converging on his ship. 'The waves stood many degrees above the water, like a highly luminous mist, and obscured by their intensity the distant horizon; and as wave succeeded wave in rapid succession, one of the most grand and brilliant, yet solemn, spectacles that one could ever think of was here witnessed.' He added: 'If the sea could be converted into a huge mirror and thousands of powerful electric lights were made to throw their rays across it, it would convey no adequate idea of this strange yet grand phenomenon.'

More accounts of lightwheels were published by scientific and nautical journals during the next half century but no organised effort was ever made to collate or analyse them. That was until 1924 when the British Air Ministry's Meteorological Committee launched a magazine dedicated to collecting empirical data on unusual phenomena at sea. *The Marine Observer* actively encouraged volunteers and junior officers to report and make detailed records of mirages, waterspouts, bioluminescence and lightwheels. Typical of the many sightings recorded by the magazine's contributors was this, logged by Captain R.R. Baxter and the crew of the MV *Scottish Eagle*, during a voyage through the Persian Gulf on the afternoon of 23 April 1955:

When approaching Jazirat Tunb Island, a bright flashing light was observed on the port box, distant about 1 mile. Almost simultaneously another was observed on the starboard bow. On approaching it was seen that these were two revolving phosphorescent wheels. The ship passed between them, the centres being about a quarter of a mile distant on either side. The wheel on the port side appeared to revolve anti-clockwise, and that on the starboard side clockwise.[20]

The reaction of the ship's crew to this incredible sight was, according to Captain Baxter, 'a feeling of weirdness, bordering on fear, similar to that experienced by people ashore during earthquake tremors'. The spokes of the wheels were between six and 12ft broad at the tips with about 15ft between them. They passed the ship with a frequency of 1.5 seconds and had a 'colour similar to that of a dull electric light'. They gradually faded but later on the observer spotted a glow on the horizon that Captain Baxter believed 'was another group of wheels covering more than a square mile'.

Data published in *The Marine Observer* was used by Robert Staples in a 1966 paper on surface bioluminescence prepared for the US Naval Oceanographic Office.[21] For his study Staples collected 85 accounts of what he called 'phosphorescent wheels' and 26 examples of other varieties of luminous phenomena at sea including undulating waves, rays extending through the water and strange luminous patterns beneath the oceans. Plotting these on a map of the world, Staples found most clustered in the southern Persian Gulf, the Strait of Hormuz, the Mouths of the Indus and the Straits of Malacca, the Gulf of Thailand and the South China Sea. He also noted there was a complete lack of reports from the Mediterranean. Although the displays were unpredictable, the US study found 67 per cent of those seen in the Persian Gulf area occurred between April and June, while three quarters of those seen in the southern hemisphere zones such as the Straits of Malacca occurred from July through to December.

Staples' study concluded 'the cause or causes of such phenomena are still unknown', but he suspected there was a link with luminous organisms in the water. Many reports came from shallow waters, such as the Persian Gulf, where extensive blooms of phytoplankton occur in large quantities on the water surface. One theory suggests plankton saturated with oxygen could be stimulated to produce formations of light when excited by shockwaves from underwater earth tremors. Seaquakes were proposed as a possible source of the lightwheels by a German scientist, Kurt Kalle, in 1960. He speculated that an expanding cone of shock waves produced by quakes might produce a series of radiating rings that rose to the surface of the ocean. These vibrations would then be reflected to the ocean floor and then upwards to the surface again to produce further sets of radiating rings. This could produce the impression of a rotating wheel on the ocean surface with a hub lying midway between two sources.[22]

Although Kalle's theory is often cited as the standard explanation for lightwheels, it falls down because few, if any, of the actual reports contain any reference to shock waves or tremors. On the contrary, a number of the accounts describe the water surface as being still 'like a mill pond' when the phenomenon occurred. The length and persistence of the intricate geometries observed seems to rule out seaquakes as a primary cause. Michael Shoemaker's study, published in 1995, considered and rejected a number of other theories including the involvement of electromagnetic forces and the striking similarity of some marine phosphorescent displays to observations of low-level auroras. Others have compared the co-ordinated movements of tiny organisms in the sea with those observed in larger animals, such as flocks of starlings. Shoemaker concluded that animal behaviour and meteorology provided the best clues towards an explanation for the mystery. To this day, however, 'we know nothing about the functional details of such patterned behaviour, which may be triggered by . . . unknown factors'.[23]

Accounts of lightwheels have continued to appear in issues of *The Marine Observer* but oddly, no good quality photographs have been obtained clearly showing the phenomenon. The most recent sightings have been made by US Navy crews on patrol in the Persian Gulf. When 30 members of the crew of the USNS *Concord* saw luminous waves and echelon shapes whilst in the Straits of Hormuz one night in May 2007, they were left so shaken by the experience that some began to suspect they may have seen a new type of secret weapon developed by Iran.[24]

Two years later, a spectacular lightwheel display was observed by Captain Kendall Gennick and crewmembers of a guided missile destroyer, the USS *Milius*, as it patrolled the Persian Gulf. A detailed report by the ship's navigator, sent by email to Kris Sherwood, said the display began at 8.30pm on the evening of 12 April 2009 after the ship passed by an oil platform. Straight waves of light began travelling towards the ship from points on the horizon and, as the captain arrived on the bridge, the patterns changed to form spirals and wheels of light that passed directly down the beam of the ship. The navigator was familiar with marine bioluminescence that glowed a bright green when it was 'split like a giant V from the ship's hull', but the speed and pattern of this display was unlike anything he had seen before. 'About fifty of our crewmembers began filing into the pilot house,' he reported. 'Their reaction and the environment it created reminded me of watching a fireworks display on the fourth of July for the first time.'[25]

One of the more unusual ideas to account for marine lightwheels is that they are caused by creatures such as the giant squid or octopus. Fishermen in south-west Madagascar believed a 'giant snake or worm' they called the *tompondrano* ('Lord of the Sea') was the source of the rotating lights they occasionally saw beneath the Indian Ocean. In 1926 a visiting French naturalist, George Petit, was told that a sighting of the *tompondrano* was a bad omen and usually preceded the arrival of a storm. Petit had been out with a group of fishermen at night when a phosphorescent trail appeared in the water that 'seemed to be coming from a body rolling on its axis'.[26] His companions believed this was the sea monster and their leader blamed it for the death of a distant relative.

THE GREAT SEA SERPENT

Water is the natural home of monsters. Mankind will always believe in the things that it cannot see. The world has been so thoroughly mapped and explored that there is no longer room for belief in monsters . . . [but] when mankind has devised some way of exploring ocean depths, and the rivers and lakes of the world have yielded up their last secrets, then, and only then, will the world-wide monster myth be settled once and for all . . .

J.P. Kay Robinson, 1934[27]

It is often said that the depths of the oceans are as unfamiliar to mankind as the depths of outer space. Given their size, our chances of coming across an example of a rare sea creature other than by accident is very small indeed. That said, large ocean-dwelling creatures long thought to exist only in the imaginations of sailors have been captured, photographed and classified as recently as the mid-20th century. A living specimen of the *coelacanth*, a prehistoric fish known previously only in fossils laid down 65 million years ago, was caught by fishermen off the South African coast in 1938. Tentacles belonging to the colossal squid (*Mesonychoteuthis hamiltoni*), the largest known invertebrate, believed to grow to a maximum length of 14m (46ft), were found in the stomach of a sperm whale in 1925.

Encounters with previously unknown sea creatures may explain the rich folklore that has grown up around legends of 'sea serpents' that date back to the earliest written records. For example, in the 16th century the Swedish archbishop Olaus Magnus wrote about a gigantic sea snake larger than a ship seen off the coast of Norway. Two centuries later, another Scandinavian cleric wrote about a similar 'monster' seen off Greenland that was 'so huge a Size, that, coming out of the Water, its Head reached as high as the Mast-Head; its Body was bulky as the Ship, and three or four times as long'.[28] Belief in the existence of sea monsters was not confined to medieval legends and traveller's tales. Sir Joseph Banks, the eminent naturalist who took part in Captain James Cook's first great voyage (1768–71) and later President of the Royal Society, went on record to express 'his full faith in the existence of our Serpent of the Sea'.[29]

FIGURE 6.3 THE GREAT NORWEGIAN SEA SERPENT ATTACKS A SHIP AT SEA, FROM
OLAUS MAGNUS, *HISTORIA DE GENTIBUS SEPTENTRIONALIBUS* (A DESCRIPTION OF THE
NORTHERN PEOPLES), PUBLISHED IN ROME IN 1555. (COURTESY OF FORTEAN PICTURE
LIBRARY)

The modern fascination with the idea of giant underwater reptiles followed the discovery of fossil plesiosaurs during the early 19th century. Some of the most spectacular examples of these aquatic dinosaurs were uncovered in the middle and lower Jurassic rocks of the south and east coast of England during the Industrial Revolution. For many Victorians, these discoveries appeared to provide an unbroken link between the dragons of myth and legend and reports of long-necked 'sea serpents' sighted in the world's oceans. In his 1886 book *Mythical Monsters*, the Victorian geologist Charles Gould declared that dragons were some kind of 'long terrestrial lizard, hibernating and carnivorous, with the power of constricting with its snakelike body and tail, possibly furnished with wing-like extensions'. Gould argued there was nothing impossible 'in the ordinary notion of the traditional dragon' and 'it is more likely to have once had a real existence than to be a mere offspring of fancy'.[30]

The word 'dinosaur' (*terrible lizard*), coined in 1842 by the palaeontologist Sir Richard Owen, was a misnomer as dinosaurs were actually a species of reptiles separate to lizards. Nevertheless the full significance of the dinosaurs' place in the fossil record was fully realised by scientists before Darwin's theory of evolution was published in 1859. Professor Owen went on to become the first superintendent of the British Museum (Natural History) at South Kensington. The museum opened in 1881 and quickly established itself as the central repository for specimens of fossil dinosaurs and other biological and geological exhibits from around the world. As a result, the museum's directors and Keepers of Zoology were frequently asked to examine accounts from people who claimed to have personally observed a species of large and hitherto undiscovered marine dinosaur.

Even before the museum was built, Owen was drawn into a furious controversy that followed one of the most famous Victorian 'sea serpent' sightings. A story that 'an extraordinary animal' had crossed the path of the 19-gun corvette HMS *Daedalus* appeared in *The Times* newspaper in October 1848, before the ship returned to Plymouth from a trip to the East Indies. Following an order from the Admiralty, its captain, Peter McQuhae, submitted a report and drawings of 'The Phoenix of the Deep' to the Second Sea Lord, Admiral Sir William Gage. McQuhae's account, published by *The Times*, said the *Daedalus*, whilst en route from the Cape to the island of St Helena, had passed within 100 yards of a strange creature that was swimming rapidly in the opposite direction, apparently propelled by submerged fins. The captain and four officers were alerted to its presence by the midshipman at 5pm on 6 August:

On our attention being called to the object it was discovered to be an enormous serpent, with head and shoulders kept about four feet constantly above the surface of the sea . . . it passed rapidly, but so close under our lee quarter that had it been a man of my acquaintance I should have easily recognised his features with the naked eye; and it did not, either in approaching the ship or after it had passed our wake deviate in the slightest degree from its course to the S.W., which it held on at the pace of from 12 to 15 miles per hour, apparently on some determined purpose'.[31]

McQuhae said sixty feet or more of the serpent's body was visible and its head resembled that of a snake: '. . . its colour [was] a dark brown, with yellowish white about the throat. It had no fins, but something like the mane of a horse, or rather a bunch of seaweed, washed about its back'.

This spectacle was visible for 20 minutes and was seen by other members of the ship's company, who were eating supper, before it disappeared astern. Yet despite the sensation his report created in England, Captain McQuhae made no mention of the incident in his ship's logbook. When in 1930 Lt Cmdr Rupert Gould tried to locate Captain McQuhae's original report and the drawings he made for Admiral Gage, he found these had been destroyed. 'At an uncertain date some clerk . . . "weeded" it out of the Admiralty records as being of insufficient importance to be kept on file,' he wrote. 'In consequence it was pulped.'[32]

Fortunately the Admiralty sent a copy of his report to *The Times* that published it verbatim. Later, an artist's impression of the drawings made by the captain appeared in *The Illustrated London News*.[33] Publication of these accounts drew a substantial response from Professor Owen. In a lengthy letter published by *The Times*, Owen said he accepted the

FIGURE 6.4 A SKETCH OF THE SEA SERPENT SEEN NEAR THE ISLAND OF ST HELENA IN THE SOUTH ATLANTIC BY THE CREW OF THE HMS *DAEDALUS* IN 1848. (COURTESY OF FORTEAN PICTURE LIBRARY)

captain and his men had evidently seen a 'large animal . . . very different from anything he had before witnessed'. But he was convinced they had been deceived by an optical illusion. In his opinion, their description of the animal was consistent not with a serpent but with a warm-blooded mammal such as a sea lion or a large elephant seal, brought to the region on a melting iceberg with its 'eddy caused by the action of the deeper immersed fins and tail of [the] seal raising its head above the surface of the water'.[34] The naturalist said he regarded the 'negative evidence from the utter absence of any of the recent remains of the great sea serpents . . . as stronger against their actual existence than the positive statements which have weighed with the public mind in favour of their existence'. In short, there was more evidence for the existence of ghosts than of the sea-serpent.

Professor Owen's intervention led Captain McQuhae to pen a furious response to *The Times*, in which he denied 'the existence of excitement or the possibility of optical illusion'. He stood by the description he gave in his official report to the Admiralty and added: 'I leave them as data whereupon the learned and scientific may exercise the "pleasures of the imagination" until some more fortunate opportunity shall occur of making a closer acquaintance with the "great unknown" – in the present instance most assuredly no ghost.'[35]

The controversy triggered by the *Daedalus* sighting continued through the second half of the 19th century. Newspapers and magazines vied with each other to publish the latest 'sea serpent' reports and zoologists responded with rational explanations for the sightings. Some typical accounts of sea serpents can be found at The National Archives among the papers of Vice Admiral Robert FitzRoy (1805–65). The meteorological section of the Admiralty appears to have kept written records of reports filed by crews of merchant vessels, but although these were occasionally passed to newspapers and journals for publication they were never subject to any systematic study.

In 1881 an Admiralty official sought an opinion on a dossier of 'sea serpent' sightings from the anatomist William Henry Flower, who took over as director of the Natural History department of the British Museum after Professor Owen's retirement. One of two detailed accounts was submitted to the Admiralty by Captain James Stockdale in of the barque *Rob Roy*. In May 1830, when the ship was near the island of St Helena, the crew heard a scuffling noise in the water. As they turned to the port bow they were amazed to see the head of 'a great thundering sea snake' that rose six feet out of the water 'as square with our topsail [and] his tail was square with the foremast'. Stockdale said his ship was 171ft long with the foremast 42ft from the stern. This would make the monster 129ft long. He added: 'If I had not seen it I could not have believed it but there was no mistake or doubt of its length – for the brute was so close I could even smell his nasty fishy smell.'[36]

A second report of an even larger sea monster came from Commander George Henry Harrington of the 1,063-ton SS *Castilan*. Once again this creature was seen near St Helena in the South Atlantic. On 13 December 1857, Cmdr Harrington and two of his officers saw 'a huge marine animal' that suddenly reared out of the water just 20ft from the ship. For a few moments its long neck and dark head, shaped 'like a long buoy' and covered with white spots, was visible 'with a kind of scroll or ruff encircling it'. The creature submerged for a moment and then reappeared, leaving the crew in no doubt they were watching a sea monster 'of extraordinary length [which] appeared to be moving slowly towards the land'. The boatswain, who watched it for some time, said that it was more than double that of the entire ship, making it 500ft in length.[37]

In his response to the Admiralty, Flower appeared unimpressed with the accounts in the dossier and 'did not think [they] were sufficient to start a scientific survey of sea-monsters or make them worthy of publication after such a length of time'.[38] Flower's lack of interest reflected a wider scepticism amongst scientists towards the 'sea serpents'. Around the turn of the 20th century, the number of detailed reports began to decline. One possible explanation was that eyewitnesses had become reluctant to report their sightings in the face of ridicule from their peers and the press. From the point of view of zoologists, sea serpents had become a 'silly season' story that re-appeared only when real news was in short supply, usually during the summer months. Even worse, a number of stories were exposed as pranks and hoaxes. For example in 1906 a solicitor and amateur fossil hunter, Charles Dawson, sent a detailed account of his own sighting to the keeper of geology at the Natural History Museum. In the letter he described seeing, from a steamer in the English Channel, a creature composed of 'a series of very rounded arched loops like the most conventional old sea serpent you could imagine'. Dawson estimated it was 60–70ft in length 'at the smallest computation'. Photographs were taken with a small Kodak camera but none showed the creature.[39]

Later in the century, Dawson emerged as the prime suspect for the man who fooled scientists with a fake skull and jawbone, said to belong to an early human ancestor, unearthed in a gravel pit near Piltdown in East Sussex. The remains were proclaimed by scientists as evidence of the 'missing link' between apes and humans. The Piltdown Man skull was not revealed as a fake until 1953 and is regarded as the most successful hoax ever perpetrated on the scientific community.

ARTHUR CONAN DOYLE'S SEA SERPENT

Despite evidence of hoaxing and misperception, a trickle of first-hand reports describing sea monsters continued to reach the Natural History Museum during the early years of the 20th century. In May 1917 the armed merchant cruiser HMS *Hilary*, whilst on anti-submarine patrol 70 miles off the south-east coast of Iceland, passed close by an extraordinary creature resting on the ocean surface. In an account published after the war, her commanding officer, Captain F.W. Dean, described it as 60ft in length with a 'black glossy head' that resembled a cow, along with a 20ft-long slender neck. The crew used this unfortunate monster as a target for anti-submarine practice and aimed shots at it from its six-pounders at a range of 1,200 yards. A direct hit was made but the creature quickly vanished without trace beneath the ocean. Soon afterwards the *Hilary* was torpedoed by a German U-boat west of the Shetlands, but fortunately Captain Dean and his crew survived.[40] After Dean's account was published in 1930, the commanders of two German submarines came forward with their own accounts of sea monsters. The wildest of all came from Commander Baron von Forstner whose submarine, the U28, torpedoed the British steamer *Iberian* in the mid-Atlantic on 30 July 1915. A violent explosion followed the disappearance of the ship and 'a few seconds later a gigantic sea monster was hurled writhing and struggling, twenty or thirty yards into the air'. He told a German newspaper: '. . . the monster was about sixty feet long, in the shape of a crocodile. Its head was long and pointed, and its four legs terminated in strong fins.' Unfortunately, it was visible for only ten or 15 seconds, 'so there was no chance of taking photographs'. Checks on the U28's war diary by historian Mike Dash found no reference to the 'creature' in the account of the sinking of the *Iberian*.[41]

Another account in the museum's file came from a soldier, John Mackintosh Bell, who saw what he believed was a sea serpent whilst visiting the Orkney Islands in 1919. Early in the morning of 5 August, Bell was out fishing for cod in the Pentland Firth when he and his friends saw 'a long neck as thick as an elephant's foreleg, all rough-looking like an elephant's hide' protruding four to five feet out of the water. On top of the neck was a small head, 'like that of a dog coming sharp to the nose' with a small black eye and black whiskers. 'The animal was very shy and kept pushing its head up and then pulling it down, but never going out of sight,' Bell wrote. 'Then it disappeared and I said "if it comes again I'll take a snapshot of it" . . . sure enough it did come but on looking at the camera shutter, I found it had not closed owing to its being swollen, so I did not get a photo.' Bell then tried to take a shot at the creature with his rifle 'but the skipper would not hear of it in case I wounded it, and it might attack us'.[42]

A pencil-drawn sketch of the creature described by Bell was examined by the museum's Keeper of Zoology, William Calman, in 1929. Soon afterwards he opened a file on sea monsters. In his response to Bell, he wrote that it was 'most unlucky that your camera jammed at the critical moment, for a photograph would have enabled us to be much more confident about the identification of the animal. All that we can say is that no animal at all agreeing with your sketches is at present known to science'. Calman displayed more of an open mind than his predecessors, noting that 'we are not so rash as to suppose that we yet know all of the inhabitants of the sea and it is within the bounds of possibility that you saw some animal that has never yet been captured or described'.[43]

Early in the previous year, workmen excavating limestone from a quarry near Harbury in Warwickshire discovered the remains of a 'sea dragon' with a long neck similar to the creature drawn by Mr Bell in his letter to the museum. The crumbling skeleton was 26ft in length and, projecting from its broad body, there were the four bony flippers that once propelled the creature through the sea. A newspaper report of the find said it had 'three eyes, the third in the middle of its small, narrow head'. Palaeontologists identified the creature as an ichthyosaur, a type of marine reptile that disappeared from the oceans 65 million years ago, when the dinosaurs became extinct.

One of the many who marvelled over the images of the Harbury ichthyosaur was the elderly Arthur Conan Doyle. His adventure, *The Lost World*, first published in *Strand* magazine in 1912, told of an expedition to a plateau hidden in a remote jungle area of South America where dinosaurs and other animals, long believed to be extinct, continued to exist. The idea may have grown from stories told by the explorer Col. Percy Harrison Fawcett, of an expedition in 1908 to a remote area of Bolivia where he found 'monstrous tracks of unknown origin'. In Fawcett's memoirs, published posthumously, he speculated

FIGURE 6.5 WORKMEN MARVEL AT THE REMAINS OF A FOSSIL ICHTHYOSAUR DISCOVERED IN A QUARRY AT HARBURY, WARWICKSHIRE, IN 1928. NEWS REPORTS OF THIS DISCOVERY LED ARTHUR CONAN DOYLE TO REPORT HIS SIGHTING OF A 'PLESIOSAUR' TO THE *DAILY EXPRESS*. (COURTESY OF WARWICKSHIRE COUNTY RECORD OFFICE)

that 'monsters from the dawn of man's existence might still roam these heights unchallenged, imprisoned and protected by unscalable cliffs'.[44] Col. Fawcett disappeared in 1925 whilst searching for the fabled lost city of El Dorado in the jungles of Brazil.

Doyle did not just imagine prehistoric monsters for his science fiction. He saw them too. In a letter published by the London *Daily Express* in February 1928, he said the discovery of the Warwickshire skeleton reminded him of a 'curious incident' that happened during a cruise near the Greek island of Aegina some years earlier.

. . . I was travelling from Alexandria to Athens in an Italian liner, and the captain had kindly made my wife and myself free of the bridge. We were off the coast of Aegina, with the famous Temple of Neptune on our port bow when, looking down from the side of the bridge, I saw a curious creature swimming parallel to the ship and about thirty feet under water. It was perfectly calm, and the creature's outline was distinct. It was about four feet long, with a long neck and large flippers. I called my wife, and she was in time to see it also. We both agree that your picture of the plesiosaurus is exactly what we saw that day. I could not connect it up with any known form of life. A very large turtle which had lost its carapace was the only other explanation I could think of. But do turtles lose their carapaces and survive?'[45]

Conan Doyle's story triggered a flurry of letters to the museum from people who wished to report sightings of sea monsters. These came from places as far apart as the English Channel, the coast of New South Wales and the Malacca Straits. Responding to a correspondent in Penang, a museum official suggested: '. . . should you ever come within range of the "Monster" I hope you will not be deterred by any humanitarian considerations from shooting him on the spot and sending the carcass to us in cold storage, carriage forward. Short of this, a flipper, a jaw or a tooth would be very welcome.'[46]

MONSTERS OF THE DEEP

In recent years some prime suspects have emerged for at least some sightings of 'sea serpents' that cannot be easily explained as mistakes or misidentifications. Reviewing the 19th century accounts for *Fortean Times* magazine, Mark Greener suggests that a number might have been caused by observations of the giant ribbonfish (*Trachipterida*), so-called because of their slim, ribbon-like appearance. Ribbonfish are rarely seen and live in deep waters, but occasionally they have been caught closer to shore. In 1854 *Scientific American* published a report describing a 16-foot 'sea serpent' caught off Caithness in Scotland. This creature may have been a ribbon-fish as it had a snake-like form and was 'covered with a long pendulous crest on the back of the head'.[47] Specimens have been found in all the areas of ocean that have generated sea serpent legends. In Taiwan they are popularly known as the 'earthquake fish' because they often turn up in fishermen's nets after major seismic events. Another inhabitant of the deep, the giant oarfish *(Regalecus glesne),* can grow up to 50 feet (15m) in length and is the longest bony fish in the world. In October 2013 two oarfish, one measuring 18 feet in length, washed up on beaches in southern California. The unusual sight of the deep-water fish so close to shore led some authorities to speculate 'they are probably responsible for sea serpent legends throughout history'.[48]

Medieval accounts of sea monsters portrayed them as dangerous predators that were capable of attacking ships and this idea re-appears in Jules Verne's novel *Twenty Thousand Leagues Under the Sea* (1870). There is no evidence that the giant squid can lift its tentacles out of water but such images are popular in the literature of science fiction and fantasy. Any unidentified giant sea monsters that continue to roam the oceans of the world remain, like the giant squid, shy and elusive creatures.

In 2010 the Royal Navy received a Freedom of Information request from an inquirer who asked if there were 'any abnormally large, or dangerous sea monsters hundreds of metres under the sea that haven't been revealed to the public'. If such creatures did exist, the inquirer argued, 'it would be in the public interest to publish the facts as the lives of marine biologists could be at risk'. The response revealed neither the Navy nor the MoD maintained 'any form of central repository of information purely devoted to sea monsters' but did encourage personnel to record sightings in ship's logs.[49]

Credible sightings of sea monsters are reported from the world's oceans occasionally and one of the most interesting was made by two fearless members of the Parachute Regiment. Captain John Ridgway and Sergeant Chay Blyth set off from England in a small fishing boat to row cross the North Atlantic in June 1966. In their book that recounts the arduous 92-day adventure, Ridgway describes a strange experience that occurred as he was rowing near midnight on 25 July. Chay Blyth was asleep at the time and Ridgway was 'lulled by the unending monotony' of his task when he was suddenly alarmed by a swishing noise to starboard: 'I looked out into the water and suddenly saw the writhing, twisting shape of a great creature,' he wrote in the book *A Fighting Chance* (1966). 'It was outlined by the phosphorescence in the sea as if a string of neon lights were hanging from it. It was an enormous size, some thirty-five or more feet long, and it came towards me quite fast. I must have watched it for ten seconds. It headed straight at me and disappeared right beneath me'. Momentarily frozen with terror, Ridgway turned his head to look over the port side of the boat but could see nothing and soon afterwards he heard 'a tremendous splash' that he thought might be the head of the monster 'crashing into the sea after coming up for a brief look at us'. When he told Blyth what he had seen, his companion said he believed him, adding 'This is a very strange ocean'.[50]

Ridgway said he searched for a rational explanation as he continued the voyage during which he and Blyth saw whales, sharks, dolphins, porpoises and flying fish. None compared to the monster that passed beneath their boat. 'I reluctantly had to believe that there was only one thing it could have been,' Ridgway concluded. 'I could understand now the tales of the ancient mariners. And like them, the memory of that incredible creature will stay with me for the rest of my life.'

GHOST SHIP

. . . Reporting the arrival [in Gibraltar] of the 'Dei Gratia' having in charge the derelict vessel (supposed to be) 'Mary Celeste', abandoned at sea under apparently singular and suspicious circumstances . . .'

Extract from Marine Registry, London, January 1873[1]

In the spring of 2012, an aircraft flying high above the west coast of Canada spotted a squid-fishing boat drifting in the vast Pacific Ocean. A boarding party discovered the empty vessel had left the Japanese port of Hachinohe one year ago, without its crew. Ripped from its moorings during the devastating earthquake and tsunami that had devastated the Japanese coast, the 150ft-long ship floated more than 4,700 miles. When news reached the media, the 'ghost ship' was immediately compared to the most famous derelict of all time, the *Mary Celeste*.[2]

The fate of the crew and passengers of the British-American cargo-carrying brigantine that bore that name remains the greatest unsolved mystery of the sea. The *Mary Celeste* was a twin-masted wooden-shelled ship, square-rigged on the foremast and fore-and-aft rigged on the mainmast. She was small, measuring just over 100ft in length, with a gross weight of 282 tons. The *Mary Celeste* was found abandoned 600 miles (1,000 km) west of Portugal on 4 December 1872. Since that time hundreds of articles and books and almost as many radio and TV programmes and films have re-told the story of this quintessential nautical legend. Along the way, almost as many ideas, theories and possible solutions – some plausible, others incredible – have been put forward to explain what happened to her crew.[3]

One central question remains unanswered: why did the experienced captain, Benjamin Spooner Briggs, abandon a well-equipped and seaworthy vessel, along with his wife, their small child and all the crew, in such haste that he failed to take with them even the most basic provisions?

The historian Charles Eden Fay, whose book is the most authoritative source for the story, wrote in 1942: '. . . for many years a considerable body of dependable factual information about the *Mary Celeste* mystery has been available for anyone diligent enough to search for it.'[4] For *The Story of the Mary Celeste*, Fay reconstructed the sequence of events that led to the disappearance from primary sources at the National Archives in Washington DC and the records of the Atlantic Mutual Insurance Company, New York, that had insured its cargo. Fay's research established the brigantine was built in Nova Scotia in 1861 and was originally christened

The Amazon. Her first captain died from pneumonia nine days after taking command and it appears the ship quickly acquired a reputation for misfortune. Initially *The Amazon* sailed under a British flag but in 1868 she took the name *Mary Celeste* and was then registered as an American vessel.

In 1872 the ship was owned by four partners that included Captain Briggs. Early in November he dined with a friend, David Morehouse, who was the captain of a British-Canadian registered brigantine, the *Dei Gratia*. Soon afterwards the two ships left New York; Captain Briggs sailed for Genoa on 7 November with a cargo of 1,701 barrels of commercial alcohol. He was accompanied by his wife and child, plus seven experienced and reliable crew. David Morehouse and the *Dei Gratia* followed on the 15 November with a cargo of petroleum bound for Gibraltar.

Almost one month later, on 4 December, the crew of the *Dei Gratia* sighted the *Mary Celeste* off the Azores, 590 miles (970km) west of Gibraltar. The vessel appeared to be in good repair, with its sails set but slightly torn. The ship was sailing so erratically with the wind that it became obvious to the crew of the *Dei Gratia* that something was amiss. Moorhouse sent a boarding party to investigate.

What had become of the crew of the *Mary Celeste*? In January 1873, the first mate of the *Dei Gratia*, Oliver Deveau, who led the boarding party, testified before a Vice Admiralty Court of Inquiry convened at Gibraltar. He said he could find no one on board and 'the whole ship was a thoroughly wet mess'. In the cabin he found the ship's papers were missing except for the logbook and 'all the Captain's effects had been left; his clothing, furniture, etc – the bed was just as they had left it'. The decks were deserted and the cabins had been battened down with planks to protect them against Atlantic storms. Although there was some seawater in the hold, Deveau was convinced it must have run off the deck from the storms. The one working pump had been dismantled and there was a small amount of water in the hold, but otherwise the ship was in good working order. In the hold, the cargo was intact 'and seemed to be in good condition'.[5]

There appeared to be at least six months' provisions on board and Deveau testified that, '. . . there seemed to be everything left behind in the cabins as if left in a great hurry, but everything in its place'. He noted the sextant and marine chronometer, along with the ship's only lifeboat, were missing. The peak halyard, used to hoist the main sail, was missing but a rope that may have been the halyard was tied to the ship and trailing in the water behind it. The final entry in the ship's logbook was made on 24 November when the *Mary Celeste* was 100 miles west of the Azores. When it was discovered, eleven days later, it was 500 miles to the east.

On 30 December 1873 *The Times* of London reported: 'The vessel was found derelict on the high seas, uninjured and with the effects of all on board apparently uninjured, on her voyage from New York to Genoa, the master, his wife and child, and the crew all having mysteriously disappeared, leaving no trace.' It added: 'They have never been heard from since, though every effort has been made by the Government to ascertain their fate.'

THE BIRTH OF A MARITIME LEGEND

The vacuum left by the absence of hard evidence about the fate of the passengers and crew of the *Mary Celeste* was soon filled by speculation. One of the earliest 'official' explanations was proposed by a US Secretary of the Treasury, William A. Richard, in a letter published by *The New York Times* on 25 March 1873. Richard said he believed the strange circumstances of the discovery 'tend to arouse great suspicion that the master, his wife and child, and perhaps the chief mate, were murdered in the fury of drunkenness by the crew, who had evidently obtained access to the alcohol with which the vessel was in part laden'.

A version of this idea came to obsess the Attorney General of Gibraltar, Frederick Solly-Flood QC, who became responsible for the inquiry held by the British authorities. Solly-Flood was described by Paul Begg, author of *Mary Celeste: The Greatest Mystery of the Sea* (2006), as 'a pompous, arrogant, excitable and very shrewd bureaucrat' who came to suspect the crew met their end through mutiny, piracy or murder.[6]

The Attorney General considered the possibility that Briggs and Morehouse had conspired together to dispose of the crew and split the salvage between them. The problem with this theory was the fact that Briggs was a part-owner of the *Mary Celeste* and his stake in the ship was far greater than anything he could expect from a share in salvage money. Despite Solly-Flood's conviction that foul play had occurred, an investigation by the US Consul in Gibraltar, Horatio Sprague, found no evidence to implicate the crew of the *Mary Celeste* or the *Dei Gratia* in a conspiracy. Papers in Lloyd's of London file on the *Mary Celeste* support Sprague's conclusion. A note in the file says: '. . . there were no signs of any violence aboard [the ship]; all sorts of valuables were left behind; the master was by reputation not the sort of man to cause a crew to mutiny; no trace of the "murderers" was ever found; had [they] been picked up by another vessel, the master would surely have at some time connected them to the *Mary Celeste* case; and had they got ashore, they would doubtless have been identified among seafaring men.'[7]

Nevertheless, rumours about mutinies, murders and hijacks continued to circulate in popular accounts of the mystery throughout the late 19th and early 20th century. As the legend evolved, the name of the ship and those of its occupants began to change. *Marie Celeste* replaced *Mary Celeste* and the numbers of passengers and crew mutated from ten into the mystical 13. Other curious 'facts' emerged, including the oft-repeated story of the boarding party's discovery on the cabin table of freshly brewed coffee, an untouched breakfast and a vial of oil sitting upright on a sewing machine. Most influential of all was the idea the lifeboat, the crew's only means of escape, had been found intact by the boarding party. As Deveau's testimony before the inquiry at Gibraltar had revealed, the lifeboat was missing.

How did these fictions become accepted as popular 'facts'? As was the case with the 'angels' that appeared at Mons, the source of the story was a piece of fiction. In 1884 *The Cornhill Magazine* published a story by an unknown author called Arthur Conan Doyle. Written anonymously, 'J. Habakuk Jepshon's Statement' was based upon the *Mary Celeste* mystery, but Doyle referred to the ship as *Marie Celeste*.[8] The narrator, Jepshon, describes himself as a Harvard doctor and specialist in consumption at a hospital in Brooklyn. He tells how the ship was hijacked by a mixed-heritage passenger, Septimus Goring, who murders the crew and sails for North Africa. Jepshon is cast adrift without food or water but is rescued by a passing ship and returns to America via Liverpool. In his account Jepshon quotes a fictional account from *The Gibraltar Chronicle* that said lifeboats (in the plural) were intact and 'slung on the davits' when the boarding party arrived on the abandoned *Mary Celeste*.

Doyle mixed together fact with fiction and, like Machen's story of the bowmen of Mons, it began to take on a life of its own. In 1927 author J.G. Lockhart wrote that '. . . it was strange that the legend that none of the boats were missing should have been so confidently and persistently repeated in subsequent re-tellings'. He speculated that story-tellers seemed content with 'slavish imitation' of second-hand stories 'without attempting to verify circumstances which undoubtedly made better part of the mystery'.[9]

J. Habakuk Jepshon's statement infuriated the authorities in Gibraltar and Washington. Solly-Flood declared it to be 'a fabrication from beginning to end'. But Fay was kinder, describing it as 'ingenious [and] wholly inaccurate, but richly meriting a high place in the category of literary entertainment'.[10] Its success as a narrative can be judged by the effect it had upon those who came to believe that it was a factual account of the crew's fate. It was reprinted widely and at least one American newspaper published it as the true story of the *Mary Celeste*. Doyle was finally credited as the author in 1890 when it re-published as part of a collection of nautical stories, *The Captain of the Polestar*.[11]

PANEL FIGURE 6.1 THE MARY
CELESTE WAS ABANDONED IN THE
ATLANTIC OCEAN NEAR THE
AZORES IN 1872. IN THE DECADES
THAT FOLLOWED MANY PEOPLE
CAME FORWARD WITH FANTASTIC
EXPLANATIONS FOR THE
UNSOLVED MYSTERY. SEVERAL
CLAIMED TO BE 'LAST SURVIVING'
CREW MEMBERS OR PASSENGERS.
ONE OF THESE, ABEL FOSDYK,
SAID THE CAPTAIN AND FIRST
MATE WERE EATEN BY SHARKS
WHILST TAKING PART IN A
SWIMMING CONTEST. HIS WIFE,
CHILD AND THE REMAINING CREW
FELL INTO THE SEA WHILST
WATCHING FROM AN IMPROVISED
WOODEN PLATFORM. (COURTESY OF
FORTEAN PICTURE LIBRARY)

Doyle's story was just the first in a long series of allegedly true testimonies offered by so-called 'eyewitnesses' and 'lone survivors' who sailed on the *Mary Celeste*. These continued to appear half a century after the discovery of the derelict ship. In 1913 *The Strand* magazine invited its readers to submit solutions to the continuing mystery. One came from the headmaster of a prep school who found an account of the *Mary Celeste* among papers bequeathed to him by Abel Fosdyk, an elderly servant, on his deathbed.[12] Fosdyk's written account has him joining the ship as a passenger in New York. During the voyage the entire crew fell into the sea from an improvised wooden quarterdeck whilst watching a swimming contest between Captain Briggs and the first mate. Everyone was eaten by sharks except Fosdyk who was rescued by a passing ship. When examined closely, Fosdyk's story unravelled as it was full of factual inaccuracies. His name does not appear in the list of passengers and crew held by the US National Archives and although his story says the crew was English, the muster shows the sailors were mostly German and American.[13] Fosdyk's story is believed to be yet another in a long series of literary hoaxes that were inspired by the *Mary Celeste* legend.

As the years passed, ever more ingenious solutions emerged to explain elements of the mystery. One of the more plausible suggested that a build-up of fumes from the cargo of commercial alcohol led the crew to believe an explosion was imminent, leading them to abandon ship. Others have suggested the ship was struck by a waterspout, the seaborne equivalent of a tornado, that can appear without warning and strike ships with violent force. A far simpler solution was that the ship was caught in a fierce Atlantic storm. Fearing it was about to sink, Briggs and his crew took refuge in the ship's lifeboat that was attached to the ship by a rope until the danger passed. But when the rope became detached the crew were lost at sea. A variation of this explanation was offered by Oliver Deveau at the Vice Admiralty Court in Gibraltar. Asked for his opinion about the cause of the abandonment, the man who was the first on board the derelict ship said he believed the crew panicked 'from the belief that the vessel had more water than had afterwards proved'.[14]

As author Francis Hitching pointed out, none of these theories can be disproved, but that does not make them any more likely to be true. 'You cannot say definitely that the crew was not captured by alien spacemen, which a number of Bermuda Triangle addicts believe,' he wrote. 'Nor is it absolutely impossible that Captain Briggs went berserk in a fit of religious fervour and slaughtered everyone before jumping overboard himself; or that a whirlwind or a giant sea serpent sucked the crew off the deck.'[15]

One curious theme emerges from the confusion of fiction and fact. As noted above, the *Mary Celeste* had been regarded as an unlucky ship long before she was discovered derelict. After the court of inquiry, she was sold at a loss by her owner, John Winchester, after his father drowned in an accident on her return to Boston, Massachusetts. The reputation of the uncanny ship led it to change hands a further 17 times during the next 13 years. Its run of bad luck ended when its final owner, Captain G.C. Parker, tried to use it to commit an insurance fraud in the Caribbean. In January 1885 the *Mary Celeste*, now in a poor state of repair, was run aground off the western coast of Haiti and set on fire. Parker was subsequently put on trial for barratry and faced the death penalty if convicted. Despite clear evidence of fraud, the jury refused to convict but Parker died three months later.[16] The wreck of the cursed ship remains to this day beneath the waters of the island.

MARY CELESTE – THE MISSING FILES

Reliance upon 'eyewitness testimony' provided years after an event, even from seemingly reliable sources, can lead researchers into blind alleys and halls of mirrors. In these circumstances the only solid ground is provided by contemporary documents. But tracing the story of the *Mary Celeste* via the evidence of primary documents is not a straightforward task. The most important source of information about the disappearance of her crew is the testimony heard before the Vice Admiralty court of inquiry held in Gibraltar during 1872–73. A transcript of the proceedings, along with extracts from the logbooks of both ships, were sent by Frederick Solly-Flood to the Board of Trade in London in January 1873. This dossier included sworn testimony from the owners, officers and crew of the British-registered *Dei Gratia*. At the conclusion of the inquiry, which lasted three months and attracted wide coverage, David Moorhouse and his crew were awarded £1,700 for the salvage of the *Mary Celeste*. Although the captain and his men were cleared of any involvement in the disappearance of Briggs and his crew, suspicion of foul play would not go away.

The mystery was resurrected in 1930 when British author Harold T. Wilkins requested copies of the proceedings from the Board of Trade in London. He was told all the records from 1872–73 had been destroyed. Even worse, the reply he received from Whitehall repeated some of the factual inaccuracies contained in Conan Doyle's fictional story. In their response to Wilkins, the authorities referred to the '*Marie Celeste*' [sic] as being an American ship 'found at sea outside British jurisdiction'. As a result they claimed that 'no inquiry was ordered or held by this Department.'[17]

Wilkins subsequently wrote to *The Times* complaining that Whitehall had not only destroyed records of their inquiry into the *Mary Celeste*, but also other important maritime papers from the 19th century and earlier. He believed the missing papers could help to clear the sullied reputations of Captains Briggs and Moorhouse (many people still believed there had been a plot to murder the crew and steal the *Mary Celeste's* cargo). In his letter, Wilkins revealed that he had corresponded with surviving relatives of Briggs and Moorhouse who 'bitterly complain of professed solutions to the mystery which blacken the good names of the two captains'.[18] Soon after *The Times* published the story, Wilkins received a letter from a Liverpool man who had access to a surviving copy of the proceedings from the Vice Admiralty court in Gibraltar. These were later used by Charles Eden Fay in his definitive book, *The Story of the Mary Celeste* (1942).[19]

PANEL FIGURE 6.2 A SURVIVING ENTRY FROM THE MARINE REGISTRY KEPT BY THE BOARD OF TRADE IN LONDON THAT REFERS TO THE ARRIVAL OF THE DERELICT *MARY CELESTE* AT GIBRALTAR IN JANUARY 1873, 'ABANDONED AT SEA UNDER APPARENTLY SINGULAR AND SUSPICIOUS CIRCUMSTANCES'. (CROWN COPYRIGHT, THE NATIONAL ARCHIVES MT 9/3491)

The British government file generated by this controversy remained open in 1950 and eventually made its way to the Public Records Office (now The National Archives). The contents reveal that Wilkins' letters were the latest in a series of requests for 'the official report' on the *Mary Celeste*. The earliest, dated 1910, provoked a weary comment from a desk officer to the effect that 'this sea mystery will apparently interest enquirers indefinitely'. In 1930, following publication of Wilkins' letter in *The Times*, officials admitted that papers in the 'Wrecks and Deaths Section' were destroyed at seven- and ten-year intervals until 1884, when protocols for their review and preservation were agreed with the Public Records Office. By that time 'the *Mary Celeste* papers may possibly already have been destroyed'. The loss of the file led officials to make suggestions for better record-keeping. An instruction was issued advising desk officers to write 'Not to be Destroyed' in red ink on the face of 'files containing precedents'. Summarising the lessons learned, a Board of Trade official wrote: 'I do not think anyone is to blame because some of the documents in the case of the "*Marie Celeste*" [sic] are not available; while the case is one of the mysteries of the sea there is nothing in the actual facts of the case, or the documents we had in regard to it, that justify it being considered of great importance.'[20]

Readers of my companion book, *The UFO Files*, may feel the sensation of déjà vu as they ponder these words. The loss and destruction of official records is a constant obstacle faced by historians who rely upon the archives to trace historic mysteries such as the *Mary Celeste* to their source.

CHAPTER 7

THE LOCH NESS MONSTER SYNDROME

The idea that marine dinosaurs, and other animals thought to be extinct, have survived to the present day in remote areas of the world has always appealed to the human imagination. The study of unknown or legendary animals whose existence is disputed or unproved has in recent years spawned its own pseudo-science dedicated to their study: cryptozoology.

The origin of belief in the Loch Ness Monster can be traced back to 1933 when there was a great flurry of press interest in sightings of a creature that resembled a 'sea serpent' in this huge body of water in the Scottish Highlands. During that year the London *Daily Mail* became so convinced of its existence that it ran the headline: 'Not a Legend – but a Fact'. The link between the monster in the loch and the 'sea serpent' was implicit in the descriptions of the 'monster'. Eyewitnesses described a small head on the end of a long neck and a body that resembled a succession of humps when seen above water.

The naturalist Richard Fitter, who became one of the leading lights in the Loch Ness Monster Phenomenon Investigation Bureau, believed the opening of the A82 road along the north shore of the loch to visitors was a key factor in the media sensation that followed. Fitter wrote that at the beginning of the 20th century Loch Ness was almost as remote to outsiders as it had been a century earlier when Robert Chambers wrote of its 'mysterious and even terrible characteristics'.[1]

Long before the sightings of the 'monster' in Loch Ness, there existed a tradition of belief in the *each-uisge*, or 'water-horse'. Alasdair Alpin MacGregor collected folk-tales about these dangerous aquatic creatures for his book *The Peat Fire Flame* (1937). He noted that until the early 20th century almost 'every locality in the Highlands and

Islands was reputed to possess a loch haunted by such a creature'. The water-horse is a shape-shifter and when in equine form can be safely ridden. When it smells or senses water, however, it dives into the deepest part of the loch, drowning and eating the unfortunate human rider. This belief existed long before the first stories were published concerning a *specific* monster inhabiting Loch Ness. In his book MacGregor linked traditions of the water-horse with 'the recent graphic descriptions given by independent eye-witnesses of the Loch Ness Monster'.[2]

Folklorist Steve Roud says there is no convincing evidence to connect the water-horse with the serpentine monster sighted in Loch Ness in 1933. In his view the lack of any mention of the monster in 19th and early 20th century accounts of the loch, such as that by Chambers, argues strongly for the legend's origin during the 1930s 'by a sort of spontaneous combustion'.[3] Another theory suggests the story was simply invented by the media. Roland Watson, who runs a website dedicated to the monster, disagrees. He believes there is a direct link between the water-horse tradition in Loch Ness and accounts of encounters with a 'real creature' that pre-date 1933.[4]

Whether ancient or newly created, all legends require a 'back story'. Many believe an episode in Adomnan's 7th-century *Life of St Columba* is the very first written reference to the 'monster'. The Irish saint was crossing the River Ness when he saw a group of people burying the body of a man who had been 'seized and most savagely bitten by a water beast' whilst swimming in the river. When one of his followers plunged into the water to fetch a boat for the saint, the beast 'suddenly swam to the surface, and with gaping mouth and with great roaring' rushed towards the helpless swimmer. As the terrified crowd watched, St Columba raised his hand and made the sign of the cross. Addressing the monster in the name of God he declared: 'You will go no further. Do not touch the man; turn back.' On hearing these words the creature retreated as if pulled back by ropes, allowing the saint's companion to reach the shore.[5]

Adomnan was the ninth abbot of Iona (679–704 AD) and he was writing about events in the life of the founder of the abbey, 150 years before his time. Accounts of encounters between holy men and water creatures are common in the medieval lives of saints, so there is nothing inherently unique about the story apart from the reference to the River Ness. If Adomnan's account is based on a generic story, there is no direct connection between it and the Loch Ness Monster. It is significant that Adomnan's story was unearthed by a correspondent of *The Scotsman* newspaper soon after the first 'sightings' in 1933, though. Steve Roud points out that once an item of lore as powerful as this is committed to print, it can be used to refresh an existing tradition or even create a new one. A transcript even found its way into a file used to brief the Secretary of State for Scotland when the subject was raised in Parliament later that year. At the time, one commentator remarked that Columba's banishment of the monster 'seems to have been fairly effective for upwards of 1,300 years'.[6]

Another influence upon the emergence of the legend in 1933 was the pre-existent belief in the existence of sea serpents that became entwined with the discovery of the fossil remains of aquatic dinosaurs during the early 19th century. In the summer of the same year, the pioneering movie *King Kong* opened in cinemas across Britain. It featured scenes in which the heroes encounter plesiosaurs and other dinosaurs who live alongside the giant gorilla on 'Skull Island' in the Pacific Ocean. The release of this film coincided with an explosion of interest in sea and lake monsters. Immediately before the Loch Ness Monster sensation, staff at the British Museum (Natural History) received a full postbag of letters reporting plesiosaur sightings in the lakes and oceans of the world. By January 1934, an official responding to a request for information on the Loch Ness mystery commented wearily: 'I need hardly tell you that we are getting a little tired of the "monster".'[7]

THE BIRTH OF THE 'MONSTER'

The idea that a 'monster' lurked in Loch Ness can be traced to a series of stories published by Scottish newspapers. Unlike Adomnan's story or traditions recorded after the legend was established, these were the first contemporaneously reported encounters with the monster. In August 1930 *The Northern Chronicle* published a story with the headline 'What was it?'. This revealed the curious experience of three young anglers, the sons of 'well-known businessmen' from Inverness. In the words of one:

> We were fishing for sea trout from a boat about 100 yards west of Tore Point. It was a fine evening and the loch was perfectly calm. About 8.15pm . . . we heard a terrible noise on the water, and looking round we saw, about 600 yards distant, a great commotion with spray flying everywhere. Then the fish – or whatever it was – started coming towards us, and when it was about 300 yards away it turned to the right and went into Holly Bush Bay above Dores and disappeared in the depths. During its rush it caused a wave about 2.5 feet high, and we could see a wriggling motion, but that was all, the wash hiding it from view. The wash, however, was sufficient to cause our boat to rock violently.[8]

The anonymous eyewitness said the three men had no idea what it was 'but we are quite positive it could not have been a salmon'. The paper said inquiries on the shores of the loch located 'a man of unimpeachable veracity', who some years earlier had observed a similar oddity in the water, 'a fish – or whatever it was – coming along the loch', dark in colour and 'like an upturned angling boat'. After the story appeared, letters followed from readers who suggested the 'fish' could have been a seal, an otter 'racing along the surface with a salmon in its mouth' or even a giant conger eel. Another reader offered an account of his own experience, whilst camping near the River Ness. Woken in the early hours by a 'tremendous splashing and snorting' in the river, he saw what he took to be a huge seal thrashing around on the surface with a fish in its mouth. The animal had a flat head and was 'a great size'. Emerging from his tent, he went to get his boots so he could go closer to the river, but when he turned around 'the monster had disappeared'.[9]

This may be the first occasion in modern times that the word 'monster' was applied to a creature in Loch Ness. Almost three years passed before a follow-up story brought the story to the attention of the national press. Published on 3 May 1933 by the *Inverness Courier*, 'Strange Spectacle on Loch Ness' used the same distinctive sub-title, 'What was it?'. This coincidence has led sceptics to suggest this was part of a desire by local journalists to keep the story running. The second story was written by a correspondent of the paper, Alex Campbell, who also worked as a water bailiff on the loch. In 1933 he began his story by referring to the folklore of Loch Ness, which 'has for generations been credited with the home of a fearsome-looking monster known as the "water kelpie", long regarded as a myth'.

Campbell then told of the experience of Aldie McKay, who was manageress of the hotel at Drumnadrochit. One night in the spring of 1933, Aldie and her husband John were driving along the newly constructed road along the north side of the loch when she saw a 'tremendous upheaval' in the water near Abriachan Pier. Previously the loch had been as calm as a millpond. Aldie cried out for her husband to stop and both watched as:

> . . . the creature disported itself, rolling and plunging for fully a minute, its body resembling that of a whale, and the water cascading and churning like a simmering cauldron. Soon, however, it disappeared in a boiling mass of foam. Both onlookers confessed that there was something uncanny about the whole thing for they realised that here was no ordinary denizen of the depths because, apart from its enormous size, the beast, in taking the final plunge, sent out waves that were big enough to have been caused by a passing steamer.[10]

The couple waited half an hour in the hope that 'the monster (if such it was) would return to the surface again', but nothing further was seen. Quizzed by Campbell as to its size, Aldie McKay said that 'judging by the state of the water in the affected area, it seemed to be many feet long'. Publication of the McKays' story led to a flood of visitors, including tourists and 'monster hunters'.

In July 1933, three months after the opening of *King Kong* in British cinemas, a couple came forward to claim they had seen the 'monster' on land. Mr and Mrs George Spicer were driving from Dores towards Foyes (again on the north bank of the loch) when, as the car climbed a slight rise, they saw 'an extraordinary-looking creature' crossing the road ahead of them in a series of jerks. Their account made headlines in newspapers across the world. Mr Spicer, a businessman from London, was quoted as saying the creature was 'the nearest approach to a dragon or prehistoric animal that I have ever seen'. No head or legs were seen, but the body was 'a loathsome-looking greyish colour, like a dirty elephant or rhinoceros'. The Spicers said they could see something like 'a long thin neck, which undulated up and down, and was contorted into a number of half hoops . . . the whole looked like a huge snail with a long neck'. The creature ambled across the road towards the loch with what appeared to be an animal its mouth.[11]

Publication of the Spicers' story was followed by other accounts from people who claimed they had seen a similar creature crossing the road in front of their cars. Soon afterwards, *The Scotsman* and the London *Daily Mail* sent 'special correspondents' to track the monster to its lair. The *Mail's* expedition was led by a big-game hunter, Marmaduke Wetherell, who took photographs of four-toed footprints found by the lochside. Casts of these were sent to the

Natural History department of the British Museum. Experts there found they had been made by the stuffed foot of a hippopotamus planted on a heaped-up bank of fine shingle.

According to Wetherell's stepson, Christian Spurling, it was this humiliation that motivated him to produce a photo of the monster that no one could disprove. In April 1934 the *Daily Mail* published what became known as 'the surgeon's photograph', depicting a creature with a snake-like neck and small head. A London gynaecologist, Col. Robert Wilson, told the paper he took the photo whilst driving along the northern shore of Loch Ness on the lookout for the monster. After setting up his camera close to the shore, he noticed a sudden commotion in the loch and then saw 'the head of some strange animal rising up out of the water' between 150 and 200 yards away. The image he captured was regarded for many years as one of the key pieces of evidence for the existence of the monster, but doubts were raised by a careful analysis of the photo in 1984. A decade later Spurling, then aged 90, confessed the 'monster' was actually a toy submarine purchased in a Woolworth's store and fitted with a plastic serpent's head.[12] According to Spurling, his step-father felt humiliated by the exposure of the hippo-foot tracks and announced, 'we'll give them their monster'. After the photograph was taken, Col. Wilson was asked to take it to the press as he appeared to be a credible 'front man' for the prank.

Lt Cdr Rupert Gould, a retired naval officer turned writer and broadcaster, was impressed by the surgeon's photograph. His book *The Case for the Sea Serpent*, published in 1930, established him as an expert on the subject of unknown or legendary animals. In his follow-up book, *The Loch Ness Monster and Others* (1934), he dismissed the possibility of hoaxing as it 'postulated many years of preparation by some obscure and affluent half-wit, the subornation and active assistance of many Loch Ness residents and visitors, and the tacit complicity of the entire Press'.[13]

In his account, Gould says he was struggling to make a living as a writer when the London *Times* commissioned him to make an 'independent investigation of the evidence'. He travelled by rail to Inverness where he hired a motorbike and set out for the hamlet of Drumnadrochit on the north shore of Loch Ness. From here he 'proceeded round the loch . . . interviewing every eyewitness I could hear of, and putting up for the night wherever I happened to be'.

Although he had no formal experience of working as a journalist, Gould was careful to ask those he met for permission to take notes and transcribed these 'never later than the evening of the same day' into a notebook. By the time his account appeared in *The Times* in December 1933, he had interviewed 51 people who said they had seen some large, unidentified animal in the loch. Yet despite keeping a constant lookout 'with camera and binoculars always handy', Gould failed to see the monster himself. At the end of his investigation he wrote there was 'little question that Loch Ness contains at least one specimen of the rarest and least-known of all living creatures'. In his article for *The Times* he put forward a bizarre theory that the monster might be 'a vastly enlarged, long-necked, marine form of the common newt'.[14]

FIGURE 7.2 THE ICONIC PHOTOGRAPH OF THE LOCH NESS MONSTER, ALLEGEDLY PHOTOGRAPHED BY A LONDON SURGEON, COL R.K. WILSON, IN APRIL 1934 AND PUBLISHED BY THE *DAILY MAIL*. (COURTESY OF FORTEAN PICTURE LIBRARY)

In 1937 he told a BBC radio audience that he changed his mind after sifting through the testimony and sketches produced by more than 60 independent eyewitnesses, 'cautious, matter-of-fact, intelligent people who generally tried to tone down their stories rather than to exaggerate'. He now believed that 'in spite of my original doubts, that Loch Ness contained – and for that matter still contains – a large living creature of "sea serpent" type'.[15] Gould's initial doubts had been based on the fact that the loch's surface is 52ft (15.8m) above sea level and its only connection with the sea was via the River Ness, which flows through Inverness to the Moray Firth. The loch itself is 23 miles in length (37km), one and half miles wide and up to 755ft (230m) at its deepest point. This made the chances of capturing the creature alive remote and Gould believed that a good quality photograph, taken from above by an aircraft, was the only satisfactory way to clear up the mystery.

NESSIE AND THE NATURAL HISTORY MUSEUM

The account of Arthur Conan Doyle's sighting of a sea serpent in the Greek islands (Chapter 6) was added to a file on 'Sea Monsters' that was opened at the British Museum (Natural History) in 1928.[16] Eighty years earlier Sir Richard Owen had been instrumental in the establishment of a separate natural history collection in South Kensington, London. Although a gifted naturalist, Owen was a controversial figure who poured scorn on the stories told by those who were convinced they had seen 'sea serpents' and other unidentified creatures not recognised by science (see p.156). It was inevitable that his successors, as scientific authorities recognised by the state, would become involved in the debate over the existence of the Loch Ness Monster.

In 1933–34 Martin Hinton, the deputy keeper of zoology at the museum, was reluctantly drawn into the public debate. Responding to Gould's article in *The Times*, he said no zoologist would deny that the discovery of a large creature of 'prehistoric type', hitherto unknown to science, was of huge importance if true. But he was not convinced by the 'evidence' of eyewitnesses alone and wanted proof. 'The observers,' he wrote, 'despite their good faith, appear to have been influenced subconsciously by three things, singly or in combination, namely, the Kelpie tradition, the sea-serpent myth, and by the picture postcards of the "Monster" on sale in Inverness'.

Hinton's theory was that observers had seen 'one or more grey seals' that were common in the Dornoch Firth and may have followed their prey (salmon) up the River Ness. He believed seals were also consistent with the descriptions of those, like the Spicers, who had seen creatures dragging themselves across the lochside road and into the water. He added: 'Accurate observation, even of familiar stationary things on land, is a very difficult art . . . these difficulties are enormously enhanced when the observation concerns an unfamiliar object seen at some considerable distance in motion in the water where light, reflections, ripple, wind and haze change from second to second.'[17]

Meanwhile, press interest continued with the Scottish *Daily Express* offering a £500 reward for the capture of the beast 'alive and unharmed'. Circus owner Bernard Mills upped this to £20,000, with the proviso that this sum would be paid only 'if it proves, on capture, to be at least 20ft long [and] weighing not less than 1000lbs and is of a species believed to be extinct'.[18] More expeditions to the loch were planned, including one organised by insurance broker Sir Edward Mountain. Having read Gould's book, he funded a team made up of 20 men, equipped with cameras and binoculars, to keep watch on the loch for a five-week period during the summer of 1934. The expedition obtained a number of inconclusive photographs and one cine film allegedly showing the 'monster'. When this was examined by the Natural History Museum, it was identified as a grey seal.

THE NESSIE FILES

The Scottish Office in Edinburgh opened a file on the Loch Ness Monster in December 1933 after they were bombarded with inquiries from the media. On one occasion, the Secretary of State, Sir Godfrey Collins, was quizzed about the 'monster of Loch Ness' when he returned to his Greenock constituency for a weekend break. The contents of the file, which remained closed until 1989, paint a colourful picture of the excitement the arrival of the monster generated across the British Isles and the rest of the world.[19]

Pressure was growing for a special act of Parliament to prevent the 'monster' from being injured or captured. This campaign was led by Murdoch MacDonald, the MP for Inverness who, in a letter, told Collins he thought the 'evidence of its presence can be taken as undoubted . . . far too many people have seen something abnormal to question its existence'. He wanted a bill to be put before Parliament for its protection and pleaded with the Secretary of State, in the meantime, to instruct the police to protect the creature from harm.

Collins' officials advised him there was 'no law for the protection of "monsters" and if the Loch Ness Monster does exist any action the police might conceivably take would have to be indirect,' such as enforcing existing legislation preventing trespass or the use of guns on private property. The Secretary of State then authorised Major A.C. McLean, the Chief Constable, to 'cause warnings to be given to as many of the residents and visitors as possible for the purpose of preventing any attack on the animal if sighted', but he felt there was no need to take any further action. This exchange was the origin of a popular belief that the monster enjoyed some form of special protection from the Scottish police force.[20]

While MacDonald was convinced the monster existed, George Hogarth, head of the Scottish Fisheries Board, disagreed. He briefed the Secretary of State that he had been assured by visiting journalists that the whole thing was 'a press stunt' and he was confident it would die down soon. As for the existence of a monster in the loch, there was no such thing.

'It is the old story of the sea serpent,' he wrote. 'Some people probably saw something, but their descriptions of what they saw differ.' He went on to present a list of possible explanations that remain popular today. These ranged from 'an optical illusion, due to the effects of light and shade, through a tree trunk, a mass of peat, otters and seals, to a plesiosaurus'. But Hogarth said he was 'sceptical about the whole business' and, in a letter dated 1938, dismissed a proposal to raise funds for a fresh investigation, writing 'personally I do not care if the mystery is never resolved and from certain points of view a continuance of the mystery might be an advantage'.[21]

FIGURE 7.3 CARTOON BY WILL DYSON ALLUDING TO A PARLIAMENTARY QUESTION ABOUT THE EXISTENCE OF THE LOCH NESS MONSTER AT A TIME OF ECONOMIC CRISIS, PUBLISHED IN THE *DAILY HERALD* IN 1933. THE CUTTING WAS PLACED IN A SCOTTISH OFFICE FILE ON THE MONSTER. (CROWN COPYRIGHT, THE NATIONAL ARCHIVES OF SCOTLAND NAS HH1/588/76)

Despite official scepticism, the monster refused to go away. In the House of Commons on 12 December 1933, William Anstruther Gray, the MP for North Lanarkshire, asked the Secretary of State for Scotland 'whether, in the interests of science, he will cause an investigation to be made into the existence of a monster in Loch Ness'. In his response, Sir Godfrey Collins said there appeared to be no reason 'to suspect the presence of any baneful Monster in Loch Ness'. He played down any potential scientific interest by suggesting that any further investigations were 'properly a matter for the private enterprises of scientists aided by the zeal of the press'.[22]

Privately, he was told scientists were unimpressed by the evidence and: 'our impression is that with them as with the public generally . . . the matter is rather one of public curiosity than of scientific interest. The first point to determine is whether the "monster" exists and this would entail the stationing of reliable observers round the loch, with equipment for proper photographs and possibly . . . arrangements for aerial observation. If the existence of the "monster" were proved the next step would be to trap it without injuring it and with a loch such as Loch Ness this would be a difficult task.'

Sir Godfrey was reassured that the Chief Constable of Inverness-shire had five police constables stationed at different places around the loch, but none had seen the 'monster'. No alterations had been made to their normal duties because of the influx of visitors searching for the monster. Even at this early stage, it seems the Scottish Office had begun to appreciate the potential of the Loch Ness Monster as a tourist attraction. Officials advised the Secretary of State that the Monster was 'providing interest and amusement and it is better to let it continue to do so than to kill it or the tales about it'. Neatly summing up the situation that would continue for the remainder of the century, they added: '. . . at the moment there hangs over the head of the "Monster" the old Scottish verdict of Not Proven . . .'.[23]

Files assembled by the Scottish Office reveal how the 'monster' quickly became a symbol of resurgent Scottish nationalism. Underlying the symbolism was a desire, shared even by sceptical politicians, not to debunk a story that had drawn international attention to the Scottish Highlands. When, periodically, announcements were made by individuals or expeditions from foreign lands that aimed to shoot or capture the creature, the Secretary of State received irate letters demanding action to stop them.

Officials took advice on the issue from the British Museum in London and the Natural History Department at the Royal Scottish Museum in Edinburgh. Both agreed that if any definitive evidence for the existence of an unknown living creature in the loch emerged, it should be 'handed over to one of our national institutions for scientific study'. They said it should not be allowed to fall into the hands of any individual determined to exploit the discovery 'for his private advantage'. However, the keeper of the museum in Edinburgh was determined that any actual remains should not leave Scotland. Although he believed the monster was either fantasy or a large beluga whale, he argued strongly for 'reversionary rights if and when its corpse or any part thereof should become available', adding that 'certainly the Monster should not be allowed to find its last resting place in England'. Such a fate, he said, would outrage Scottish Nationalism which was 'thriving greatly under the monster's beneficient influence'.[24]

When early in 1938 a big game hunter, Peter Kent, arrived in Fort Augustus and declared he intended to catch the monster 'dead or alive', there were fresh demands from Scottish MPs for it to be given some kind of legal protection. Kent said he was having a special harpoon gun made and he planned to return in August with '22 experienced men for the purpose of hunting the Monster down'. On reporting this development to the Scottish Office, the Chief Constable of Inverness, William Fraser, revealed he was a believer in the monster. 'That there is some strange fish [creature] in Loch Ness,' he wrote, 'seems now beyond doubt but that the Police have any power to protect it is very doubtful'. Fraser arranged for Kent to be 'warned of the desirability of having the creature left alone', but he had to admit that he had no real power to stop anyone who wished to hunt the 'monster'.[25]

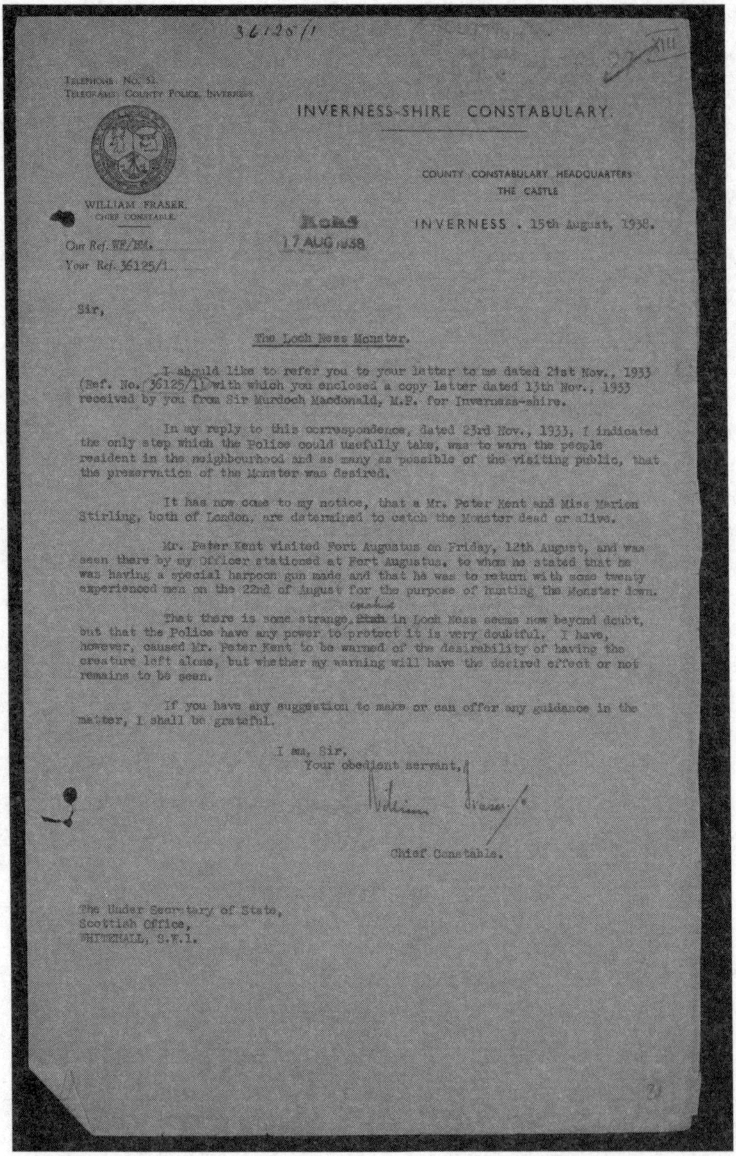

FIGURE 7.4 A LETTER SENT BY THE CHIEF CONSTABLE OF INVERNESS, WILLIAM FRASER, TO THE SCOTTISH OFFICE IN 1938 IN RESPONSE TO CALLS FOR OFFICIAL PROTECTION OF THE 'MONSTER' FROM BIG GAME HUNTERS. FRASER SAID 'THAT THERE IS SOME STRANGE FISH 'CREATURE' IN LOCH NESS SEEMS NOW BEYOND DOUBT'. (CROWN COPYRIGHT, THE NATIONAL ARCHIVES OF SCOTLAND HH1/588/31)

Despite the wealth of eyewitness testimony that was enough to convince Gould and the Chief Constable of Inverness-shire, according to the *Daily Herald*, 'officially, as far as any government department is concerned, it [the Monster] does not exist'. Privately some government officials were less dismissive. In the files of the Department of Agriculture and Fisheries for Scotland, one official admitted that, '. . . in common with many others, I have talked to a number of people who claim to have seen Nessie, whose good faith I would not doubt. The descriptions are always the same in all essential points'. The difficulty was that 'people resident in our area are very chary of discussing the thing with strangers as they feel they leave themselves open to ridicule'.[26]

MORE THAN A LEGEND?

The arrival of the Second World War brought a temporary halt to planned expeditions at the loch and during this time it was patrolled by the Royal Navy. Interest began to grow again from 1957, which saw the arrival of an annual monster hunting 'season' with new expeditions to explore the mysterious waters every summer. For the first time there was renewed interest from naturalists who were prepared to declare their belief in the possibility that some mysterious creature *might* be found in the loch. The potential damage to the reputation of scientists who declared an interest, and the institutions that employed them, is evident from a terse memo issued to staff by the Trustees of the Natural History Museum in 1959. This informed them the museum authorities did not approve of the use of time or paid leave for work on 'the so-called Loch Ness Phenomenon'. It qualified this advice as follows: '[although we] have no intention of curtailing the granting of special leave for approved purposes, nor of interfering with the manner in which members of the staff . . . spend their private leave, they take this opportunity of warning all concerned that if as a result of the activities of members of the staff the Museum is involved in undesirable publicity, they will be gravely displeased.'[27]

Despite the disapproval of their peers, some naturalists were prepared to go public with their faith in the existence of Nessie, as the 'monster' was called by the media. Possibly the best known 'convert' was Sir Peter Scott (1908–89), the son of the explorer Captain Scott of the Antarctic. Sir Peter was an Olympic yachtsman who became Vice-President of the World Wildlife Fund and founder of the Severn Wildlife Trust. In an article published by *The Sunday Times* in 1960, he declared that he was convinced not one but a whole family of plesiosaurs inhabited the loch.[28] He was influenced, as were some of his peers, by the publication in 1957 of *More Than a Legend* by Dr Constance Whyte. Whyte lived near Loch Ness and her husband was engineer and manager of the Caledonian Canal. Her book updated the stories collected by Lt Cdr Gould, who had died in 1948, and presented a renewed case for the existence of the monster.[29] It also gave impetus to enthusiastic individuals and groups – including students from Cambridge and Oxford universities, who were sponsored by television stations – to mount fresh investigations and expeditions to the loch.

This period of renewed public attention reached a peak in 1960 when Tim Dinsdale, an aeronautical engineer, obtained what is probably the best known film footage of the Loch Ness Monster. Dinsdale became interested in the mystery after reading an article by Alex Campbell and, at the age of 36, he decided to devote his life to solving the mystery.[30] In April 1960 he left his home in Reading in a small car loaded with equipment to spend a week observing the loch. On the last day of his trip, at 9am on 23 April he was eating breakfast when he was amazed to see what he believed was a creature in the water near Foyers. According to his story, it was moving directly away from him across the loch at a range of nearly a mile from his roadside vantage point, which was some 300ft above the surface of the loch. Grabbing his camera, he managed to film the beast for almost a minute and noticed it appeared to turn slightly to the right before submerging. It continued to move parallel to the shore. The excitement felt by Dinsdale can be detected in the telegram he sent to 'the directors of the British Museum, London' from the Post Office in Fort Augustus later that afternoon.

Gentlemen . . . I wish to record that on [21st and] 23rd April I exposed approximately 70ft of a 16mm film through a 135mm lens on the phenomenon known as the Lochness Monster . . . my camera is now sealed and the film will be developed under independent control in due course . . . when I have studied this I will present my report in detail . . . until then I must ask for your complete confidence.[31]

Dinsdale's confidence was not shared by senior staff at the museum. Upon arrival in Bloomsbury, the telegram was discussed with the museum director, Sir Gavin de Beer, who declared 'Resolved – no action'. Having heard nothing by 1 May, Dinsdale wrote again, saying the film had been developed in the Kodak laboratory and he had 'watched its projection a number of times'. He was convinced that the museum's official position on the 'phenomenon' would now have to change.[32]

THE MP AND THE MONSTER

All these events culminated, in 1961–62, in Peter Scott, Richard Fitter and Constance Whyte coming together to form a limited company called the Loch Ness Phenomena Investigation Group. One of their greatest achievements was to bring into their fold one of

Scott's wartime friends as one of the four directors, the Conservative MP David James. During the Second World War, James famously made two daring escapes from German prison camps and in the 1950s took part in expeditions to the Antarctic. James was initially reluctant to get involved in promoting the Loch Ness project at Westminster. When approached by Scott, he told the group 'he had entered the House to make a reputation and not destroy one'. Nevertheless, he changed his mind after reading Whyte's book and went on to become one of the most energetic and committed promoters of what he referred to as 'the Loch Ness syndrome'.

Although his constituency was in Brighton, James owned a house on the Isle of Mull and the long journey between the two places allowed him to make frequent visits to the loch. Like Lt Cdr Gould before him, James interviewed eyewitnesses who had seen unidentified creatures in Loch Ness. James came out publicly as a believer in a Christmas article 'Time to Meet the Monster', published by *The Field* in 1961. In this article the MP declared that 'unless one is prepared to brand more than 3,000 people, whose names and addresses are available, as either fools or liars, it is hard to see how any unbiased person can disregard this sheer weight of evidence', adding that 'having interviewed nine witnesses of eight separate sightings, [I] have no doubt as to their veracity, and that the circumstances do not permit of mistake'. He went on to declare his belief in the existence of 'an unidentified species in Loch Ness' and his intention to convince others this conclusion was 'inescapable'.[33]

James' friend and biographer John Robson explained his decision to take a lead role promoting the Loch Ness project because it appealed to his 'sense of romantic adventure and exploration, coupled with curiosity'. The campaign drew upon his establishment contacts, ranging from the royal family to the Ministry of Defence, but led some to doubt his credibility as a politician. In the 1964 general election James lost his seat, after a record seven recounts, to Labour's Dennis Hobden by just seven votes. The result was a shock to James and led to speculation that his obsession with the hunt for the monster had been a factor in his defeat at the ballot box.[34]

Undeterred, James was returned to Parliament as Conservative MP for North Dorset in 1970, but he used the hiatus in his political career to devote much of his time and energy to establishing the Loch Ness Phenomena Investigation Bureau as a serious, scientific fact-gathering organisation. In March 1962 the Bureau was established as a charity, with its main aims being to act as a clearing house for information and to promote active research at the loch itself. James lost no time in drawing up plans for a major expedition and in October of that year he and 26 volunteers set up camp at Achnahannet on the west shore of the loch, south of Drumnadrochit. Equipped with cameras and two searchlights, on loan from the War Office, the first of what would become annual expeditions was fortunate in experiencing warm and calm weather. During the fortnight a number of sightings of what James called 'somewhat striking phenomena' were made, including a 'long dark shape, divided into humps and undulations', a vertical finger shape and a 'dome' seen in daylight on 22 October. On three occasions unusual phenomena were captured on film and four still photographs added to the dossier of evidence. This was submitted to a panel of independent experts chaired by a barrister, Adrian Head, in 1963. It concluded that: 'there is some unidentified animate object in Loch Ness which, if it be a mammal, amphibian, reptile, fish or mollusc of any known order, is of such size as to be worthy of careful scientific examination and identification.' If it could not be identified as an animal known to science, it represented a challenge 'which is only capable of being answered by controlled investigation conducted on careful scientific principles'.[35]

So far so scientific, but despite having considerable reserves of enthusiasm James encountered a brick wall when he tried to attract funding to continue his investigations. Copies of his report were submitted to the Scottish Office, who passed them to scientists at the Department of Agriculture and Fisheries Marine Laboratory in Aberdeen. A marine scientist there, after reading the dossier, said it was 'interesting . . . but it is difficult to avoid the impression that they [the observers] have been "seeing things" that were not there'.[36]

James was unfortunate in the timing of his expedition. Despite the backing of ATV, which ran a short programme on the expedition, there was little public or media interest in the findings. The entire nation, and the world, was holding its collective breath as a result of the Cuban Missile Crisis and the very real possibility of a nuclear war. Undeterred by this setback, within weeks of leaving his camp on Loch Ness, David James discussed his plans with the Duke of Edinburgh, who was well known for his interest in a range of fringe phenomena such as flying saucers. Prince Philip advised him to pass the panel's report to Solly Zuckerman (see Chapter 4) who, as well as being Professor of Anatomy at the University of Birmingham, acted as Chief Scientific Advisor for the Ministry of Defence.[37]

Early in 1964 Zuckerman responded cautiously, noting that as a scientist it would be impossible for him to regard the panel's view as definitive as it was based purely upon witness testimony. Nevertheless, he confessed at being 'fascinated that after all these years . . . the issue of the existence or non-existence of a "monster" is still open'.[38] James followed this up a year later when he sent Zuckerman a report on his second expedition to the loch, which resulted in further sightings and film footage. The MP asked for advice on where he might obtain funding for further investigations and equipment, which, up to that point, had been paid for entirely by voluntary contributions.

James explained that 'we are trying to identify a syndrome, rather than to photograph a "monster"' and because many of the sightings had been clustered in the Urquhart Bay area of the loch, he felt there was a link with local blasting activities. 'It is well known that reports reached a crescendo during the years 1933–35 when the new road was being built down the north shore,' James wrote. 'It may be significant that there had been very few reports in the last few years, until this last summer when the Forestry Commission resumed blasting to

make a track to extract timber for the new pulp mill at Fort William and that, throughout the blasting period, there were once again three or four reports per week.'[39]

With his natural curiosity piqued, Zuckerman took advice from the Royal Navy's Chief Scientist, Sir John Carroll, noting that 'if a sonar investigation – or any other kind of investigation – were to reveal something extraordinary in the Loch, it could be of considerable scientific interest'. Zuckerman's enthusiasm was not shared by his advisors, who believed 'it would not be sensible to contribute anything which did not involve a new systematic approach offering a reasonable hope of reaching some definite conclusion'. The Navy wanted to avoid any suggestion of committing MoD scientific resources to a 'full scale scientific investigation of Loch Ness in search of a monster' and advised that '[we] do not think this could possibly be justified at least at this stage'.[40]

THE JARIC REPORT

In what appeared to be a buck-passing exercise, James was advised to submit his best evidence to 'the junior service', the Royal Air Force. In December 1965 he sent Dinsdale's

16mm film of the 'monster' to Eddie Shackleton, another son of a famous Antarctic explorer, who was minister for the RAF in Harold Wilson's government. Shackleton asked the RAF's Joint Reconnaissance Intelligence Centre (JARIC), which was at that time based at RAF Huntingdon near Cambridge, to examine the film. JARIC had an international reputation as the world's leading photographic interpretation agency; it was the expertise of their staff that led to the identification of Hitler's secret weapon, the deadly V2 missile, from aerial photographs taken by RAF crews of the Peenemünde weapons plant in 1943.

A lesser-known function of JARIC – now known as the Defence Geographic and Image Intelligence Agency (DGIA) – has been to assist MoD branches in the interpretation of other unusual images, including some contributed by members of the public. On rare occasions, photographs and film of 'UFOs' have been sent to the agency for an expert opinion.[41] Today much of the DGIA's work involves advanced computer enhancement, but in 1966 frames from the Dinsdale film were enlarged by a factor of 20 and then carefully scrutinised by RAF analysts. Almost every aspect of the content and conclusions in the resultant JARIC report on the Dinsdale film remains controversial. In summary the findings stated that it was a 'reasonable assumption' that the speed of the object 'may be as high as 10 mph'. This appeared to rule out the possibility of it being a small boat. However, it later emerged that JARIC may have over-estimated the speed of the 'object' in the water because they did not take the winding time of Dinsdale's cine camera into account. If that was indeed the case, then a boat cannot be ruled out.

The speed of the 'object' was not the only source of contention. JARIC decided the object filmed had some 'body' that appeared to have a height above the water of around 3ft. While not ruling out the possibility of a boat, they wrote 'these craft are normally painted in such a way as to be photo visible at any time, and in any case the existence of such a craft on the loch would scarcely be missed by an observer . . .' The report continued: 'The interpretation is a more difficult problem, but first consider whether this [object] may be a surface vessel of any kind. The object appears to submerge, but it can readily be argued that under certain conditions of light, reflectivity and aspect angle, etc., objects may NOT be visible on the photography.'[42]

Despite these caveats, in his covering letter to Derek James, Shackleton pointed to one line in the JARIC report that appeared to provide the breakthrough James had hoped for. The defence minister told the MP: '. . . I think you will find this extremely interesting. The report comes to the conclusion that "it probably is an animate object" . . . this is indeed fascinating and will no doubt encourage you in your efforts.'[43]

In retrospect, while the author of the report was careful to qualify all his statements, he was reliant upon the information provided by James and Dinsdale. If the object was not a boat or a submarine, then the only conclusion he could reach was that 'it probably is an animate object' – in other words a living creature of some kind. Dinsdale had taken a control film of a boat 'of known size and speed' one hour after the footage in similar conditions, yet oddly this does not appear to have been submitted to JARIC for direct comparison. If both films had been scrutinised together, the conclusion could have been very different. In recent years, fresh analysis of the report and the images has led a number of researchers to conclude the 'object' is indeed a boat.[44]

At the time Lord Shackleton insisted that James kept news of the JARIC report secret as he did not wish 'to find the Ministry of Defence taking sides in a first-class public argument about the possible nature of the underwater population of Loch Ness'. Unfortunately the Loch Ness Phenomena Investigation Bureau was a leaky organisation and within a few days, news of the report was splashed across the national press. Peter Vane, writing in the *Sunday Express*, announced that 'experts [at] the Ministry of Defence say that the Loch Ness Monster could be a giant living creature nearly 100ft long'.[45] The Bureau subsequently published the report as a leaflet, complete with an introduction from Derek James, priced at sixpence, to raise funds for their investigations.[46]

NOT A FACT – MORE OF A LEGEND?

The late 1960s was a heady time for the Loch Ness syndrome and, throughout the decade that followed, armed with the JARIC analysis, Derek James and Sir Peter Scott continued to apply pressure on their contacts in government to have the monster officially recognised. The Loch Ness Phenomena Investigation Bureau folded in 1972 through lack of funds but the legend refused to go away. In the same year an American inventor, Dr Robert Rines, reported seeing 'a large darkish hump covered . . . with rough, mottled skin, like the back of an elephant' in the loch. Rines, who died in 2009, mounted numerous expeditions to Scotland and employed sophisticated electronic and photographic equipment to search its depths. Among the underwater photographs that resulted was one that appeared to show the flipper of the monster and a close-up portrait of its neck and head. When news of the Rines photos leaked to the press in 1975, the British Museum (Natural History) were once again drawn into the media feeding frenzy. Pressed for an opinion, the Keeper of Zoology, Dr Gordon Sheals, issued a press release that said 'none of these photographs is sufficiently informative to establish the existence, far less the identification, of a large animal living in the loch'.[47]

Undeterred by the Museum's scepticism, Sir Peter Scott took the opportunity to give the creature a Latin name. In a paper published by the journal *Nature*, he christened the monster *Nessiteras rhombopteryx* ('the Ness monster with diamond fin'). Unfortunately, his attempt to bring scientific credibility to the syndrome ended in farce when a columnist for the *Daily Telegraph* pointed out this was an anagram of 'monster hoax by Sir Peter S'.[48]

David James had no more success in a fresh attempt to persuade the government to officially recognise the existence of the monster. In January 1976, he asked the Secretary of State for Scotland 'what powers he has under statute to protect *Nessiteras rhombopteryx*' and asked him to state what 'standard of proof he would demand' to exercise such powers. Privately, he briefed the minister that 'while scientific proof was lacking there was such a high degree of probability attached to the evidence, which had such distinct scientific support, it would be better to be safe than sorry'. But the Nature Conservancy Council advised the Scottish Office that protection could not be granted without agreement of the 'authoritative taxonomic authority', which was the British Museum (Natural History).[49]

Despite the lack of any hard evidence for its existence, the Loch Ness Monster has become an asset for the Scottish tourist industry. The contents of the Scottish Office files on the phenomenon at the National Archives in Edinburgh imply that some officials preferred the mystery to continue. Although publicly politicians refused to provide a grant of £2,000 to Derek James' investigation bureau, privately the Secretary of State, George Younger MP, told officials: 'From a tourist point of view, it would be equally disastrous if they found the monster or proved it didn't exist.'[50]

The monster's iconic status as the quintessential Scottish legend led the Department of Agriculture and Fisheries Division to become 'reluctant experts' on the subject. Like their counterparts on the MoD's UFO desk, scientists at the department's Marine Laboratory continued to receive reports of sightings and responded to letters from monster hunters across the world.[51] In September 1985 a local authority in Sweden contacted the British Embassy in Stockholm 'for help in dealing with pressure for the protection of the Storsjö Monster, whose status is similar to that of our own Loch Ness Monster'. After taking advice from Scottish officials, the Foreign Office advised the Swedes that perhaps the 'best protection the monster has is itself', adding:

> If it has evaded capture, injury or even positive identification for so long, it is not necessarily complacent to envisage it continuing to do so for the future. But we should certainly welcome teams of Swedish scientists, amateur and professional, bent on establishing Nessie's identity and [we] can assure them that there is ample accommodation in the Highlands and plentiful supplies of the national beverage which will help them to see her in the dark.[52]

CAT FLAPS

From rumours of large black creatures haunting the moors of Cornwall to reports of a lion roaming a holiday resort in Essex, sightings of 'big cats' have become a persistent part of the British landscape. Although there have been stories about 'out of place' big cats throughout recorded history, the number of reports that reach police, journalists and naturalists appears to have increased towards the end of the 20th century. In 2006, a survey by the British Big Cats Society (BBCS) listed 2,123 sightings of 'big cats' during the preceding two years.[1] Merrily Harpur, author of *Mystery Big Cats*, says there may be as many as 2–4,000 sightings every year, of which around 75 per cent are of 'black cats', commonly described as large, glossy and muscular. The remainder describe brown or sandy-coloured pumas and a smaller number refer to smaller lynx-like cats.[2] Many witnesses describe the larger animals as resembling black leopards or pumas, but in fact these species are very rare, even in captivity. Adult melanistic leopards are ten times the size of a domestic cat. The lynx is much smaller and was once native to Britain but became extinct some 4,000 years ago.

The iconic black colour and elusiveness of the British 'big cats' has led some folklorists to link them with legends of the demonic black hound, such as that said to haunt Dartmoor and which inspired Arthur Conan Doyle's 1902 story *The Hound of the Baskervilles*. Devon emerges from figures published by the BBCS as the county that generates the highest number of sightings annually, closely followed by Yorkshire, Scotland, Wales and Gloucestershire.

Since the late 1950s, when sightings of the 'Surrey Puma' and 'Fenland Tiger' first captured the imagination of the national media, tens of thousands of pounds in public money have been spent on fruitless searches of the countryside by armed police. In 1988 the government took the unusual step of sending soldiers from the Royal Marines on a five-week hunt for an elusive creature called 'the Beast of Exmoor'. One farmer claimed to have lost 100 sheep in a few months from violent injuries inflicted by what he believed was a big cat. Although some of the soldiers, who were armed with high-powered sniper rifles, claimed to have occasionally glimpsed the creature, nothing larger than a fox was found.[3]

In August 2012 more than 30 officers, along with specialist marksmen and two helicopters equipped with heat-seeking cameras, searched fields near St Osyth in Essex after a lion was spotted by holiday-makers in a caravan park. Residents were asked to stay indoors while checks were made on Colchester zoo and local circuses, but all captive big cats in the area were accounted for. It was estimated the operation cost £25,000 but no lion was found and, at the end of the two-day operation, Essex police said it believed 'a large domestic cat or a wild cat' was responsible.[4]

During the last 60 years hundreds of photographs have been published allegedly showing 'big cats' prowling the fields and gardens of Britain, but none has provided conclusive evidence. Many have been proved to show domestic cats while others are so vague or blurry they could show almost anything. Other hard evidence, such as droppings, corpses or captured specimens, are non-existent. Although the majority of 'big cat' reports are made in good faith by honest people, pranksters have muddied the waters occasionally. A leopard skull discovered by a 14-year-old boy in the River Fowey, Cornwall, in 1995 was proclaimed as definitive evidence for the presence of non-native big cats in Britain. However when this was examined at the Natural History Museum, the egg-case of a tropical insect was found in the naval cavity, leading scientists to conclude it 'could not have died on Bodmin Moor [and] must have originated from the tropics'. The museum believes the leopard had been killed possibly as a trophy abroad and its skull was later dropped in the Cornish river as a prank, where it was eventually found and brought to the museum.[5]

Nevertheless, claims that big cats are living and breeding in the British country-side have led to demands for government investigations. In 1998 Elliot Morley, then parliamentary secretary for the Ministry of Agriculture, Fisheries and Food, said his prime concern was the potential threat big cats, if they existed, might pose to livestock. Elliot said his officials received many such reports every year and although the 'vast majority of reports are not genuine sightings of big cats', the subject was regarded as 'a serious issue' by the government.[6]

In 1995 Morley's ministry commissioned its first formal investigation into 'the possible existence of one or more large exotic cats' on Bodmin Moor in Cornwall, where many sightings had been made. The inquiry was launched in response to 'continued concerns expressed by people living in the area, that such animals might become established and pose a significant threat to livestock'. The study was widely publicised, with farmers and members of the public invited to submit evidence to inspectors. From the outset, the environmental consultancy that carried out the investigation admitted it would never be possible to prove that such an animal, or animals, did not exist. That said they were sure that if a creature of this type *was* at large, hard evidence would be found and the team spent six months collecting sightings, videos and still photographs and reports of suspected livestock kills and injuries.

Detailed analysis of the videos and still photographs were summarised in a short but thorough report published in 1995.[7] It proved a devastating blow for those who believed the Beast of Bodmin Moor was a real big cat. The team used large measuring poles to demonstrate the heights of walls and other natural features against which some of the creatures had been photographed. One classic image of the 'Beast of Bodmin Moor', taken by a press photographer using a long focus lens, appeared to show

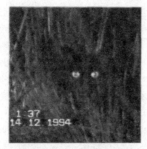

PANEL FIGURE 7.1 A PAGE FROM A
REPORT ON THE BEAST OF BODMIN MOOR
COMMISSIONED BY THE MINISTRY OF
AGRICULTURE IN 1995 AFTER A SERIES
OF SIGHTINGS OF A BIG CAT IN
CORNWALL. (CROWN COPYRIGHT: MAFF/
DEFRA)

a) A colour copy of a single frame from a video taken by a farmer on 14 December 1994. Note that the pupils are narrowing to a vertical slit. (Mrs R. Rhodes)

b) A photograph of a melanistic leopard showing that the pupils constrict in a way similar to humans; in a circular fashion. In this photograph they have closed to a very small circular opening. (ARDEA)

two 'big cats' posing on a stone wall, with one balanced upon a gatepost. When this was re-photographed with a one metre tall ranging pole providing scale to the gatepost, the 'beast' was clearly shown to be no taller than 30cm (12 inches) at the shoulder. It was, in fact, a domestic cat. Several other still photographs and video sequences, taken in daylight, were subjected to the same technique. In each case, the black animals depicted were revealed as no larger than domestic felines.

One sinister night-time shot that claimed to show the eyes of a young leopard in close-up was compared with an image of a real black leopard. The pupils of the 'beast' photographed in Cornwall could be clearly seen in the light of the farmer's lamp as narrow vertical slits. This type of constriction is not found in the pupils of larger cats like leopards and pumas. The investigators concluded again that the animal in the photograph was a domestic cat.

Examination of footprints and alleged big cat 'kills' were equally disappointing. Three plaster casts of prints taken on Bodmin Moor were examined and it was concluded that two belonged to an ordinary cat and the third to a dog. Of the small number of livestock kills that were followed up by the team, none produced any evidence for the presence of big cats. Traces of indigenous predators, such as badgers, crows and foxes were found, however, in most cases as scavengers after sheep had died from natural causes.

Based on this, and earlier investigations, the current position of the British authorities is that, 'based on the evidence . . . [we] do not believe that there are big cats living wild in England'.[8] The remit of the team that investigated the Bodmin Moor flap was restricted to answering two very specific questions: firstly, was there any evidence for the existence of a big cat and, if so, did it pose a threat to livestock on the moor? Although the answer to both questions was an emphatic 'no', the report did not explain *why* people continue to believe such a creature exists. Ultimately, the 'evidence' for 'big cats' living wild in Britain relies almost entirely upon the testimony of eyewitnesses. In this respect the phenomenon resembles other intractable modern mysteries such as the Loch Ness Monster and UFO sightings.

In his book *Feral* (2013), the journalist and environmental lobbyist George Monbiot asks why there has been so little discussion of the big cat sightings in the scientific literature. Monbiot interviewed a number of people near his home in West Wales who have seen a large black cat, said to be six feet long and three feet high, that has been dubbed 'the Pembrokeshire Panther'. He became convinced of their sincerity and their claim to have no prior knowledge or interest in the subject before their personal experience with the big cat. Nevertheless, he found it impossible to accept such creatures could be so common without hard evidence emerging of their existence. After consulting psychologists, he began to realise how witnesses could turn ordinary cats into extra-ordinary ones by magnifying their size out of the context of their surroundings, as the analysis of photographs taken on Bodmin Moor proved.

Monbiot speculated 'whether there might be a kind of template in our minds in the form of a big cat' that we have inherited from our ancestors. When we are confronted with something 'that vaguely fits the template', in sudden and unexpected circumstances, 'the template triggers the big cat alarm'. The influence of media stories and images of big cats from zoos and films may also play a part in shaping how such 'sightings' are interpreted by eyewitnesses. But Monbiot admitted this theory fails to explain why sightings of big cats appear to have become more abundant in recent years.[9]

One popular explanation for the increase is that a number of exotic cats were released into the wild by owners of private menageries after the government enforced the Dangerous Wild Animals Act of 1976. Figures published by the Department of Environment, Fisheries and Rural Affairs in 2006 listed 27 examples of escapes since 1975, including leopards, lynx, jaguars, puma and a lion. Most were quickly recaptured, shot or were killed on the road.[10] In another case a live puma was captured near Cannich, in Inverness-shire in 1980 where it had been living wild for a long period of time. Cross-breeding of big cats does occur in captivity, but puma, lynx and leopard are not closely related within the cat family. Naturalists believe that big cats are unlikely to breed in the British countryside given the massive behavioural, biological and logistic barriers that escaped individual animals would have to overcome.

One of the first academic studies of the 'big cat' phenomenon appeared in 2013 when a multi-disciplinary team of scientists studied the remains of a Canadian lynx that died near Newton Abbot, Devon, in 1903. The creature was shot by a local man after it killed two dogs and its skin and skeleton were presented to the Bristol Museum, where they were stored for decades. Tests on the animal's remains revealed that it had probably spent some time in captivity before it escaped, or was set free, but the team were unable to discover any record of its fate in local newspapers. The authors believe this Canadian lynx is the earliest recorded example of an exotic cat living wild in the UK. If that is correct, the Devon specimen takes the history of alien big cats way back into recorded history, long before the Dangerous Wild Animals Act came into force. They concluded: 'It seems more likely that escapes and releases have occurred throughout history, and that this continual presence of aliens explains the "British big cat" phenomenon.'[11]

NOTES AND REFERENCES

References to recurring archive sources are abbreviated as follows:
BL: British Library
IWM: Archives of the Imperial War Museum
M-OA: Mass Observation Archive, University of Sussex
NAS: The National Archives of Scotland
NHM: Natural History Museum
TNA: The National Archives (UK)

INTRODUCTION

1. Eden Fay, Charles. ([1942]1998) *The Story of the Mary Celeste*. Originally published by the Peabody Museum, Massachusetts. New York: Dover, p. vii.

2. http://www.nationalarchives.gov.uk/ufos; the story of the British government's UFO investigations can be followed in my 2012 book *The UFO Files* (London: Bloomsbury).

3. Mass Observation Archive online: http://www.massobs.org.uk/index.htm

4. M-OA DR 1263 'Belief in the Supernatural', report on replies to April directive, 16 May 1942.

5. M-OA FR Bulletin No. 5, January 1947: 'The Supernatural'.

6. Trubshaw, Bob. *Seeing and Believing: applying developments in cognitive research to understanding the perception of anomalous phenomena*. Unpublished paper, 2012.

7. Degh, Linda. (1991) 'What is a Legend After All?' *Contemporary Legend*, 11: 19.

8. Rubinstein, William D. (2000) 'The Hunt for Jack the Ripper.' *History Today*, 50(5).

9. Knight, Stephen. (1976) *Jack the Ripper: The Final Solution*. London: Harrap.

10. *Daily Express*: 7, 9, 10 March 1931.

11. TNA MEPO 3/142, released in 1988.

12. Evans, Stewart P. and Keith Skinner. (2001) *Jack the Ripper: Letters from Hell*. Stroud: Sutton, pp. 143–48.

13. MoD Guidance for Record Reviewers, June 2011 (Annexe S), released to the author in December 2013 under the Freedom of Information Act.

14. Clarke, David. (2012) *The UFO Files*. London: Bloomsbury, Chapter 1.

1 WAR AND THE WEIRD

1. Macdonald, Lyn. (1987) *1914: Days of Hope*. Harmondsworth: Penguin, pp. 137–38.
2. Taylor, A.J.P. (1963) *The First World War: An Illustrated History*. Harmondsworth: Penguin, p. 29.
3. Ellis, Phillip. (2005) 'Spectral Soldiers: Possible literary antecedents for "The Bowmen".' *Studies in Weird Fiction* (winter 1999); Wood, Scott. (2005) 'The Angels of Mons and Elsewhere.' *The Skeptic*, 18(2).
4. Hole, Christina. (1965) *Saints in Folklore*. London: G. Bell & Sons, pp. 23–24.
5. Many of the lesser-known booklets and pamphlets concerning the Angels of Mons that were published during the First World War can be consulted in the reading rooms of The British Library and the archives of the Imperial War Museum in London. Some of these are listed on the IWM information sheet, The Angels of Mons (No. 24, 1256A, undated).
6. Clarke, David. (2004) *The Angels of Mons: Phantom Soldiers and Ghostly Guardians*. Chichester: Wiley. Chapter 2 provides a detailed account of the battle of Mons and the stories that grew from the retreat to Le Cateau.
7. *Sunday Times*, 30 August 1914.
8. Machen, Arthur. (1915) *The Bowmen and Other Legends of the War*. London: Simpkin, Marshall & Co., p. 8.
9. *The Evening News* (London), 29 September 1914.
10. Gawsworth, John. (1930) *The Life of Arthur Machen*. Unpublished MS, University of California, Chapter 15.
11. 'The Invisible Allies: Strange Story from the Front.' *Light: A Journal of Psychical, Occult and Mystical Research*, 24 April 1915.
12. Papers of the Drury-Lowe family, Dr 4F 3/1–10, letters from Captain John A.E. Drury, University of Nottingham Manuscripts and Special Collections.
13. *Daily Mail*, 24 August and 2 September 1915.
14. Machen, 1915, pp. 24–25.
15. Machen, *op. cit.*
16. Begbie, Harold. (1915) *On the Side of the Angels: An Answer to Arthur Machen*. London: Hodder & Stoughton.
17. Harris, Melvin. (1986) *Investigating the Unexplained*. New York: Prometheus.
18. Campbell, Phyllis. (1915) *Back of the Front*. London: George Newnes & Co.
19. See, for example, the articles and correspondence published on 'The Angels of Mons', *This England*, Summer & Winter 1982.
20. Charteris, Brigadier General John. (1931) *At GHQ*. London: Cassell & Co., p. 25.
21. This argument was central to the account presented by Kevin McClure in *Visions of Bowmen and Angels* at: http://magonia.haaan.com/2009/visions-of-bowmen-and-angels-kevin-mcclure/
22. Papers of Brigadier General John Charteris, GB0099 KCLMA Charteris 2/22: Liddell Hart Centre for Military Archives, King's College, London.
23. Charteris, 1931, p. v.
24. Hayward, James. (2002) *Myths and Legends of the First World War*. Stroud: Sutton, p. 34.
25. IWM Archive. 'The Angels of Mons' booklist 1256A, undated.
26. Salter, W.H. (December 1915) 'An Enquiry Concerning the "Angels at Mons".' *Journal of the Society for Psychical Research*, pp. 117–18.

27. Machen, Arthur. (1938) 'The True Story of the Angels of Mons', in Sir John Hammerton (ed)., *The Great War: I Was There*, Vol 2. London: Amalgamated Press.

28. Brittain, Vera. (1933) *Testament of Youth*. London: Victor Gollancz, pp. 144–45.

29. Text from BBC DVD version of *All The King's Men* (BBC Worldwide 2005), produced by Gareth Neame. A BBC documentary on the vanishing battalion, 'A Matter of Fact', was transmitted on 7 November 1999.

30. (1965) 'Incident at Gallipoli: Was the Regiment Abducted?', *Spaceview*, 45: 6–7.

31. *Spaceview, op. cit.*

32. Vallée, Jacques. (1968) *Passport to Magonia: From Folklore to Flying Saucers*. London: Neville Spearman. Earlier references in the UFO literature include Steiger, Brad and Joan Whritrenour. (1966) *Strangers from the Skies*. London: Tandem; *Flying Saucers* magazine No. 46 (March 1967), Palmer Publications, Wisconsin; Steiger, Brad. (1967) *Flying Saucers Are Hostile*. London: Universal-London.

33. For full accounts of the Suvla campaign and the 'disappearance' of the Norfolks, see Rayer, Dick. (2000) 'The Sandringhams at Suvla Bay.' *Stand To!*, 58: 5–9; Dutton, Philip. (2000) 'Suvla: The attack of the 163rd Brigade, 12th August 1915'. London and Canberra: Joint Imperial War Museum/ Australian War Memorial Battlefield Study Tour to Gallipoli, pp. 1–10.

34. TNA WO 95/4325.

35. Travers, Tim and Birten Çelik (2002). '"Not one of them ever came back": What happened to the 1/5th Norfolk Battalion on 12 August 1915 at Gallipoli?' *The Journal of Military History*, 66: 389–406.

36. Aspinall-Oglander, Brigadier General Cecil F. (1932) *Military Operations, Gallipoli*. London: Heinemann, pp. 317–18.

37. Sir Ian Hamilton, 'Third Gallipoli Despatch', published in *The London Gazette*, 6 January 1916.

38. McCrery, Nigel. (1992) *All The King's Men: One of the Greatest Mysteries of the First World War Finally Solved*. London: Simon & Schuster.

39. Travers and Çelik, 2002, p. 406.

40. TNA AIR 2/19117; AIR 20/12966.

41. IWM Archive Information Sheet 6, 'The Vanishing Norfolks', updated 1992.

42. *Spaceview, op. cit*, p. 6.

43. (1966) 'Research on "Incident" at Gallipoli.' *Spaceview*, 47: 9.

44. McCrery, *op. cit.*, p. 112.

45. TNA AIR 1/2326/223/53/1: *Final Report of the Dardanelles Commission*, Cmd 371. HMSO London, 1917.

46. Begg, Paul. (1979) *Into Thin Air*. London: David & Charles, p. 50.

47. McCrery, *op. cit.* p. 113.

48. Begg, *op. cit*, p. 51.

49. BBC productions, *All The King's Men* (November 1999).

50. Dutton, *op. cit.*, p. 1.

51. Quoted in Travers and Çelik, p. 391.

THE PHANTOM MENACE

1. TNA KV 1/2.

2. *The UFO Files*, pp. 6–10.

3. Hayward, James. (2003) *Myths and Legends of the Second World War*. Stroud: Sutton, p. 3.

4. TNA KV4/28; WO 199/1982.
5. TNA KV 4/185.
6. TNA KV 4/28.
7. *The UFO Files*, pp. 11–12.
8. TNA KV 4/28.
9. TNA KV 4/190.
10. Jones, R.V. (1978) *Most Secret War*. London: Hamish Hamilton, p. 114.
11. TNA KV 4/11: B3C report in connection with suspected fifth column activities, includes sections on suspicious ground markings, suspicious pieces of paper, messages and marked maps found. A separate file, KV 4/12, deals with 'suspicious markings on telegraph poles'.
12. *The Huffington Post* (UK edition), 29 January 2013.

2 THE DEATH RAY

1. Wells, H.G. ([1898]1993) *The War of the Worlds*. London: Everyman, Chapter 5.
2. Booth, Jenny. 'Historians prize uncovered Churchill letters predicting First World War.' *The Guardian*, 6 February 2004.
3. Zimmerman, David. (2001) *Britain's Shield: Radar and the Development of the Luftwaffe*. Stroud: Sutton, pp. 36–7.
4. TNA AIR 5/179.
5. 'New Riddle of the Air', *Daily Mail*, 8 September 1923.
6. 'Ray to Disable Planes', *Daily Mail*, 10 September 1923.
7. *Daily Mail*, 10 September 1923.
8. TNA AIR 5/179.
9. TNA AIR 5/179.
10. Owen, Gari. (1997) 'Directed-energy weapons: a historical perspective.' *Journal of Defence Science* 2(1): 89–93.
11. Owen, *op. cit.*, pp. 89–90.
12. Barwell, Ernest H.G. (1943) *The Death Ray Man*. London: Hutchinson; a more recent biography is Jonathan Foster's *The Death Ray* (Inventive Publishing, 2008).
13. TNA AIR 5/179.
14. *Daily Mail*, 5 April 1924.
15. TNA AIR 5/179.
16. TNA AIR 5/179.
17. *Daily Sketch, Daily Mail, Daily Express*, 28 May 1924.
18. Hansard (House of Commons), 28 May 1924.
19. AIR 5/179.
20. *New York Times*, 3 November 1924.
21. Littlewood, S.R. (1924) 'The Art of the Cinema.' *The Sphere* (London).
22. *New York Herald*, 7 August 1924.

23. Jonathan Foster: http://www.harrygrindellmatthews.com/theDeathRay.asp

24. TNA BT 226/4670.

25. Swansea County Archives: Harry Grindell-Matthews;
     http://www.swansea.gov.uk/index.cfm?articleid=23083

26. TNA AIR 5/179.

27. Owen, pp. 90–91.

28. Barwell, p. 65.

29. Owen, p. 91.

30. Swansea County Archives, D/D Z 346/118, Grindell-Matthews Collection.

31. *Sheffield Independent*, 25 September 1924.

32. TNA AIR 5/542.

33. Jones, R.V. 1978, pp. 63–4.

34. TNA AIR 20/181.

35. TNA AIR 20/181.

36. 'Mr Baldwin on Aerial Warfare – A Fear for the Future', *The Times* (London), 11 November 1932.

37. TNA AIR 20/80.

38. Jones, R.V. 1978, pp. 16–17.

39. Jones, R.V. (1968) 'The Natural History of Flying Saucers.' *Physics Bulletin*, 19: 226.

40. Kinsey, Gordon. (1983) *Bawdsey: Birth of the Beam*. Sudbury: Terence Dalton, pp. 44–5.

41. Churchill Archives Centre, University of Cambridge, papers of R.V. Jones, RVJO GCHQ letter dated 2 January 1969, D13C.

42. Jones, 1968, p. 226.

43. Craig, Roy. (1968) 'Indirect Physical Evidence' in Edward Condon & Daniel Gillmor (eds), *The Scientific Study of Unidentified Flying Objects*. Boulder: University of Colorado, p. 115.

44. *Eastern Daily Press* (Norwich), *The Guardian*, 22 February 2006.

45. BBC News online, 2 November 2006.

46. Owen, p.89.

47. TNA PREM 19/972.

ANGELS IN THE CLOUDS

1. London *Daily News and Leader*, 17 February 1930.

2   London *Daily News and Leader*, 28 February 1930.

3. Barwell, *The Death Ray Man*, 1943, pp. 123–4.

4. TNA FO 898/6.

5. Maskelyne, Jasper. (1949) *Magic: Top Secret*. London: Stanley Paul & Co.

3 PHANTOMS IN THE ARCHIVES

1. M-OA DR 1263 'Belief in the Supernatural', replies to April directive, 16 May 1942.
2. Sidgwick, Henry, *et al.* (1894) 'Report on the Census of Hallucinations.' *Proceedings of the Society for Psychical Research,* 10: 345.
3. Thomas, Keith. (1971) *Religion and the Decline of Magic.* Harmondsworth: Penguin, p. 719.
4. Ipsos MORI survey for *The Sun* newspaper, February 1998: http://www.ipsos-mori.com/polls.1998/s980205.shtml
5. Ipsos MORI survey with *Schott's Almanac*, October 2007: http://www.ipsos-mori.com/polls/2007/schottsalmanac2.shtml
6. Bennett, Gillian. (1987) *Traditions of Belief: Women and the Supernatural.* Harmondsworth: Penguin.
7. Bennett, *op. cit.*, pp. 16–17.
8. Thomas, 1971, pp. 701–11.
9. BL MS 1103.e.53. *A Great Wonder in Heaven.* 1642.
10. BL James I, King of England, *Daemonologie.* Published in Edinburgh, 1597; London: W. Apsley & W. Cotton, 1603.
11. *The Guardian*, 3 January 2004.
12. Davies, Owen. (2007) *The Haunted: A Social History of Ghosts.* Basingstoke: Palgrave, pp. 51–2.
13. *The Times*, 6 January 1804.
14. Tatton Law Library: *The Complete Newgate Calendar vol IV: Francis Smith* [account of trial]: http://tarlton.law.utexas.edu/lpop/etext/newgate4/smithf.htm
15. TNA HO 47/32/12.
16. Murdie, Alan. (2003) 'The Hammersmith Ghost.' *Justice of the Peace,* 167: 975–77.
17. Williams, Professor Glanville. (1949) 'Homicide and the Supernatural.' *Law Quarterly Review,* 65.
18. Williams, p. 492: Reg v. Machekequonabe (1894), 28 Ontario 309.
19. Murdie, 2003, p. 977.
20. Murdie, 2003, p. 976.
21. *The Times*, 16 January 1804.
22. Larwood, Jacob. (1874) *The Story of the London Parks.* London: Chatto & Windus, p. 479.
23. Larwood, *op. cit.*, p. 480.
24. *The Times*, 24 January 1804.
25. TNA HLG 121/70.
26. Underwood, Peter. (1973) *Haunted London.* London: Harrap, pp. 144–5.
27. Chief Fire Officer's report, 5 April 1968: TNA HLG 121/70.
28. TNA HLG 121/70.
29. Transcript of judgement by Lord Parker CJ, *Rating and Valuation Reporter*, 22 May 1969, pp. 343–5.
30. *Daily Mail, The Guardian*, 19 January 1999. According to the Listing Section of Derby County Court, 'the original file on the Lowes Cottage case' was destroyed some years ago. Personal communication 2 September 2013.
31. A full account of the Solway case can be found in Randles, Jenny. (1997) *MIB: Investigating the Truth*

Behind the Men in Black Phenomenon. London: Piatkus, pp. 75–88; a letter from Jim Templeton summarising the story was published by the *Daily Mail* on 13 December 2002.

32. 'Solway "Spaceman" poses picture puzzle for police experts', *Cumberland News* (Carlisle), 12 June 1964.
33. Cumbria Constabulary, response to Freedom of Information request from author, dated 9 March 2012.
34. *Cumberland News*, 12 June 1964.
35. *Cumberland News*, 19 June 1964.
36. TNA AIR 2/17526.
37. *Cumberland News*, 19 June 1964.
38. Transcript of interview with Jim Templeton, Carlisle, 9 July 2001.
39. Randles, 1997, p. 205.
40. *Cumberland News*, 4 September 1964.
41. BBC 2 *Tales of the Paranormal*, April 1996.
42. TNA DEFE 24/1983/1.
43. IWM Archive COI 1125X (1964); British Pathé Archive: http://www.britishpathe.com/video/blue-streak-two-one-zero
44. Chalker, Bill. (11 December 2010) '1964 Woomera UFO movie solved – cold case', UFOs: scientific research blog at: http://ufos-scientificresearch.blogspot.co.uk/2010/12/1964-woomera-ufo-movie-solved-cold-case.html
45. Clarke, David and Andy Roberts. (2012) 'Farewell to the Solway Spaceman?' *Fortean Times*, 286: 28–9.
46. http://rationalwiki.org/wiki/Solway_Firth_Spaceman

THE LAST WITCHCRAFT TRIAL?

1. Gaskill, Malcolm. (2001) *Hellish Nell: Last of Britain's Witches.* London: Fourth Estate, pp. 181–4.
2. TNA DPP 2/1204: Details of prosecution by Edinburgh Police in 1933.
3. Transcripts of Helen Duncan's trial at the Old Bailey in 1945: TNA CRIM 1.1581; CRIM 4/1709; CRIM 2/256.
4. Gaskill, 2001, pp. 215–16.
5. Gaskill, 2001, p. 183.
6. TNA CRIM 1/1617.
7. TNA MEPO 2/9158: Confidential Memo to Chief Constables, 9 March 1945.
8. TNA HO 144/22172.
9. TNA HO 144/22172.
10. Transcript of Court of Appeal judgement before The Lord Chief Justice, Mr Justice Oliver and Mr Justice Birkett, 8–10 June 1945, TNA HO 144/22172.
11. 'Campaign to pardon the last witch, jailed as a threat to Britain at war.' *The Guardian*, 13 January 2007.
12. TNA HO 144/1806.

4 SPECIAL POWERS

1. TNA HO 199/480: report by Sgt J. Hall, 19 May 1941.
2. TNA HO 199/480: 'Corpse Divining', file note by Professor W. Curtis, 15 June 1941.
3. TNA HO 199/480: 'Drowning Fatality in River Avon', report by Inspector W. Drakeley, 4 July 1941.
4. *Ibid.*
5. TNA HO 199/480: Note of interview with Dr E.J. Dingwall, Cambridge, by R.E. Stradling, 16 July 1941.
6. TNA MEPO 2/8800.
7. TNA AY 10/14: Papers read at the Bombay Engineering Congress, Nov–Dec 1923.
8. TNA WO 195/16653: Unexploded Bomb Committee, Ministry of Supply, 6 September 1941.
9. Churchill Archives Centre, University of Cambridge, papers of R.V. Jones, RVJO D399, copy of MEXE report dated March 1968.
10. TNA WO 195/16653: 'Some Recent Dowsing Experiments', MEXE report by R.A. Foulkes, March 1968.
11. Foulkes, R.A. (1971) 'Experiments organised by the British Army and Ministry of Defence suggest that results obtained by dowsing are no more reliable than a series of guesses.' *Nature* 229: 168.
12. 'Water worker's divine job.' BBC News Online, 27 July 2001; Pilkington, Mark. 'Water witching.' *The Guardian*, 16 June 2004.
13. 'The dangerous lie that went around the world', *The Guardian*, 24 April 2013; 'Officials promoted bogus bomb detectors', *The Guardian*, 22 August 2013.
14. Wood, Dr Bruce. (2013) 'Woo Bomb detectors – the End of Dowsing for Death.' *Huffington Post Science*, 22 August.
15. *Daily Express*: 7, 9 and 10 March 1931.
16. Harris, 1986, pp. 59–65, 207–9.
17. Information on the results of an examination of the stone and chair in 1996 is summarised in Rodwell, Warwick. (2013) 'The Coronation Chair: Anatomy of a medieval throne.' *Current Archaeology*, 283: 34–40.
18. Pennick, Nigel. (1996) *Celtic Sacred Landscapes*. London: Thames & Hudson, p. 45; Rodwell, Warwick. (2013) *The Coronation Chair and the Stone of Scone: History, Archaeology and Conservation*. Oxford: Oxbow.
19. TNA MEPO 2/8800: Chief Superintendent's report, 5 February 1951.
20. TNA MEPO 2/8800: report from Newark CID, 11 January 1951.
21. TNA MEPO 2/8800.
22. Tullett, E.V. (1951) 'Coronation Stone Surprise.' *Sunday Express*, 21 January.
23. TNA MEPO 2/8800: *Sunday Express*, 28 January 1951.
24. TNA MEPO 2/9152: letter from J.S. de Long of Apeldoorn Police to Scotland Yard, 18 January 1951.
25. TNA MEPO 2/8800.
26. TNA MEPO 2/9152: memo from the Chief Inspector CID, 24 April 1951.
27. TNA MEPO 2/10554: murder of Thomas 'Ginger' Marks in Bethnal Green, January 1965.
28. 'Marks Gang Shooting Remains a Mystery', *The Guardian*, 31 October 1975.
29. TNA MEPO 2/10554: letter dated 1 February 1965.
30. Moran, Sarah. (1999) *Psychic Detectives*. Godalming: Bradley Books, pp. 47–52.

31. BL Sound Archive 69/01/01, formerly TNA MEPO 2/10558.

32. *Daily Express*, 29 March 1965.

33. *Daily Express*, 1 April 1965.

34. *The Independent*, 28 December 1999.

35. Harris, 1986, pp. 43–57; *The Guardian* G2, 9 June 2011.

36. *New York Times*, 8 June 2011.

37. *Daily Telegraph* (London), 5 November 2009. In response to a FOI request in 2010, Dyfed–Powys police said: 'as a matter of policy, mediums, clairvoyants or other psychics are not used by the force' (Dyfed–Powys Police FOI reference 427/2010).

38. Barnes, Hannah. (2009) 'Can psychics help to solve crime?' BBC News Online, summarising content of Donal MacIntyre show, BBC Radio 5 Live, 22 November.

39. Hansard (House of Commons), 28 October 2005: response from Home Secretary Hazel Blears to Lynne Featherstone MP.

40. Silence, Eddie. (2006) 'The Police and Psychics.': http://www.ukskeptics.com accessed July 2012.

41. Response by ACPO to Freedom of Information request from the author, 14 November 2013.

42. DI51/8/5/3/1 dated 6 November 2001, released to the author under the Freedom of Information Act, November 2013.

REMOTE VIEWERS

1. M-OA DR 1263 'Belief in the Supernatural', report on April directive, 16 May 1942.

2. Chambers, Paul. (1998) *Paranormal People*. London: Batsford, pp. 99–103.

3. The best account of the US remote viewing programme is given in Schnabel, Jim. (1997) *Remote Viewers: The Secret History of America's Psychic Spies*. New York: Dell.

4. Targ, Russell and Harold Puthoff. (1974) 'Information transmission under conditions of sensory shielding.' *Nature*, 251: 602–7.

5. Schnabel, Jim. (2011) 'Psychic Spies.' *Fortean Times*, 272: 30–35.

6. Interview with former CIA Director Stansfield Turner, *The Real X-Files: America's Psychic Spies*, Channel 4 documentary shown in 1993, directed by Bill Eagles and narrated by Jim Schnabel.

7. Marks, David F. (2000) *The Psychology of the Psychic*. New York: Prometheus, p. 92; see also Blackmore, Susan. (2010) *Consciousness: An Introduction*. 2nd ed. London: Hodder, section 7: p. 21.

8. Mumford, *et al.* (1995) *An Evaluation of Remote Viewing: Research and Applications*. Prepared by The American Institutes for Research for the CIA, 29 September 1995: http://www.lfr.org/lfr/csl/library/airreport.pdf

9. Ronson, Jon. (2004) *The Men Who Stare at Goats*. London: Picador.

10. TNA KV 2/2821 describes how from 1940 MI5 hired a Hungarian/British astrologer, Louis De Wohl, who claimed he could use horoscopes to influence Adolf Hitler and his advisors.

11. Gaskill, 2001, p. 289.

12. TNA FD 23/896.

13. TNA DEFE 24/1973/1.

14. TNA DEFE 24/1978/1.

15. Irving, Rob. (1996) 'Watching the Dream Detectives.' *Fortean Times*, 86: 23–8.

16. Personal communication, December 2006.

17. The titles of two MoD files released following a FOI request from the author in 2008 are DI51/GPO

28 Novel Phenomena, Remote Viewing and DI51/GPO 21 Novel Bio-effects, Psychotronics, Remote Viewing.

18. DI51/5/03/10 dated 10 October 2001, released to the author under the Freedom of Information Act, November 2013.

19. A redacted version of the DI51 report on Remote Viewing, completed in 2002, was released by the Ministry of Defence via its Freedom of Information publication scheme. It was not available at The National Archives at the time of writing.

20. DI51/8/5/3/1 dated 6 November 2001, released to the author under Freedom of Information, November 2013.

21. DI51 Remote Viewing report, Ministry of Defence 2002.

5 THE INEXPLICABLE SKY

1. Conan Doyle, Arthur. (1913) 'The Horror of the Heights.' *Strand Magazine*, 46 (275).

2. Parker, Bev. 'A Great Victorian Adventure.' Wolverhampton History and Heritage website: http://www.historywebsite.co.uk/articles/BalloonFlight/Flight.htm

3. Conan Doyle, 1913.

4. Ward-Jackson, C.H. (1943) *It's a Piece of Cake: RAF Slang Made Easy*. London: Sylvan Press, p. 33.

5. For details of the foo-fighter sightings, see Clarke, *The UFO Files*, 2012, pp. 16–27.

6. Fort, Charles. ([1923]1974) *New Lands*, New York: Dover edition, p. 324.

7. BL US Department of Defense, Office of Public Information. (1949) 'A digest of preliminary studies made by the Air Material Command of the US Air Force on "Flying Saucers".' Washington DC.

8. Williamson, Jack. (1931) 'Through the Purple Cloud.' *Wonder Stories*, 12 (2).

9. Gaddis, Vincent. (1964) 'The Deadly Bermuda Triangle.' *Argosy*, 358: 29.

10. Gaddis, Vincent. (1965) *Invisible Horizons: True Mysteries of the Sea*. New York: Chilton Books, pp. 174–5.

11. US Navy Historical Center factsheet, 'The Loss of Flight 19', Washington DC, March 1998.

12. Gaddis, 1965, p. 184.

13. Begg, 1979, pp. 145–67.

14. TNA BT 217/2041; TS 52/11: Report of Court of investigation of the accident to the Tudor IV Aircraft *Star Tiger* G-AHNP on 30 January 1948. See also Tom Mangold's investigation for BBC News Online, 13 September 2009, 'The Bermuda Triangle Plane Mystery Solved'.

15. Begg, 1979, pp. 167–73.

16. Kusche, Lawrence David. (1973) *The Bermuda Triangle Mystery – Solved*. London: New English Library.

17. US Navy Historical Center factsheet, 'The Bermuda Triangle', Washington DC, December 1998.

18. Interview with Dennis Plunkett, Bristol, 2005.

19. Gaddis, 1965, p. 184.

20. TNA BT 220/1.

21. TNA BT 220/1: Accident Investigation Branch report CA 106: loss of *Star Dust*.

22. BBC News Online, 26 January 2000.

23. TNA AVIA 13/1363.

24. Clarke, *The UFO Files*, 2012, p. 134.

25. Clarke, *op. cit.*, pp. 57–61.

26. TNA BJ 220/108: transcript of public inquiry into loss of Comet aircraft G-ALYP near Elba on 10 January 1954 and G-ALYY near Naples on 8 April 1954.

27. Good, Timothy. (2006) *Need to Know: UFOs, the Military and Intelligence.* London: Sidgwick & Jackson, p. 155.

28. Extracted from the executive summary of the Ministry of Defence report, *Unidentified Aerial Phenomena in the UK Air Defence Region*, completed 2000. A redacted version was uploaded to the MoD Publication Scheme in 2005. It was not available at The National Archives at the time of writing.

29. MoD UAP report, 2000, executive summary.

30. TNA AIR 2/19174: RAF Aircraft Accident Report by Air Commodore F.O. Barrett, Director of Air Safety, 30 June 1972.

31. TNA DEFE 24/1972/1 contains facsimiles of the articles published by the *Evening Telegraph* (Grimsby), 10–13 October 1992.

32. Versions of the bogus transcript appear in Pat Otter, 'Captain Schaffner's Last Flight', *Flying Saucer Review* 39/1 (Spring 1994), pp. 16–21; See also Dodd, Tony. (1999) *Alien Investigator: The Case Files of Britain's Leading UFO Detective.* London: Headline, pp. 189–92.

33. BBC 1 North *Inside Out*, 16 September 2002; BBC News Online, 17 September 2002.

34. TNA AIR 2/19174.

35. TNA DEFE 71/95: Board of Inquiry file on crash of Lightning F6 XS894, 8 September 1970.

36. TNA DEFE 71/95: accident investigation report, 30 June 1972.

37. TNA DEFE 71/95: transcript of Captain Schaffner's conversation with ground controller 1970.

PHANTOM HELICOPTERS

1. Five files covering the FBI's investigation of the animal mutilation phenomenon are available via the agency's Records vault at: http://vault.fbi.gov/Animal%20Mutilation

2. Rogerson, Peter. (1976) 'A Panorama of UFOlogical Visions.' *MUFOB*, 3: 12.

3. Personal communication from Simon Crowe, 12 December 1988.

4. MEPO file 371/74/94 'Low Flying Helicopters 1973–74' released to the author in August 2005 under the Freedom of Information Act.

5. Personal communication from Andrew Brown, Metropolitan Police, 30 November 2004.

6. 'Police appeal over Mystery Helicopter.' *Staffordshire Evening Sentinel* (Stoke-on-Trent), 15 January 1974.

7. 'On the trail of the Phantom Flier.' *Daily Mirror*, 18 January 1974.

8. *Manchester Evening News*, 17 January 1974.

9. MEPO file 371/74/94: Letter from Assistant Chief Constable, West Yorkshire Police to Commissioner of Police, New Scotland Yard, 18 July 1974.

10. MEPO file 371/74/94: Memo to Chief Supt 'B' Squad, 22 March 1974.

11. MEPO file 371/74/94: Memo, Commander Ops, 20 March 1974.

12. Personal communication from John Warwicker, December 2013.

13. MEPO file 371/74/94: Unauthorised helicopter flights, 9 July 1974.

14. *Daily Mail*, 21 January 1974.

15. Randles, Jenny. (1983) *The Pennine UFO Mystery*. London: Granada, pp. 29–30.

6 MYSTERIES OF THE SEA

1. Moore, Thomas. (1806) *Epistles, Odes, and Other Poems*. Philadelphia: John Watts.

2. Lockhart, J.G. (1924) *Mysteries of the Sea: A Book of Strange Tales*. London: Philip Allan & Co., pp. 45–6.

3. Barrington, George. ([1795]2004) *A Voyage to Botany Bay*. Sydney: Sydney University Press, Chapter VI.

4. Lockhart, 1924, pp. 53–4.

5. (1821) 'Vanderdecken's Message Home.' *Blackwood's Edinburgh Magazine*, 9 (50): 127–31.

6. (1877) *Public Ledger*. Memphis, Tennessee. 6 September.

7. de la Croix, Robert. (1956) *Mysteries of the Sea*. London: Muller, p. 139.

8. Underwood, 1973, p. 106.

9. Haining, Peter. (1974) *Ghosts: The Illustrated History*. London: Sidgwick & Jackson, p. 67.

10. Dalton, John. (1886) *The Cruise of Her Majesty's Ship* The Bacchante *1879–1882*. London: Macmillan & Co., Vol. 1, p. 551.

11. TNA ADM 53/11664: HMS *Inconstant* logbook 1881.

12. Staples, Robert F. (March 1966) 'The distribution and characteristics of Surface Bioluminescence in the oceans [technical report].' Washington DC: US Naval Oceanographic Office.

13. (1880) 'A Strange Phenomenon.' *Nature*, 21: 409–10.

14. Sherwood, Kris. (1997, updated 2001) 'Marine Lightwheels: Crop Circles of the Sea?' http://www.cropcirclesanswers.com/marinelightwheels.htm

15. Shoemaker, Michael T. (1995) 'The Lightwheel Wonder', in Steve Moore (ed.) *Fortean Studies* 2. London: John Brown, pp. 8–63.

16. (1790) 'Memoirs of Navigation and Commerce from the Earliest Periods.' *The Naval Chronicle* 1: 190.

17. TNA ADM 53/11327: HMS *Vulture*, logbook May 1879.

18. Pringle, J. Eliot. (1879) 'Report of an unusual phenomenon observed at sea.' *Nature*, 20: 291.

19. (1880) 'A Strange Phenomenon.' *Nature*, p. 409–10.

20. Baxter, R.R. and J.A. Gilchrist. (1956) 'Phosphorescent Wheels.' *The Marine Observer*, 26: 78–9.

21. Staples, 1966, pp. 38–43.

22. Kalle, Kurt. (1969) 'Wheels of Lights.' *Sea Frontiers*, 15: 116; Shoemaker, 1995, p. 9.

23. Shoemaker, 1995, pp. 45–6; see also 'Marine Phosphorescent Wheels' (1892) in William S. Corliss (ed.), *Lightning, Auroras, Nocturnal Lights and Related luminous phenomen*. Glen Arm, Maryland: The Sourcebook Project, pp. 180–199.

24. Sherwood, Kris. (2007, updated 2008) 'Spectacular lightwheel display witnessed by navy crew in the Straits of Hormuz, May 19, 2007': http://www.cropcirclesanswers.com/marinelightwheels.htm

25. Sherwood, Kris. (2009) 'Astounding new Marine Lightwheel sighting by US Navy ship in the Arabian Gulf': http://www.cropcirclesanswers.com/marinelightwheels.htm

26. Heuvelmans, Bernard. (1968) *In the Wake of Sea Serpents*. New York: Hill & Wang, pp. 421–2.

27. Letters, *The Field* (London), 10 February 1934.

28. Kingshill, Sophia and Jennifer Westwood. (2012) *The Fabled Coast*. London: Random House, pp. 348–9.

29. Heuvelmans, 1968, Chapter 1.

30. Hoare, Philip. (2013) 'Enter the Dragon.' The *Guardian G2*, 10 December.

31. 'The Great Sea Serpent', *The Times*, 14 October 1848.

32. Gould, Rupert T. (1930) *The Case for the Sea Serpent*. London: Philip Allan, pp. 96–7.

33. 'The Great Sea Serpent', *Illustrated London News*, 28 October 1848.

34. Letter from Richard Owen, *The Times*, 14 November 1848.

35. Letter from P. McQuhae, *The Times*, 21 November 1848.

36. TNA BJ 7/49: 'Sea Serpent'.

37. TNA BJ 7/49: 'Sea Serpent'.

38. TNA BJ 7/49: Letter from William Henry Flower, Royal College of Surgeons, 18 February 1881.

39. Walsh, John Evangelist. (1996) *Unravelling Piltdown*. London: Random House, pp. 195–6.

40. Gould, 1930, p. 397.

41. *Deutschen Algemeine Zeitung*, 19 October 1933; also Dash, Mike. (2009) 'Baron Forstner and the U28 Sea Serpent of July 1915.' CFI blog, 11 December.

42. NHM DF 200/195: Statement of Mr John Mackintosh Bell, 1929.

43. NHM DF 200/195: letter from Keeper of Zoology, 8 January 1929.

44. Fawcett, Percy and Brian Fawcett. (1953) *Exploration Fawcett*. London: Hutchinson, p. 122.

45. 'Plesiosaurus Not Extinct.' *Daily Express*, 7 February 1928.

46. NHM DF 200/195: letter from Keeper of Zoology, 9 March 1934.

47. Greener, Mark. (2010) 'The Golden Age of Sea Serpents.' *Fortean Times*, 260: 38.

48. *The Guardian*, 19 October 2013, quoting Associated Press in Oceanside, California.

49. Response from Royal Navy, 29 March 2010 to FOI request from Sebastian Darby to MoD; *Daily Telegraph* (London), 16 May 2010.

50. Ridgway, John and Chay Blyth. (1966) *A Fighting Chance*. London: Hamlyn, pp. 131–3.

GHOST SHIP

1. TNA MT 9/3491: Marine Registry M1803/73.

2. 'The ghost ships that haunt the oceans.' *The Guardian*, 27 March 2012.

3. The most reliable sources for the *Mary Celeste* story include: Eden Fay, Charles. ([1942]1988) *The Story of the Mary Celeste*. Originally published by the Peabody Museum, Massachusetts, New York: Dover Edition; Begg, Paul. (1979) *Into Thin Air*. London: David & Charles, Chapter 8; and Begg, Paul. (2006) *Mary Celeste: The Greatest Mystery of the Sea*. Harlow: Pearson.

4. Lloyd's of London file (Guildhall Library): also Eden Fay, Charles. (1950) 'The Greatest Sea Mystery.' *Sea Breezes* (Aug–Sept): 1.

5. Fay, 1942, pp. 62–71.

6. Begg, 1979, p. 102.

7. The *Mary Celeste* is mentioned in Lloyd's list for Gibraltar, 13 December 1872; a copy of the Lloyd's of London file on the ship was provided by Valerie Hart of the Guildhall Library, London, September 2013.

8. See J. Habakuk Jepshon's Statement in *Cornhill Magazine*, new series II (January 1884), pp. 1–32.

9. Lockhart, J.G. (1927) *A Great Sea Mystery: The True Story of the Mary Celeste*. London: Philip Allan & Co., p. 128.

10. Fay, 1942, p. 141.

11. Conan Doyle, Arthur. (1890) *The Captain of the Polestar, And Other Tales*. London: Longman & Co.

12. Linford, A. Howard. (1913) 'Abel Fosdyk's Story.' *Strand Magazine*, 46: 46.

13. A reproduction from the original 'list of persons composing the crew of the *Mary Celeste*', from The National Archives, Washington DC, appears as Appendix J in Fay, 1942, p. 209–10.

14. Fay, 1942, p. 124.

15. Hitching, Francis. (1978) *The World Atlas of Mysteries*. London: Collins, p. 218.

16. Fay, 1942, pp. 137–40.

17. TNA MT 9/3491: letter from Board of Trade to H.T. Wilkins, 20 January 1930.

18. 'Destruction of old documents.' *The Times*, 10 March 1930.

19. Fay, 1942, p. 61; a complete reproduction of the Vice Admiralty court proceedings appears as an appendix in Begg, 2006.

20. TNA MT 9/3491: file note, 21 March 1930.

7 THE LOCH NESS MONSTER SYNDROME

1. Fitter, Richard. (1988) 'The Loch Ness Monster: Saint Columba to the Loch Ness Investigation Bureau.' *The Scottish Naturalist: Journal of Scottish Natural History*, XX: 44–5.

2. MacGregor, Alasdair Alpin. (1937) *Peat Fire Flame: Folk-tales and Traditions of the Highlands & Islands*. Edinburgh & London: Ettrick Press, p. 67.

3. Westwood, Jennifer and Sophia Kingshill. (2009) *The Lore of Scotland: A Guide to Scottish Legends*. London: Random House, p. 441–2.

4. Roland Watson's 'Loch Ness Monster' blog: http://lochnessmystery.blogspot.co.uk/

5. NAS AF 62/5101: newspaper cutting 18 October 1933.

6. NAS HH1/588: extract from 'The Life of Saint Columba', copy sent to the Scottish Office on 11 January 1934.

7. NHM DF 200/195.

8. 'What Was It?' *Northern Chronicle* (Aberdeen), 27 August 1930.

9. *Northern Chronicle*, letters, 3 & 10 September 1930.

10. *Inverness Courier*, 3 May 1933.

11. 'Strange Spectacle on Loch Ness.' *Inverness Courier*, 4 August 1933.

12. 'West End Surgeon's Photo of the Monster.' *Daily Mail*, 21 April 1934.

13. Gould, Lt Cdr R.T. (1933) 'The Loch Ness "Monster". ' *The Times*, 9 December.

14. Gould, Lt Cdr R.T. (1933) 'The Loch Ness Monster – A Survey of the Evidence', *The Times*, 9 December.

15. Gould, Lt Cdr R.T. (1943) *The Stargazer Talks*. London: Geoffrey Bles, p. 86.

16. NHM DF 200/195.

17. NHM DF 232/7/1/3: Hinton, Martin. (1934) 'Summing up the Loch Ness Monster.' *The Field*, 27 January , pp. 107–8.

18. NAS HH55/1395: Scottish *Sunday Express*, 13 December 1933.

19. NAS HH1/588: Loch Ness Monster 1933–8.

20. NAS HH1/588: Notes for Parliamentary Questions, December 1933.

21. NAS HH1/588: letter from George Hogarth, Fishery Board for Scotland, to the Scottish Office, Edinburgh, 26 October 1933.

22. NAS HH1/588: extract from Hansard (House of Commons), 12 December 1933.

23. NAS HH1/588: briefing for PQ, December 1933.

24. NAS HH1/588: minutes summarising advice from the Natural History Museum (London) and the Natural History Department of the Royal Scottish Museum (Edinburgh), 3 January 1934.

25. NAS HH1/588: Letter from the Chief Constable of Inverness, 15 August 1938.

26. NAS AF 62/4398 – letter from Stephen Drummond to David James MP, 29 May 1962.

27. NHM DF 1004/510: 'Loch Ness Phenomena', memo to NHM staff, 21 October 1959.

28. Scott, Sir Peter. (1960) 'The Loch Ness Monster: Fact or Fancy?' *Sunday Times*, 14 August.

29. Whyte, Constance. (1957) *More Than A Legend*. London: Hamish Hamilton.

30. 'Obituary: Tim Dinsdale 1924–1987': *The Scottish Naturalist: Journal of Scottish Natural History* (1988), pp. 209–11.

31. NHM DF 1004/510: cable from Tim Dinsdale to NHM, 23 April 1960.

32. NHM DF 1004/510: letter from Tim Dinsdale to NHM, 1 May 1960.

33. James David. (1961) 'Time to Meet the Monster.' *The Field*, 23 November, pp. 951–2.

34. Robson, John. (1998) *One Man In His Time*. Pen & Sword Books, p. 204.

35. NAS AF 62/4398: 'Report on Loch Ness Expedition 1963' by David James.

36. NAS AF 62/4398: DAF (Scotland) memo, 15 May 1963.

37. University of East Anglia, Zuckerman Archive, SZ/CSA/152/2 letter from David James to Solly Zuckerman, 12 February 1963.

38. University of East Anglia, Zuckerman Archive, SZ/CSA/152/4 letter from Solly Zuckerman to David James, 17 February 1963.

39. University of East Anglia, Zuckerman Archive, SZ/CSA/152/14 letter from David James to Solly Zuckerman, 3 January 1964.

40. University of East Anglia, Zuckerman Archive, SZ/CSA/152.15 & 37, note from Solly Zuckerman to Chief Scientist (RN), 7 January 1964. MoD CSA draft, 'Investigations in Loch Ness', dated 12 April 1966.

41. See Clarke, 2012, *The UFO Files*, pp. 147–9.

42. NAS AF 62/4398: JARIC report 66/1: Loch Ness; NHM DF 933/25.

43. NAS AF 62/4398: letter from Lord Shackleton to David James MP, 7 February 1966.

44. See for example 'Analysis of the Tim Dinsdale Film':
http://www.nessie.co.uk/htm/the_evidence/analysis.html

45. Vane, Peter. (1966) 'Loch Ness monster may be real, say RAF experts.' *Sunday Express*, 21 February.

46. *Report on a film taken by Tim Dinsdale* (with introduction by David James), (1966) Loch Ness Phenomena Investigation Bureau.

47. NHM DF5014 (Press Cuttings, 1975–1983): 'Loch Ness Monster' British Museum (Natural History) press notice, 24 November 1975.

48. NAS AF62/4939: Scott, Sir Peter and Robert Rines. (1975) 'Naming the Loch Ness Monster', *Nature*, 258, pp. 466–68.

49. NAS HH60/1208/1: letter to Scottish Office from W. McKenzie, Nature Conservancy Council, 29 March 1976.

50. NAS AF 62/4939: memo from George Younger MP, 8 December 1971.

51. NAS AF 62/4939: DAF (Scotland), memo, 26 November 1971.

52. NAS DD37/234: letter from M. Bradfield, British Embassy, Stockholm, 6 November 1985.

CAT FLAPS

1. 'New evidence for big cats in Britain', *BBC Wildlife* magazine, April 2006; http://www.britishbigcats.org

2. Harpur, Merrily. (2006) *Mystery Big Cats*. Loughborough: Heart of Albion, Chapter 1.

3. Beer, Trevor. (1986) *The Beast of Exmoor: Fact or Legend?* Barnstaple: Countryside Books.

4. *Daily Mirror, The Sun, Guardian*, 28 August 2012.

5. NHM Nature Online (Mammals): 'The Beast of Bodmin Moor': http://www.nhm.ac.uk/nature-online/life/mammals/beast-of-bodmin-moor/

6. Hansard (House of Commons), debate 2 February 1998.

7. Baker, S.J. and C.J. Wilson. (1995) *The evidence for the presence of large exotic cats in the Bodmin area and their possible impact on livestock*. ADAS report produced for the Ministry of Agriculture and Fisheries, London.

8. *Ipswich Star*, 16 March 2008.

9. Monbiot, George. (2013) 'Beast Fever.' *The Guardian* G2, 22 May.

10. 'Report received by Defra of escapes of non-native cats in the UK', response from Defra Countryside following a Freedom of Information Act request, 2006.

11. Blake, Max, *et al*. (2013) 'Multidisciplinary investigation of "British Big Cats": a lynx killed in southern England c.1903.' *Historical Biology*, 23 April.

IMAGE CREDITS

CHAPTER 1

1.1 Fortean Picture Library
1.2 Fortean Picture Library
1.3 Mary Evans Picture Library
1.4 The National Archives
Panel Figure 1.1 The National Archives

CHAPTER 2

2.1 The National Archives
2.2 West Glamorgan Archive Service
2.3 Mary Evans Picture Library
2.4 The National Archives
2.5 The National Archives

CHAPTER 3

3.1 The National Archives
3.2 British Library
3.3 The National Archives
3.4 Jim Templeton
Panel Figure 3.1 The National Archives
Panel Figure 3.2 The National Archives

CHAPTER 4

4.1 The National Archives
4.2 The National Archives
4.3 Edinburgh Castle
4.4 Mary Evans Picture Library
Panel Figure 4.1 Author's collection/Crown copyright

CHAPTER 5

5.1 Mary Evans Picture Library
5.2 The National Archives
5.3 The National Archives
5.4 The National Archives
Panel Figure 5.1 Author's collection/Crown copyright
Panel Figure 5.2 Author's collection

CHAPTER 6

6.1 The National Archives
6.2 Fortean Picture Library
6.3 Fortean Picture Library
6.4 Fortean Picture Library
6.5 Warwickshire County Record Office
Panel Figure 6.1 Fortean Picture Library
Panel Figure 6.2 The National Archives

CHAPTER 7

INDEX